Conquering
Me

Conquering *The*

A Memoir Of Courage, Faith, And Transformation

By Dr. Jolinda Wade
as shared with Arthur Samuel Joseph, M.A.

Foreword By Dwyane Wade, Olympic Gold Medalist And
Member Of The Naismith National Basketball Association
Hall Of Fame

INDIE BOOKS
INTERNATIONAL

Conquering Me
A Memoir Of Courage, Faith, And Transformation

ISBN 13: 978-1-966168-56-0

Designed by Melissa Farr, Back Porch Creative, LLC

INDIE BOOKS INTERNATIONAL®, INC.
2511 WOODLANDS WAY
OCEANSIDE, CA 92054
www.indiebooksintl.com

And do not be conformed to this world,
but be transformed by the renewing of your mind,
that you may prove what is that good and acceptable
and perfect will of God.

ROMANS 12:2

Table Of Contents

Foreword

There's something remarkable about watching someone become the hero of their own story.

My mother didn't wait for rescue. She didn't pretend the hard parts didn't happen. She met them head-on—with honesty, with faith, and with a love that refused to give up. Her life has taken her through trials that would've broken many: addiction, prison, pain. But somehow, through it all, she kept looking up. And in looking up, she found a way forward—not just for herself, but for those of us lucky enough to walk behind her.

This book is her voice. Her truth. Her story told in her own words. You'll hear about the love she's always had for God—not rooted in fear, but in grace. You'll see the lessons she's learned as both a mother and a grandmother. You'll feel her faith in action—even in the loneliest moments.

When she was in prison, I only saw her once. My sisters, not many times. And yet, she never stopped seeing us. She held on to our faces—visualizing them, leaning on them—when it would've been easier to give up. That mental picture of her children helped pull her through, and that kind of love? That kind of love is not ordinary. It's Agape!

My mom has enhanced my life in ways I'm still learning to name. She's taught me about real love, real care, real strength. And I like to think I've given her a little something back too—maybe a lesson or two, maybe just a reason to keep going.

This isn't a story wrapped in a bow. It's raw. It's detailed. It's honest. But that's exactly why it matters. Because someone out there needs to know that redemption is real. That healing is possible. That your past doesn't disqualify you from purpose.

Read these pages, and you'll meet a woman who turned pain into power, mistakes into ministry, and faith into forward motion. She is, without question, the hero of her story. And I couldn't be prouder to call her Mom.

Dwyane Wade,
Olympic Gold Medalist, NBA All-Star,
and member of the National Basketball Association Hall of Fame

Preface

This book is an opportunity for me to share the various experiences of my life through the arc of my Journey to this point in time. I want you to take away from your reading of my story insights that may inspire you and may enable you to empower yourself. My tale starts with experiencing my life through the prism of my pain and struggles, continues onward to my victories, and shares my ever-present courage for survival that led to my ultimate success. I "made it out!"

However, for so many years it was virtually impossible for me to "see the light of day," as the tunnel I was buried in was so very deep and dark until—finally—at 10:30 a.m., October 14, 2001, when God's voice awakened me. Frankly, I'd heard His voice before, but this time I listened. God asked me to get dressed—and go to church. With that simple act, I changed my life and claimed my power.

Please note: I did not say, "*My life changed.*" I clearly said, "*I changed my life.*"

I fervently believe that when you read this book, you will not simply be motivated to take action in your own life; you will be *inspired* to do so. I share this because the root of the word *inspire* means to "breathe into" someone. As God breathes the breath of life into me, I want to breathe my very soul into you. Through this passionate commitment to give all that I can, if I can help save one life by publicly sharing my story, I will have fulfilled the mission of this book.

We are living in a time when people truly need inspiration. We are living in a time when we need to experience hope and possibility. *Conquering Me* is, on the one hand, the story of my life, but beyond this, it is an exploration of faith, courage, resilience, will, and ultimately—freedom.

I was a broken vessel that I had to piece back together for God's purpose. Faith without work is dead. One must really put forth an effort to come through those things that we fear the most. Until that day of my awakening, I firmly believed that fear had conquered me—that I had no control over my situation in life.

The word *conquer* means to "overcome"—to "take control of"—and that day, on October 14, 2001, God came to me and told me that I could now take control of my life. Simply by *letting go* of my crippling fear and *letting God in*, I would be reborn. Not simply "reborn" in the evangelical sense, but I would be fully responsible for rebirthing myself.

I had been swimming alone against the tide—going nowhere. The Creator did not give me my fear; I created it. After my awakening, I heard the Creator say, "I didn't give you a spirit of fear, but the power of love and a sound mind."

Fear sucks the life right out of us. It takes our power from us, crushes our belief system. Fear controls when we laugh, whom we laugh with, and whom we love. When we are in fear, we are not of sound mind. Fear is the mind killer.

When God spoke to me that day, except for the births of my beautiful children, it was the most remarkable moment of my life, for, in an instant, I released my fear. God did not release my fear; God gave me the power to release my own fear, and in that moment, I knew that all would be right.

I had heard God's voice many other times in my life and generally ignored it. This time was different. Through letting go and letting God in, I immediately felt God's reassuring presence that I was not alone. God was my partner. The comfort and security this knowledge brought was an epiphany. In choosing to listen, in choosing to act, I climbed out of the tunnel to emerge into the light of day. Literally, each day ever since has been amazing.

I *am* my own hero. What an astonishing thing to say. I began writing this book when I was sixty-six years old and completed it when I was seventy. Given the circumstances of my life over the previous several decades, I never thought that I could be anyone's hero—let alone my own. As the chapters unfold, you will be able to discover how I am actually able to acknowledge this truth. It is not an aspirational truth—*it is the truth*. I am my own hero and I know it.

My belief is that, if you, too, have taken a wrong turn in life as I did and have gotten lost, you can learn from my story and, hopefully, it can lead you to *your* right path.

Chapter 1

The Beginning

*L*et me take you back to where this all began.

I was born on the South Side of Chicago, the fifth of nine children, five girls and four boys, to our single mother, Willie Mae Morris. My father had left us but continued to live in the neighborhood and only occasionally visited us. So, it became my mother's responsibility to raise seven of us as well as manage to support us on the meager wages she earned cleaning houses, among other jobs she held.

I knew she loved us. She showed us her love every day by faithfully working diligently to make sure that we always had a roof over our heads, food on the table, and clothes on our backs.

At the same time and for many years as we were growing up, my mom was an alcoholic. Sometimes she'd go out and party, and often, she held card games in our home. Although she drank and enjoyed the company of men, she didn't allow any of the men to mess with us. This was the lifestyle we were exposed to—in fact, my older siblings also abused drugs and alcohol. We didn't see it as being such a bad thing. It was our normal.

Even when my mother was drinking and partying, she still continued to put our welfare first. She continued to love us, provide for us, and care for us. In this respect I now recognize that she was very special—in fact, exceptional.

When I was twelve or thirteen, Mom said, "My kids are growing up." And, with the realization of how her behavior was affecting us, she gave up her drinking and partying life—just like that. A number of years later, she did tell me that a couple of years after she stopped drinking, she tried to sneak a beer and it just "froze in her mouth." She never touched another drop again.

That took grit and willpower. For that reason, as well as for the powerful love and devotion she had for all of us, plus her courageous work ethic, her unwavering faith in God and the Holy Spirit, my dear mother is my first hero.

One theme woven throughout this book is heroism. As I just stated, my mother is my first hero. My grit and determination come from my mother. I am forever in her debt for being such a powerful role model. She accepted whatever life gave her and always remained a woman of faith, steadfast and upright.

Another theme that will run throughout this book is an exploration of fear. One thing that I discovered in crafting this memoir was how, for so many years, fear and my lack of self-worth and self-esteem were inextricably linked, and I asked myself, "Where did my fear, my lack of self-worth, and belief in myself begin?"

One thought that occurred to me is that I was a very sensitive child. I felt every single thing so intensely. In this context, one recognition that emerged is that I simply needed more affection, more hugs, more personal time with her than my loving mother could provide.

I now recognize that this longing for more nurturing than my siblings required was due to my emotional sensitivity and to the fact that I had contracted rheumatic fever, which clearly depleted me physically as well as emotionally and spiritually. I was weakened in every way.

Because of my illness, Mama wouldn't let me go outside and play with the other children. Consequently, I spent a great deal of time alone. This, in turn, was scary as I didn't know what was happening to me, or where to go to feel safe and know that everything would be "all right." I didn't know how to share what I was feeling or even who to share it with.

As I spent a good deal of time by myself, I created a rather elaborate fantasy world where I would stage my dolls, shoes, and anything I could find to interact with and tell them stories that I created from my rather remarkable imaginary life. I would speak out loud. I would envision what the people in my stories looked like, where they lived. I saw everything, and it was very real to me.

I have always loved reading and, during these solitary times, I retreated into the world of books. I even used to hide under the bed or find anywhere I could to hole up and escape into the world of stories. They transported me into a realm of fantasy, adventure, and romance.

The tales I read became my reality. I simply did not have to be here—I was transported to a better place. And, because of my passion for reading and my inability to express my feelings, I discovered that, in solitude, my books and my hiding places became a sanctuary, a safe place for me to be.

However, this behavior led my family to think I was strange. My dad often said, "There's something wrong with this child," and that I needed to be in a hospital. My siblings would sometimes say to me, "Girl, you're strange." But, truth be told, I didn't want to be "different." I didn't want to be more "strange" than I already was perceived to be.

Even at that early age, I recognized that I wanted to be like everyone else—but I wasn't. I didn't know how to process my feelings, so I shut down and didn't share what was going on with me. I later realized that this, in turn, contributed to my isolation and lack of self-confidence.

It may sound silly or trivial, but another fear was a fear of scary movies. They terrified me! I couldn't watch anything scary as it really messed me up. We only had one TV, and those scary movies were what my family liked to watch, so if I wanted to watch TV, I had to watch them too. It was all very real to me—even *Frankenstein* was terrifyingly real.

One movie in particular I clearly remember watching was *Children of the Damned*. I was ten years old. It was movie day, and my mother let my siblings take me to see it at the movie theater. Of course, I couldn't watch it; I peeked at it, hiding my face as best I could. When we left the movie, I thought I would be OK—until bedtime, when I tried to lie down and I saw the images all over again in the shadows our clothes made on the bedroom walls.

These shadows were so real, I just went off. My sister had to call my mama, who was at a party, to come home and calm me down because I was so upset that I screamed and hollered. As she had done before, Mama left the party and came home to take care of me.

She would always do that, or if she planned to go out, she would delay leaving whenever I became so distraught that I needed her to comfort me. She would let me climb into bed with her and, literally, hold me until I felt safe. It was her spirit that created this feeling of security and sanctity for me. Nobody else could calm me down except my mother.

My fear of scary movies continued. Even as late as when I was in the eighth grade, I still couldn't watch them. Of course, to this day, I'll never see a horror film.

Throughout my childhood, my favorite day of the week was Sunday. That's when my mother would have us all dress in our Sunday best, and we would go to church. I loved church. I loved Bible study. I loved hearing the songs and, when I was old enough, I loved reading the Bible and singing the songs.

Whatever reality existed Monday through Saturday, Sunday was its own reality. During the week, my family life was busy and more chaotic. On Sunday, we were together as a family. In this way, the church became like another sanctuary for me, as we were all together and we felt embraced by God's loving and nurturing presence. And, throughout the rest of my life, even in my darkest days, when I go to church alone or take my friends along, whenever I am in church, I feel safe and I love being there.

I first heard God's voice when I was twelve years old. I remember where I was when I first heard His voice. I shared a room with my sisters and one of our brothers, Eddie, who was nine. I was sitting on the side of the bed and, as I often did, was writing in my "journal." What I called my journal were simply random pieces of paper where I shared my most personal thoughts, then stored them in a purse I hid under my mattress.

On this particular day, I was sitting alone in my room, writing something deep and heartfelt, when I heard a soft, gentle Voice say, "It's OK. I love you. You're special." When I heard this, I immediately felt reassured and comforted.

As this Voice emerged within me, it blocked out everything else in my external reality. In this moment, I was not aware of anyone or anything else. I don't know exactly what I was writing that brought the Voice to me to tell me I was special and that I was loved.

It was over in a few seconds. After this extraordinary experience had passed, I stayed on the side of my bed for some time, grabbed a book, and just started reading. Afterward, I felt truly special—for the first time in my life, I felt like I did matter.

As I told you, my dad said, "There's something wrong with this child." So, when I first heard God's voice, not knowing it was His voice, I too began to doubt what I was hearing and think maybe I was crazy, really crazy. I knew this wasn't simply me talking to myself; the experience was too profound, but I was terrified that, if my family found out I was "hearing voices," they would send me away for sure! So, I never shared with anyone that I heard this voice. I kept it to myself.

I was fourteen the next time I heard the Voice. I was alone outside playing hopscotch by myself, and in this episode, it was like I suddenly traveled in time to a foreign place. When I returned to myself and looked around, I found I was still playing hopscotch. The Voice then said, "You're safe."

Now, I didn't know where I had been taken, but later, as an adult living in Panama with my husband, I experienced a feeling of déjà vu when one of my friends took me into Panama City. I was standing on the American side of the street, listening to Spanish being spoken. When I looked, it was exactly where I had "traveled to" when I was fourteen. I recognized it and said to myself, "I've been here before." I knew this was not a hallucination, as I was not on drugs or doing them at the time. It was then that I recalled the Voice and what it had said to me.

So, from the age of twelve through the rest of my life, I heard this Voice. I never knew when or why it would emerge; it simply appeared. Interestingly, it never scared me—it was simply a voice to me. As I've said, I never shared with anyone in my family, and one of the principal reasons was, besides not wanting them to think me crazy, that I felt it would give my family another reason to think I am strange.

This sentence is important for the reader to understand. This fear of being strange, of being different, is what was about to lead me down a very dark path for the next thirty-one years of my life—trapped in a living nightmare. So, even though for years I continued to hear the voice, I didn't know where it came from, what it even was, or what it meant; I didn't know why it came to me.

It wasn't until 2001 that I *knew* it was God's voice. It was simply a voice that I didn't understand, and I ignored it. I buried it. Whenever I heard it, I would once again close my mind and heart to it—until that fateful day years later at the age of forty-six, when I could no longer deny that it was the voice of God I'd been hearing throughout my life—and I finally chose to listen.

The notion of *choice* is a critical metaphor for all of us. A friend recently said to me, "Every single thing in life revolves only around two things: to choose to do something or to choose not to. It doesn't matter how seemingly daunting, how scary. All that matters is how badly you want it."

In Oakland Elementary School, in the fifth grade, I made the choice to stand up to fear. At recess, there were always a lot of students on the playground, and I might have played with one or two of them, but more often, I wound up by myself just observing. Believe it or not, I didn't even know how to jump rope, and I was afraid if I attempted to, students would laugh at me.

There was one particular student, a Native American girl, who was a loner like me. I used to watch a handful of girls bullying her every time we went to recess. They didn't seem to have anything else to do but bully her, and the teachers in the yard never intervened.

One day, I became so upset that I couldn't take it anymore as I watched them pulling her hair and shoving her. I said aloud to myself, "Enough. Enough in my spirit." I marched right up to them and said, "If you don't stop hitting her, then you're going to have to fight me,"—like I was the toughest person there. Of course, I was afraid they would turn and come after me, but they didn't. The fact that I had sisters who also went to this school gave me a reputation that I played to the hilt, and perhaps this was the reason they backed off.

Even though crippling fear was connected to me and traveled with me until 2001, in this one moment when I was ten years old, fear did not stop me. I was able to summon my courage in spite of it and then found I could simply walk past the fear—because I had to be there for someone else, someone who was more unfortunate than I was—and, in the process, I conquered me as well.

As I write this chapter, aside from the fear that controlled me until I was forty-six years old, it is gratifying for me to realize that one of my strong character traits is that I have always wanted the best for everyone and have often stood as a protector of those less fortunate and those confronting impending danger. I find it rather quixotic that, while I could be there for others, I could not be there for myself—until I was forty-six years old.

From the age of fourteen, my lack of self-esteem, fear of being different, craving and wanting to be like everyone else, my unquenchable fear, and my need to belong drove all of my choices—my initial fear and the choices that ensued ruined and ruled my life for the next three decades.

Up until my life drastically changed in the spring of the eighth grade, when I was fourteen, I'd been very active at school. School had always been my refuge. I loved school; I loved my teachers. I was a good student and had a wonderful reputation. In fact, I even wanted to be a teacher when I grew up. If you had asked my teachers, "Who will be the one to succeed?" they would have all said, "Oh, Jolinda is going to succeed." But then, during my final year in middle school, driven by my desire to belong, I began hanging around with the "in crowd."

When I first began making ill-informed choices for myself, I was a "follower" and I wanted to follow the in crowd. This particular group was, how can I say it, wild, independent, and didn't follow the rules. I knew, of course, that I wasn't allowed to drink at school, but as I was a follower, not a leader, one day at lunch, my friends offered me peppermint schnapps and I took a sip. They said, "When we go back to class, the teacher won't be able to smell it." But I reeked of it.

Whenever a student told me to "Try this," or "Try that," I did. It began with peppermint schnapps, the next was marijuana, and then dropping acid. I even tried cocaine, and a hallucinogen they called "tack." This all led to my experimenting with heroin. Before long, I was drinking even before school and, on occasion, would go into my mother's medicine cabinet, identifying the particular pills that would give me a sense of euphoria. My next youngest sister had more street smarts than I did, and I would ask her, "What is this?" She'd tell me, I'd take it, and that way I thought I could get high without Mama smelling it on my breath.

Well, that was my thinking. I said to myself, "You can't smell pills, but alcohol she could smell." I regularly began dropping these pills before going to school. We called it "doing a Belushi."

As I began using pills, drugs, and alcohol, I became less focused on school and just wanted to hang out with my friends. My teachers clearly began to see me changing; certainly, they could smell alcohol on my breath, and, of course, saw that I was hanging out with the wrong crowd. Clearly, it was not the "in crowd" after all. The teachers cared about me and let my mom know that I was abusing alcohol, so that she could try and catch me before it was too late. However, it was already too late.

Then, in the ninth grade, I was admitted to Dunbar Vocational High School in Chicago. It was a difficult school to get into, but I was accepted. They had a rigorous academic program, and students at Dunbar often went on to college—and some of the better colleges as well—and still I squandered the opportunity due to my poor choices.

I began ditching class and learned that, if you showed up in homeroom, they marked you "in." Then, I wouldn't go to my classes after that. So, for stuff like that, I "beat myself up" and, the more I beat myself up, the more I drank, the more I used drugs. It was a vicious downward spiral.

Even so, I couldn't see how serious my situation was. All I cared about was wanting to be with my friends who were in the "cool group." I so yearned to be popular, to be liked. I wanted to be "that girl"—but I wasn't. I was what we called an "L-7," a "square from Delaware"; nevertheless, I forced myself into their world, and I was *accepted*.

For the last few years, I've been able to gain greater insight and have more perspective about my life. I've often looked back at my childhood, my school years, and seen the extraordinary lack of self-confidence and self-esteem that might have been evident to anyone who knew me, but perhaps I hid it well. Remember, I had become very proficient in burying my feelings.

In hindsight, I now realize I was craving attention, acceptance, affection, and love. Perhaps, I was also hoping my peer group would become a second family, providing me with the affection and acceptance that I didn't feel I always received at home. Again, not because my mother didn't love me, of course she did, but because she simply didn't have the time to fill the void I felt within.

So, at fifteen, not thinking very highly of myself, somehow I noticed that one of the most popular boys on the block was attracted to me—in fact, he lived in my building. Remember, I wasn't street smart, so I didn't know his rep.

Later, I learned that he had a very, very bad reputation, but I was blind to it. My mother hadn't really let us go out in the neighborhood too much because of the type of neighborhood it was, so I was shielded from the reality of my block.

My first boyfriend was seventeen, and I had known him since we were in grammar school. We had always lived in the same building, and my mama knew his mother, and sometimes Mama would babysit for her. When I was twelve and thirteen, he always used to watch me when I was coming home from school, but I didn't know this then. I wasn't interested in boys; I was far too innocent. Maybe that's why Mama protected us, but it made me want to break out of her protective bubble, and I began hanging out with him.

So, when one of the most popular boys in the neighborhood was attracted to me, it did something to me, and I became infatuated with my "first love," who ended up becoming my lover. He was very popular; all the girls liked him and wanted to be with him. None of that mattered—he liked *me*. And, because I was so naive, so innocent, I couldn't see that he was playing me—he was playing on my naivete. I used to say to him, "You've got me wrapped around your little finger." You see, I never knew that, with all the affection he was showing me, he had only one thing in mind.

When I wrote earlier about choice, here was the choice that would change my life forever: At fifteen, I chose to give myself to him because I believed I was in love with him and he with me. This was the man I was going to marry.

I had images of the white picket fence, all that stuff. This was my fantasy world, my romantic books, come to life. This was it! The fairy tale world I had been living in for so many years was now real. I even named all the kids we could have. I was going to have about twelve kids, and I wrote all their names down. There was Ardella, Bidella, etc.—all of them were going to be named after him.

The day came when I decided to give over my bodily treasure, my most precious jewel, to this young man I was in love with, believed I would marry, and spend the rest of my life with. Talk about naive. Oh my god, I was the poster child!

Whenever we had sex, I used to ditch school to be with him. That first time was not at all like I thought it would be. It hurt! He was rough. There was no compassion. There was nothing. In fact, it hurt me so bad, we had to call it off. I didn't enjoy anything about it!

I didn't know about how to protect myself from disease and pregnancy. I never thought about asking him to wear a rubber—he didn't have one anyway; also, we didn't talk about such things. All I thought about was "I'm giving my virginity over to my dream come true"—to the man who loved me. I can tell you I have no fond memory of losing my virginity.

We began having sex in January of that year. We were not intimate that often. I didn't like it and it scared me, but because he was my "dream come true," I continued to give myself to him. Then, in July of that same year, I discovered I was pregnant, and my doctor said I had conceived in March.

When I learned that I was pregnant, I also learned that he was a player. In that one year, he got three other girls pregnant as well. Imagine!

I always thought he was all mine. I had no idea that people could be this mean.

When I found out that there were three more girls who had gotten pregnant by him that same year, I went to see one of the mothers with her baby, which he denied up until the time I went and saw the baby. He couldn't deny it after that. He was seventeen years old and I later learned that he was what we called a "cherry popper." His goal was to have sex with as many virgins as possible, and he didn't care about the consequences to any of us. Again, I never knew anybody could be that mean.

Even though he could no longer deny that he was that baby's father and had gotten me pregnant, he still took no responsibility for any of us. My baby was the last of his babies born that year. My first child, whom I named Deanna, was born in December. I don't know if that relationship defined the rest of my relationships, but I can definitely say it truly damaged me and made it far more difficult for me to trust anyone.

While pregnant, I continued going to school but had to leave Dunbar and went to a continuation school for pregnant girls. After delivering Deanna, my beautiful baby, I was able to return to Dunbar, where I remained until I dropped out in January of my senior year.

Mama watched Deanna during the day while I went to school because she was then working evenings. When I got out of school, I had to come straight home in order to take care of Deanna myself. I was supposed to graduate in June 1973, but had been demoted to the junior division because of my lack of credits. All I needed to do was make up the credits, but that demotion made me feel ashamed and humiliated that I was a senior but in class with juniors. I made another egregious choice, left school, and began working in a factory.

Even though I dropped out of school, education was important to me, and receiving my diploma was important to me. Finally, thirty-two years later, at the age of forty-nine, I earned my high school general equivalency diploma (GED).

The path to earning my GED was like all the convoluted, circuitous paths of my life's Journey. I had begun pursuing my diploma as early as my early twenties, and attended various schools, but never achieved my goal because using and selling drugs was the world I was in.

When I added drinking into this mix, I was definitely no longer interested in getting my GED. One reason was that when I was in this place, I often felt more of a failure and did not want to confront the truth of having dropped out of school. I didn't want to acknowledge yet another failure.

Still, one thing that kept me going was that I wanted it as much for my mother as for myself. So, finally, in 2004, the third time I was released from prison, I was determined to graduate and went to Olive-Harvey College in Chicago.

One amazing teacher that God sent me was my son Dwyane's high school basketball coach, Coach Fitzgerald, who came late at night to my home to help me study for the GED exam. I thought he was the craziest person I'd ever met in my life, coming into this Black neighborhood late at night, but he didn't care. He was committed to helping me pass the GED test, and nothing was going to prevent that.

Once again, as I've already said, God never left my side. He sent Coach Fitzgerald to help me with English, history, and other subjects, but math was challenging for me. So, God sent me the perfect math teacher who really helped me to understand math through his dedicated way of teaching.

Throughout the years of failed attempts, I never gave up the belief that I would finally accomplish my goal; and, when I received my diploma, it was one of the most fulfilling moments of my life. I recognized I had truly accomplished something.

I am not sure my family knew how proud I was of myself, but I was. My mom was still living, and she had never stopped believing in me. So, to see her beaming with pride from ear to ear when she saw my diploma filled me with immense joy. Yes, I was that girl who got pregnant and dropped out of school, but I was also that girl who never stopped dreaming, never gave up, and finally accomplished my goal of graduating from high school.

Up until the time I made that first cataclysmic choice that changed my life and took me on the path to the dark side, I never thought I would wind up being "that one"—the girl who got pregnant and dropped out of school. No teenager ever thinks anything bad can happen to them; certainly, that was true for me. I never thought that I'd be the girl who got pregnant and dropped out of school, made the decisions that I began making, and started going downhill.

I never imagined I would travel the road I did, which would take me to such a perilous world. But I did. Yet, despite it all, God never left my side. I did not know that He protected me until the day I awakened and joined with Him to protect myself.

Please understand: *Everything* we do is wrapped up in the choices we make—*everything*.

Chapter 2

Becoming A Mother
Fear, Discovery, And My Evolution

ear can have such a grip on you. It will suffocate you and make it impossible for you to develop emotionally and intellectually. This stultifying fear prevents you from becoming who you may have been destined to be. Fear can feel like a weight on your chest and make it almost impossible to breathe.

Interestingly, when I looked up the root of the word "fear," one of the Old English definitions is "danger." Fear can awaken so many feelings: distress, apprehension, alarm, and, as I learned while writing this book, danger.

But "fear" can also mean "fear of God," which, in a biblical sense, reflects a reverence or awe. Even though, in this chapter, I'm referring to fear as in "terror," I am gratified to be reminded that fear can also be positive. I will share more of this in the final chapter. For now, I simply want you to know I was not able to transform myself until I recognized and fully accepted God's immense love for me.

In this moment, the only fear I am speaking of is the paralyzing fear I first experienced in July 1970 when I was fifteen years old and my doctor told me I was pregnant.

I had watched my mom take on this responsibility and, at fifteen, I was still not emotionally mature enough to see myself as a mother. In many ways, I was still a child. So, thinking about having a baby was *really scary*.

When I was twelve and thirteen, I used to write stories about getting married, having twelve children, living in a house with a white picket fence, just like what I saw when I watched *Father Knows Best* on television. I never realized that, of course, this was a sanitized white American version of family life. This was not my reality, living in the ghetto on the South Side of Chicago.

In the spring of that year, when I began to feel my body change, I didn't even know I was pregnant. That's how naive I was.

When my older sister, Diann, who had recently had a baby, told me I was pregnant, the first fear that came wasn't that I was pregnant; it was fear of my mom finding out. I knew how sad I would make her, and how disappointed in me she would be. I had watched what my mother went through with my older sister's pregnancy and saw her sadness and disappointment—but I also saw the love my mother showed my sister and her first grandchild.

When I finally told my mom I was pregnant, she must have wondered how it had happened, as, because of my heart condition caused by the rheumatic fever, I was the child she had always had under her protective wings, the innocent one, the one she least expected to get into trouble, to get pregnant.

As a matter of fact, after I told her, my mother's only words to me were, "You're just the sly and the slick," which came from a popular song called "The Sly, The Slick and The Wicked." What she meant by that came from the song lyrics, which, in part, read:

the sly, the slick, the wicked, child
No, no, no—they all try to fake ya'
'Cause the sly—he's got a fly, fly alibi…
…he'll try to pull the wool over your eyes
But remember—there's one more
And he's the wicked—he *shows you a good time*
He's gonna gain your confidence, baby—*and he'll leave you behind*

It was her way of telling me I'd been used, taken advantage of by this man.

She *was* so disappointed in me.

So now, a baby was growing inside me, but I wasn't mature enough to understand anything that was going on. I mean anything! A pregnancy should be wonderful and beautiful—experiencing a human being growing inside of oneself; but, for me, this was not my experience. I was getting bigger by the day and knew nothing about becoming a mama. I still liked my dolls. I never considered abortion—first, my mother would never have allowed it; but, second, part of me knew it was a choice I would never make.

At fifteen, when I gave myself to the man who I thought was going to be my husband, was going to be my whole world, as I've already said, it was true love—but only in my eyes. By the time I was ready to deliver in December of that year, my baby's father was no longer in the picture.

I went on to become pregnant three more times, and I can honestly tell you that the best thing that happened to me with the three men in my life, which I came to understand after my awakening, was the privilege of giving birth to my amazing children.

Over the next several years, each time I got pregnant, I immediately stopped using drugs and also became sober. I had no physical withdrawals. I just made up my mind that I knew alcohol and drugs would hurt my babies, and I wanted my body to be pure for them.

I learned that my babies were attached to me through the umbilical cord, and whatever I took in, they ingested as well. I never wanted to damage them in any way, so each time I simply stopped all drugs, alcohol, and smoking cigarettes. In this way, I was able to protect my babies who were all born drug- and alcohol-free. I am proud of myself for at least doing that right.

That said, as soon as the birthing period and the early months of feeding and caring for my babies were complete, I drifted back into my old lifestyle, casually drinking and smoking. Before I knew it, I was back to the races—drinking, smoking marijuana, and using cocaine.

What caused me to drift back to my old life each and every time, after having been clean and sober for over a year each pregnancy, was that I still lacked self-esteem and self-confidence, and did not particularly like myself. I was not comfortable being me, and using drugs and alcohol helped me mask all of this.

When I was in the throes of my addiction, I would simply "ignore" everything else about myself. I knew *exactly* how I was going to feel once I ingested one or both of them. Whether it makes any sense or not, when I was high, I tuned out reality and hid in an alternate one.

I knew Mom had made the decision for herself to stop drinking, but somehow, her taking responsibility was something I could never connect with for myself. I never knew why she used to drink and party the way she did, but, as I've already said, I knew for me, drugs and alcohol helped me *avoid* being myself. (Once again, as I am writing this, I am struck by the very fact that I never thought about who I already was before drugs and alcohol took over my life. I didn't know I was *already good enough*.)

In this period of my life, I thought drugs and alcohol actually enabled me to cope. Of course, the complete opposite was true. They made it impossible for me to cope. Mom continued to always say to me, "You can do better, Jolinda. You need to put that s.h.i.t. down. You need to be more of a mother to your kids."

I thought about this so many times over the years: If I was so determined to stop drugs and alcohol each time I was pregnant and abstained for up to a year, why did I choose to return to the lifestyle of substance abuse and hanging out with the people I hung out with?

I've come to understand that, from about the age of fourteen, when I started to mess up, the catalysts were my loneliness and my complete lack of self-esteem/self-confidence. Every time I returned to the group I was with, using and dealing drugs again, there was at least some vague sense of belonging. But the most important element was when I was using, I was numb. I didn't feel my grief, my guilt; I didn't have to feel my crippling lack of self-esteem. I could simply stay in my drug-addled world.

Deanna

My firstborn, Deanna, though perfect in every way, had complications at birth. My water began leaking two days before I went into labor, and because of this, my baby contracted an infection in utero. She had to stay in the hospital for two weeks.

Even though I did not feel connected to my baby when she was growing inside of me, after she was born, I immediately started feeling connected to her. I was proud to be Deanna's mother. I wanted to be with my baby every moment; I needed her and, also, believed she needed me. Those first two weeks in the hospital, when I couldn't bring her home because she was so sick, made me very sad.

Deanna's father's mother had been close to our family for many years and went with me to the hospital the first time I visited my baby. The first thing we recognized was that she had been neglected. She had not been properly cared for, not properly cleaned. She had on a dirty diaper. It was pure negligence. But, my friend, her grandmother, didn't play around. She got on those nurses and said in no uncertain terms, "The next time we come here, y'all better be taking care of her."

I cried when I saw Deanna because she looked neglected and in need of love. I visited her every day for two weeks, and was taught how to hold her and change her, but, interestingly enough, I did not need to be taught how to love her. I simply did. Finally, I was allowed to bring her home. She was so small; she was like a little doll.

My love for Deanna made me try to be the best mother I could be. In the beginning, when I brought her home, I was terrified as all outdoors. I didn't know anything about becoming a mother. Yes, I was raised by a loving mother who truly cared for me to the best of her ability, but of course, I never saw her do this with infants. I had never seen any family, friends, or neighbors care for infants or toddlers. What a time this was in my life.

Even so, I was learning how to pick her up properly, and learning how to bathe her, diaper her, and provide her with all the sustenance she needed. To say that I was ill-equipped is an understatement. Even though my mother and the nurses were teaching me and trying to help me, I simply didn't trust myself. I wasn't confident enough to know that I could properly care for Deanna. I was constantly living in fear that I was incapable of being a mother to this perfect human being. It was all coming at me so very, very fast. I was overwhelmed. The fear almost completely paralyzed me.

Deanna was seven or eight months old when one night I looked in on her in the crib and she just didn't look right. She was listless, wasn't moving, and didn't want to eat. So, I called my mother, who was working, and she said, "Get a jitney and take her to the hospital." I wrapped her up, went downstairs, and, holding Deanna with my right arm, hailed a jitney with my left.

I arrived at the hospital and told the nurses at the emergency desk my baby wasn't well. They took her from me and found that she had a very high fever—103 to 104 degrees. So they immediately put her into an ice bath. Once they got her temperature down, they released her to me and said to go back home. I did as I was told. I didn't ask, "What is wrong with her? Doesn't she need to stay longer? Shouldn't she have more tests?" They simply said, "Your baby can go home now."

The next morning, she was just lying there and actually looked dead, and I was terrified. So, I took her back to the hospital. This time, they paid more attention and told me she needed a spinal tap.

Of course, I didn't know what that was, and it sounded so scary. I said, "I'm only sixteen, I don't know what you need to do to her—I don't know anything." They then asked, "Is there anyone that you can call?"

I said, "Yes, my mama." It was about eight in the morning, and I woke her up. As you'll recall, she worked nights. We spoke for a moment—she said, "I'll be right there." Half an hour later, she was holding me while I was shaking and crying as the doctor explained to my mother what was wrong and what they needed to do. After Mama spoke with them, she, in turn, explained everything to me.

When they were examining Deanna, they asked me to leave the room, but my mother stayed while they performed the spinal tap on her. It hurt my baby so much, I could hear her screams in the waiting room, which sent shudders through me. Following the examination, they came out and told me she had contracted spinal meningitis and had to remain in the hospital under quarantine.

Once again, my beautiful little baby was separated from me. Once again, I visited her every day. Sometimes my mother and father came, sometimes I was there by myself. Holding her and stroking her soft, baby skin, comforting her fragile body, nurtured me as much as it did Deanna.

It's a bit of an oxymoron to me. As I've said, I was so emotionally immature. I dropped out of school and still felt like a child myself: insecure, lacking any real confidence; yet, I had innate maternal instincts that enabled me to do three very important things that Tuesday night when I recognized there was something desperately wrong with my baby.

As I had been bonding with her over all those months, I immediately knew I needed to do something *right away.* So, first, I took control. Next, I had the presence of mind to call my mother. Third, no matter how traumatized I was, I was not paralyzed and had the courage to take immediate action, which saved her life.

Another critical health crisis with one of my children came a few years later following the birth of my fourth child, Dwyane Jr. When he was three years old, he contracted such a serious ear infection that he had to be hospitalized for two weeks—and, as with Deanna's life-threatening moment, except for the loving support of my mom who was there every day at the hospital, I had to also handle this crisis on my own.

My son's ear infection was so severe that it caused a kind of short-circuit in his brain. The ear infection threw off his equilibrium, and he also lost certain bodily functions, had to wear diapers, and struggled to learn to walk again. Of course, I didn't know at this time that God was preparing Dwyane Jr. to be a warrior—to be the champion he has become, overcoming any obstacle, no matter how severe.

When, once again, I had to rush my child to the hospital, my emotions were all over the place. At this point, I was a true drug addict and alcoholic. I was thirty-one years old, confronting the guilt of being the type of mother I was, seeing my baby in agony in the hospital, and I vividly remember asking God not to take him from me. Clearly, God heard my prayer.

Keisha, Tragil, Dwyane Jr.

Following Deanna's birth, the doctors started me on birth control pills, but my body rejected them. Then, they taught me how to use and encouraged me to use a diaphragm, but my body wouldn't tolerate that either.

When Deanna was about a year and a half old and I was sixteen or seventeen, I met the boy who was to become the father of my second daughter, Keisha. He and Deanna's father were friends. He lived with his sister in a building around the corner from where I lived with my mother.

I had returned to Dunbar High School and took the bus each day to get there. One day, he was in the window of his apartment and called out to me as I passed by on my way to the bus stop, "Hey, where you goin'?" I said, "I'm going to school." Then, he said, "Come here for a minute."

So, I went over—he invited me upstairs where we talked for quite a while, then he offered me a joint. Once I smoked that joint, I didn't go to school. We simply sat and talked for the next few hours.

After that fateful day, I never went back to high school, even though each day my mother thought I was going to school. Instead, I went to his apartment and hung out all day.

A few weeks after we began meeting regularly, he came on to me for the first time, sweet-talking me, telling me how pretty I always looked and how he had always liked me. One thing led to another, and once again, it became all about the sex, and I acquiesced—but it didn't mean anything to me either physically or emotionally. We were physically intimate a few more times, but there was never an emotional connection for me—and, when I told him I was pregnant, he immediately became very cold toward me.

After his reaction, once again, I felt like a fool. I felt used and refused to feel used anymore. So, I ended the relationship—but a few months later, he begged me to come back. I told him, "No," because the way he treated me felt like he kicked me to the curb. There'd never been any love, there had never been any true emotional connection; I was just giving myself to him in the heat of being upset with Deanna's father, my first love.

As I've already said, I was so terrified when I felt my first child growing inside of me, but I was thrilled to discover that, as my second child began to blossom within, I was not terrified. I was excited and actually looking forward to my baby's birth.

Two and a half years after I had Deanna and at eighteen years old, I gave birth to my second daughter, Keisha, on September 30, 1973. I was at home with my family when I went into labor around noon, and labor began accelerating very quickly, so much so that my mother said, "Get to the hospital right now, and I'll meet you there," as she was not yet dressed and ready to go with me.

My family called a cab for me, but didn't accompany me. It was just the cab driver and me, and all the way there, I was in excruciating pain. I tried to be "an adult" and not scream out in agony, but my contractions hurt a lot. The ride lasted about thirty minutes, and once we arrived at the emergency entrance, the pain became much worse as my baby was already coming.

I somehow managed to pay the cab driver, but I remember latching on to him to help stabilize me while, at the same time, he tried to pull away, saying, "Let me go! Let me go!" And I was crying, "No, no."

Somebody from within the hospital saw my struggle and immediately brought out a wheelchair and wheeled me into the emergency room. They put me on a gurney and wheeled me into an examination room where they discovered that my baby was already crowning. They said, "Oh my God, she's coming!" and, at that same moment, my water broke.

I was in such pain, and just as I had grabbed the cab driver, I reached out and grabbed a nurse's arm for security, and she then hit me on my hand. I shouted at her, "Why did you hit me?" The doctors saw this and immediately sent her out of the room. Mom still hadn't arrived when they took me into the delivery room.

Keisha was born in a hurry! She came out hollering and screaming, and all that pain that I had been feeling for the last few hours was immediately a distant memory because the moment they put her on my chest, it felt so wonderful. She was beautiful, had a head full of hair, and, even as fussy as she was, it was love at first sight.

My older sister Rosalyn didn't have children of her own, and, prior to Keisha's birth, she asked if I would give her my baby when my second child was born, and I promised to do so.

This may seem like a very odd thing to do. In creating these memoirs, I shared this with a friend who said, "Jolinda, this is an example of your pure love. You didn't offer your child because you didn't want to raise two children or abandon your child in any way. You offered your child because your sister did not have one, and out of your love for her and her desire to have her own family, you simply told her she could have your baby and raise your baby as her own. It was a remarkable act of generosity."

I had never thought about it in this way, but he was right. I loved Rosalyn so much, I wanted her to be happy and more complete. But, when I saw Keisha, the immediacy of my love for her was so strong, I simply could not release her to my sister.

When Rosalyn came over with new clothes for "our baby," ready to take Keisha home, I told her I had changed my mind. She said, "But you promised!" I said, "I know, but I can't give my daughter away." When we sat and talked it over for a few minutes, she understood and forgave me. When she looked at Keisha, she simply said, "I understand, Jolinda."

A few years later, Rosalyn went on to have her own children. Her family was raised in a home with a backyard where we had barbecues, and our whole family used to go over there a lot. Before I got lost on drugs, I hung out with her more than with anyone else.

It was 1973. I was nineteen when I first saw Dwyane Wade, "the boy next door." Right from the beginning, I was attracted to Dwyane. Even though we lived on the same block, I didn't know him at all, and he didn't even know I existed.

From my apartment window, I used to see him skateboarding up and down the block, and he was always smiling. When I looked at that smile, I thought he had the prettiest teeth. I remember saying, "Hmm! He'd make some pretty babies." He was still in high school. I was nineteen, two and a half years older, and pregnant.

In 1974, when Big Wade came into the picture, I was working in a factory and selling drugs on the side, earning enough to support my children. I was twenty and Dwyane was still in high school. Keisha was one, and I was living at 54th and Calumet.

When Dwyane and I began dating, his mother put him out, and he came to live with Deanna, Keisha, and me. Dwyane immediately became a part of our lives. From my apartment, we then moved into a two-bedroom apartment, but only stayed there a year. We didn't know it at the time we moved in, but this apartment was in a condemned, rat-infested building. I swear these rats were as big as cats. When we moved in, we were young and needed a place to live—and we didn't know any better.

After that year, we needed to move out because we were concerned the rats would harm our children. We then found a real apartment west of there, off of Halsted, and stayed until 1976 when Dwyane enlisted in the army.

When Deanna was born, I had an understanding with her father that he could be in her life, and I kept the same kind of agreement with Keisha's father. I had learned that from my mother—she kept our fathers in our lives even though they ceased being in hers. So, I didn't see any reason to exclude my daughters' fathers from their lives. Their fathers wanted to meet Big Wade to check him out once he moved in with me. They were all cool with each other. There was a mutual respect among all of us, and there was no judgment.

In 1976, we moved into our own apartment. I was twenty-two and Big Wade was nineteen. Shortly after he moved in, we had a very bad falling out. He left. A few months later, we decided to get back together and were married in 1977. On the day we were married, we left the courthouse arguing, and I was ready to get an immediate annulment.

I don't know exactly why we decided to marry, although I later found out that Dwyane said he married me out of respect for me. We were and still are very, very good friends.

Dwyane was young; we were both young and partying people, just doing what we thought we were supposed to do when in a relationship. Big Wade was also a very responsible young man. After graduating from high school, he worked at a regular job and then, at nineteen, decided to join the army. He was looking for direction and stability in life. When he came into my life, I had two kids already, and he contributed to their support and really cared about Deanna, Keisha, and me. Big Wade was also a really good athlete. He played basketball, football, baseball—even boxed. He always loved sports.

In 1976, I found out that I was pregnant with my third child. Dwyane was now stationed in Panama while I was still living in Chicago. On July 18, 1977, when I was twenty-two years old, I gave birth to my third daughter, Tragil.

Big Wade was twenty-three when he was honorably discharged from the army in 1981 after serving four years. We discussed the idea that he might reenlist, but I didn't want to go back in with him. Once again, we were on good terms and decided to make our marriage work. Then, I became pregnant with my fourth baby.

In 1982, when I was twenty-eight, my last child, our son, was born. As with my three daughters, his birth day was *intense* and unexpected. I was at my doctor's appointment for my regular examination. As he examined me, he calmly said, "You're going to have this child today."

"I can't—I'm not due yet. I haven't even packed my suitcase."

He replied, "I want you to go directly from here to the University of Illinois Medical Center." He didn't want me to go to Michael Reese Hospital, the same hospital where my other three children were born, because there were complications, and, as I was high risk, he wanted me to get the best care possible. He called ahead to the hospital and told me, "Tell the cab driver to take you to the main entrance."

I did as I was told and didn't even have time to go home and pack. Once again, I hailed a cab and, all by myself, headed off to the hospital—just as I had with Keisha and Tragil. When I arrived at the main entrance and got myself into the hospital, they were ready for me—wheeled me right into delivery, put me on the table, and told me I was going to have a cesarean section. I didn't even know what that was. They induced labor in order to perform the C-section. My other three children were born naturally, but my fourth could not be.

When I got to the hospital, I overcame all that was going on for me physically and emotionally, and called my husband, who worked as a driver for a transportation company called Alexander Smith, to tell him I was in labor. He left work and was at the hospital when I was in the recovery room. Dwyane said I could name the baby, and I had all kinds of really interesting names for him, but I finally chose to name him Dwyane Wade Jr.

In the recovery room, I was drifting in and out of the anesthetic. In one lucid moment before going back to sleep, they placed my son in my arms, and I heard a Voice from within me say the word "Blessing." I didn't yet know God's voice, so I did not know where the sound was coming from—I simply heard the Voice say, "Blessing," and went back to sleep.

A Moment Of Reflection

Since the birth of my first child, Deanna, I have never felt confident as a parent. Then, after Big Wade and I divorced and my addictions took over, I really felt as though I was always parenting on eggshells.

Even though I had little confidence in myself as a mother, I did have confidence in my ability to give my children as much love as I could—and that was a lot. I had nothing else, but I had that. The desire to be a better mama was always there. It was a deep, deep yearning that, in fact, helped keep me alive and helped guide me toward salvation.

I loved my children a lot, but when I reflect on this period of my life, I also beat myself up for being such a mess as a mother. But, someone once told me, "Jolinda, you gave them something at the beginning of their lives that no one or nothing could take from them, which was love. You showed them what love felt like; even through your addiction, it was love."

From this one insight, I began to understand and recognize that I definitely had maternal instincts, which were a combination of some innate ability I had been unaware of and, also, what I now realize I had learned from experiencing my mother care for all of us.

However, over the next couple of decades, during my addiction, my children, along with my mother, loved, cared for, and looked out for me as much or more at times than I did for them. Their unconditional love and acceptance of my plight enabled me, ultimately, to become the parent they deserved.

In 1982, three or four months after Dwyane Jr. was born, Big Wade and I started to go out partying again, taking a little sip here and there—then everything started back up again. However, with Big Wade, we were always doing it casually, recreationally, and it was limited.

Several months later, Big Wade and I decided to separate. We had been together for eight years, but we no longer worked well together. Sometimes in our relationship, there were moments when I didn't feel emotionally safe. Part of it came from the way Big Wade would occasionally treat me, which I didn't like, but, truth be told, another reason was that, at the deepest of levels, I was also afraid to let anyone in.

I had survived to this point in my life by "keeping my guard up" and not allowing anyone to penetrate my shield so that I could "never be hurt." But, emotionally, I was hurt. But that was not only on Dwyane, it was also on me. Sometime later, after we'd been separated, we did mend our friendship.

When I left Dwyane Jr.'s dad, I returned to my mom's home, taking my four children with me, and continued on the path I had previously been on with my old friends who were doing and dealing drugs. I was twenty-eight years old.

Chapter 3

Addiction—
Drugs, Alcohol, And Fear
The Impact On My Life
And My Children's Lives

Before continuing with my personal narrative, I want first to set the backdrop for the story of my life as it unfolded within the context of this time.

The 1960s and '70s were an unprecedented period of social activism and the push for change. President John F. Kennedy's Peace Corps helped open the door to peace movements in America. Then, fueled by opposition to America's military involvement in Vietnam, the era was marked by organized nationwide protest movements designed to awaken the nation to the systemic racism and inequality in our country and help to establish greater equal rights and opportunities for all disenfranchised citizens.

Dr. Martin Luther King Jr.'s civil rights movement forged a pivotal role both as a cause for social justice and as a model for peaceful protests and marches. Among the more prominent of those other quasi-political movements were CORE, the Congress on Racial Equality; the Black

Panthers; the gay rights movement; the women's liberation movement, which was driven by the efforts of Gloria Steinem, among other leading feminists; and more.

All of this together formed a counterculture challenging America's traditional norm and, out of this extraordinary cultural melting pot, drugs, for the first time in American history, emerged as a mainstream pastime. LSD and other psychedelic drugs, along with marijuana, cocaine, hashish, and even heroin, became infused in every aspect of our popular culture, including film, literature, art, and music. Artists across all genres, who famously and infamously used and abused drugs, became media celebrities, all of which helped popularize drug use.

In the process, artistic expression based on drug experiences created new artistic movements, such as pop art popularized by Andy Warhol. In pop music, this was the period of the Beatles, Motown, and the popularization of folk music led by the Kingston Trio, Peter, Paul, and Mary, Bob Dylan, and Joan Baez. It was the era as well of the emergence of hard rock bands, including the Rolling Stones, the Grateful Dead, and Jimi Hendrix, who lived and sang about their drug-fueled lives.

Drugs were ubiquitous. Even though drugs remained illegal, they became socially sanctioned, and their availability proliferated in all strata of our society; rich, poor, young, and old began to use them recreationally.

Drugs do not discriminate.

Prior to this, drugs had always been a personal and private affair, kept behind closed doors. Still, as far back as the late nineteenth century, Sir Arthur Conan Doyle wrote about Sherlock Holmes's cocaine habit. During the nineteenth century, laudanum, which was an opium derivative, as well as cocaine, were prescribed to "cure" all types of ailments. In 1880, when it was first marketed, the original Coca-Cola contained cocaine as one of its ingredients.

Historically, however, alcohol had been the most widely available, socially acceptable, mainstream, recreational drug of choice. During the

'60s and '70s, because it was legal, it continued to be used and abused as well.

During the counterculture revolution of the '60s, the popularization of marijuana and hard drugs initially spread primarily on college campuses nationwide, and then, its tentacles reached into the larger cities and suburban communities.

As during Prohibition in the 1920s, when alcohol was forced underground, the spread of illegal drugs was swiftly followed by organized crime taking over its production and distribution, leading to violent gang warfare over territorial disputes.

Three generations later, when illegal drugs were in demand, organized crime again commandeered these same communities—including the South Side of Chicago, where I grew up. The illicit drug trade was everywhere; drugs were sold openly on street corners in the neighborhoods in which I grew up and on the blocks where I walked to school.

For the first time, drugs even became available on junior high and high school campuses, where I was introduced to them in junior high school. This is where my story continues.

My Story

Fear is the path to the dark side. Fear leads to anger.
Anger leads to hate. Hate leads to suffering.
GEORGE LUCAS, IN *STAR WARS: EPISODE I—THE PHANTOM MENACE*

Fear is a disease that eats away at logic
and makes man inhuman.
MARIAN ANDERSON

I came across these two quotations while doing research in preparation for my memoir. They very clearly encapsulate the grip that fear had on me and how, if left unchecked, can dehumanize people.

In 1982, when I moved back to live with Mom, she was living in a four-bedroom apartment at Fifty-Ninth and Prairie with my little brother Roderick and one of our nephews. My mother's house was always open for anyone who needed a place to stay. She would just open the doors for all of us. This was also the apartment where I was living when both Keisha and Tragil were born, and it was where I lived when I met Big Wade.

In 1982, Deanna was eleven, almost twelve; Keisha was nine, almost ten; Tragil was five, and Dwyane was a baby, about six months old. Keisha often slept on the sofa or stayed with her father's family, but the rest of us slept together in one bedroom.

This was also the time when my life began to spiral out of control. I had become close to my neighbors from Fortieth Street when we all lived there. They also sold drugs on Fortieth Street, but at this point, I wasn't selling drugs. They then moved to Fifty-Ninth Street into the same building I lived in. They lived on the first floor, and we lived on the third floor. They began using their apartment as a place to sell drugs and worked the streets as well.

I saw them selling weed, pills, and all that stuff, and asked how much money they made, because I was looking to bring in additional income, because my children's fathers were providing no additional support. When Big Wade and I separated, I applied for Aid to Families with Dependent Children (AFDC) and the government garnished a portion of his wages, and I received $100 a month from him.

The additional welfare subsidy helped me support my other children. And, just as my mother never asked the fathers of my siblings and me to provide any additional support, I never asked my children's fathers either. Although I was able to supplement the AFDC with my work at the One Stop grocery store in our neighborhood, I simply could not effectively support all of us on my income.

So, eventually, I made the decision to begin selling drugs and became connected with my drug-dealing neighbors, and started selling drugs on Fifty-Ninth Street. My neighbors hooked me up with their supplier, and I began dealing weed and pills, while also using these and other products on the side. I will always mark 1982 as the beginning of the next chapter of my life, when selling drugs and that whole lifestyle began to permeate every aspect of my life.

When I was with Mama, I never sold out of the building; I just sold drugs out on the street. She knew I was dealing, but she never questioned it. I began having real financial success selling drugs. All of my sources of income enabled me to eventually get my own apartment on the first floor in the same building. The reason I wanted the apartment was simply to have a place to live. However, shortly after moving in, I began selling drugs out of my apartment in addition to selling them on the street.

By 1984, I had been dealing and using for about a year and a half. My children were young and still lived with me. I was their primary parent, and took care of them and provided for them. I made sure they had their own food stamps. They told me when I needed to go to their school for parent conferences or any events. We would enjoy watching television sitting together on the sofa in our living room.

When Tragil was around ten, she took an interest in cooking, so I began to teach her; and, at seven, Dwyane always wanted to do what Tragil was doing. So, I began teaching them both how to cook. A favorite meal we liked to prepare was rice from scratch, which I taught to Dwyane. I didn't allow Dwyane to use a knife, but I did teach Tragil how to use a knife to slice and dice onions and peppers. Given my circumstances, I was doing all I could to be the best mother possible.

However, my drug abuse was so bad that I needed drugs before I needed food. I couldn't even eat unless I had dope in me, and once I had the dope in me, then alcohol followed. Because my children lived with me, I knew I couldn't just lay in my bed and be sick because their needs, to the best of my ability, always had to come before mine. And, as far as meals were concerned, even though I wouldn't necessarily eat, I made sure that they did.

During the day, they'd go to my mother—she was the strength of our family. When Dwyane was small, he actually called her his "Mom." Deanna wasn't always around as she would go and hang with the friends she'd made in the projects.

I kept Tragil and Dwyane together. Because Tragil was older, she'd often look out for him, which is why they continue to be so very close. I got this from my mother, because she used to make us take care of one another while she worked. So, it was natural for me to ask Tragil to, when necessary, take care of Dwyane as well.

I was locked in a vicious cycle: I needed to use drugs so I wouldn't get sick and be unable to take care of my children. And, while in my full-blown habit, whenever I went to see my mother or my children, I always wanted them to see me "at my best." Maintaining this facade meant that I had to continue shooting up whenever I was going to be with them. In chapter 2, where I spoke about Dwyane being hospitalized with a serious ear infection, whenever I went to see him, I first needed to put heroin into my bloodstream. Without the heroin, I would risk letting him see me as I would be without it—very sick from the painful withdrawal.

The kind of person I became when I didn't have drugs was reflected in my appearance. I looked horrible. When I had the drugs, I'd wash myself up, comb my hair, and look presentable for my children. Even though they knew what was happening to me, I didn't want them to see me looking "horrible." I was trying to hold on to as much of me as I could. As I say in many different ways throughout this memoir, they really kept me alive because I knew I had to take care of them.

During 1985, I obtained the drugs I needed from my friends and, also, ultimately from a young man named Greg I had casually met one night in the Jamaica Club, a lounge where my friends and I hung out.

Although I didn't know it at the time, he had just been released from jail. He was hanging out with another group and they were making a lot of noise. I looked over and saw this very attractive, dark-skinned young man who had very beautiful hair. Beyond that, I paid no attention as I was heading out to go to the store to buy a bottle of liquor to sneak into the bar so that we wouldn't have to spend any more money there. We would just pour it from the bottle into our glasses.

Coincidentally, Greg came into the store while I was there and was standing a little way away from me, looking at me, smiling. Turns out his friends also wanted him to go to the store to buy some liquor for them. We briefly looked at each other—he smiled and I smiled back. Once again, a man's smile hooked me.

We each bought what we came for and, separately, returned to the lounge. Then, we wound up seeing each other again about a week later, back at the lounge, and that's when we began speaking.

As I add up the years, Greg entered my life when I was about thirty years old and disappeared from the story in 1999. We began living together on and off in my first-floor apartment with my children for the next few years. These ten years were the most volatile of my life, but sharing this story will have to wait for the next chapter.

Greg and I were street workers, so we'd get packs and, when we got packs from the suppliers, they gave us ours off the top. When we sold everything, we got our pay at the end of the night. This was how I was able to keep up my habit. Also, I was on public assistance and, whenever I got the monthly check, first I made sure that my children had everything they needed—food, clothes, materials for school—then I would also spend some of it on drugs to support my addiction. When

I worked at One Stop, I spent my salary on my children and also spent some for myself. But with all this, I still never got ahead.

Even though the drug world I lived in was a very dangerous one, I never felt threatened by any of the suppliers I dealt with, but Greg was another story. He would "mess over the people's products"—in other words, he would get high and spend the money he was supposed to deliver to our suppliers, and trust me, these were big-time drug dealers. They would occasionally come looking for him and, since I was so close by, they came looking for both of us. However, God protected me because the dealers didn't see me as the threat; they only wanted him.

I believe this was another reason I wasn't beaten up or even killed. Living in this world, I didn't have time to be scared. I actually never really thought about it. I was an addict. Another reason I wasn't afraid was my own sense of shame, which made me feel they would say to one another, "Don't bother with her." In my mind, I was just someone I called "the thing."

In my mid-thirties, I didn't care whether I lived or died. There were countless times, countless nights, that I hated myself even more than I would ever have thought possible and was so ashamed of who I had become—this emaciated, horrible-looking person.

In spite of the terrible life I was trapped in, once I fixed my hair and put on clean clothes, I cleaned up pretty good. However, I was also fooling myself because people who knew me, people who loved me—my mother, my children, my siblings—knew there was something very, very wrong with me. But the other people who were around me were just like me, so none of us really noticed or cared what we looked like when we were with one another. By this time, my drug of choice was heroin.

This was my reality.

I remember one particular time when the people we hung out with came over to the house, and we were in the front part of the house, drinking and already high on dope. Deanna was about fifteen at this time and, one afternoon, she was in her room when one of the young men I was partying with saw her and said, "Ooh, your kid's sure growin' up." And I stopped and looked at him with a rage in my eyes and a roar in my voice and said, "If you ever look at my child at any time, in any way, like that again, you'll meet a side of me you don't want to meet. Don't look at my children like that ever again." And, I physically put him out of the house, telling him I never wanted him around my children again.

This was another moment in my life when the lioness in me awakened. I will describe her roar a few other times in these pages, but this was the first time I was called on to literally and physically protect my children.

Greg and I continued to live together. But about a year into our relationship, his violent nature began to emerge, but only directed toward me—never toward my children. I continued to always draw the proverbial "line in the sand" that I dared anyone to cross when it came to them. I was still that person who would lose my mind if anyone even looked inappropriately at my children. Sometimes I would kick Greg out of the house when I recognized his volcanic behavior, which often frightened Tragil and Dwyane.

One time after I had kicked him out, he found a way in through a window in their bedroom and my children were really scared.

Previously, an older woman in our building had told me how to protect myself from intruders by creating a concoction containing ammonia and keeping it by the door. Should I, as a single mom, ever have to confront one of these intruders, I should simply throw it into their eyes.

So, on that day when Greg had climbed in through their bedroom window and I saw the terror on my children's faces, I picked up the ammonia and said, "You're going to get out of here! I don't want you scaring my children anymore," and I threw the container in his face.

He started screaming, "I can't see. I can't see."

Then, I picked up a two-by-four I also kept by the door and said, "You're going to see your way out of here!" The kids opened up the door, and we cast him out. My children—Deanna, Tragil, and Dwyane—and I literally, physically, pushed him out the door.

After that, my mom and my children were in fear for me to even go to the corner store because of what I did to Greg. For days, Mom wouldn't let me go out of the apartment. One day, I said to Mom, "I'm tired of sitting on this porch worried about what he is going to do. So, I'm going to the store to buy a bottle of Wild Irish Rose red wine. If something's going to happen, it's going to happen. I can't sit here in fear anymore. I just can't do it."

So, I walked up the street to the store by myself. My mom was so worried that she got word to the family that I was going there on my own. I didn't know this but my family followed me there. I went into the store and ordered a pint of wine.

Somebody ran in and said, "Greg's out there." I'm not going to tell you that my heart didn't go boom, boom, boom, boom, as I didn't know what was going to happen.

But I simply said, "Oh well," grabbed my bottle, walked out of the store, and saw him standing nearby.

His eyes were really messed up—and he said, "B———, you got a lotta nerve comin' up here. I'm gonna kill you." He was ready to hurt me.

By this time, my niece and her friends came out of nowhere and said, "You talkin' about takin' her down, you gotta take us down too." This force of people came on him and he ran.

The fear just left me, and I walked home.

Throughout all the years of our life together, I'd kick him out, let him back in—kick him out and eventually let him back into my life. One of the reasons I continued this "revolving door" relationship with Greg was that, with him, I didn't have to do the things other people had to do to get drugs, as he supplied me with them. In addition, he would occasionally do some kind things when he bought clothes for my children and contributed money for food.

Addictions: My Origin Story

Looking back on it now, it all began when I was a young child sheltered from my friends because I contracted rheumatic fever. My mother never explained to me why I couldn't go out and play or live a normal life, which left me to question what was wrong with me. I know now there was nothing wrong with me besides having had rheumatic fever, but I was simply lonely—very lonely.

However, as I grew older, the idea that there was something wrong with me led to the cataclysmic choices I began to make when I was fourteen. Because of this belief and without anyone to help me understand what was going on, I always felt I never fit in. Even after I recovered from rheumatic fever, the conviction that there was something wrong with me, not because of my illness but because of who I was, caused me to miss out on having a normal childhood. While my friends were socializing, running around, playing games, I was living in my isolated world, shut out from everyone.

In writing this paragraph, I find myself attempting to come to grips with the choices I made and why I made them. Until the age of fourteen, I had been considered a model student, the one most likely to succeed, but for some reason, that was not enough for me. I wanted to be accepted by my peers; I wanted to be part of the group, but I suspect that was, in part, because I never had the opportunity to have that sense of belonging, being part of something, when I was a younger child.

I realize now that I was an extraordinarily sensitive young girl and teenager, a model student, and intellectually bright. But, as I've already said, I never felt that I could belong *anywhere*. So, when I was fourteen and presented with options as to what clique I wanted to join, I chose the one where the girls were pushing boundaries, not following social norms but creating their own rules. Observing these girls being a bit more defiant than other girls—that became the group I wanted to belong to.

Up until this time, I was always the "good girl" following the rules, never taking risks. I had never challenged concepts of right and wrong. I also never had role models that I could emulate. My teachers were not my role models, they were my teachers. So, my role models became "the bad girls" who always looked like they were having a good time, and they let me become part of their group.

Another insight revealed by my reflections and research in preparation for writing my story—and, my family doesn't mind my sharing this—is that, along with my mother's partying, my other family members, to lesser or greater degrees, were also using drugs and drinking, and it was rampant throughout the neighborhood we lived in as well—all of it contributed to my sense that this was *normal.*

Another fascinating discovery was my curiosity. When my mother and her friends partied in our home, everyone seemed to be jolly—and I wanted to *feel jolly* just like them. I now recognize that I saw the jolliness, the good times everyone was having, as a way of relieving my abject loneliness and the sense of never fitting in. Perhaps I thought that partying would make me feel part of the group, which meant I would no longer feel so alone.

In my mid-teens, when school friends offered drugs, I experimented. My point in part is, whether observing it among my family or with my school friends, drugs and alcohol were always a part of my life.

Of course, I never knew that all of this could ever harm me in any way. No one ever told me this was harmful. It was just the world in which I lived. My mom's side of the family drank, and my dad's side of the family drank. Everyone around me drank and used recreational drugs. That's just the way it was.

Alcohol and drugs have always been a place of comfort and odd security for me. Once I used drugs or alcohol, I knew exactly how I was going to feel and how I would respond to this big world that I was always so very uncomfortable in.

I knew I was making really terrible choices. But even though I was the mother of four beautiful children, living with my mother and the rest of my family by my side, I continued to make terrible choices.

I was an addict and could not stop.

When I was in the drug world, drugs numbed me to the reality of my life. It was as though I lived in some perverse chrysalis cocooned from the rest of the world.

In addition, it made me feel like I was somebody. Except for creating my beautiful children, I felt I never did anything else right. I had nothing to offer society. I had dropped out of school, had gotten various jobs, but didn't succeed there either. So, the only thing that seemed to offer me any hope of livelihood was selling drugs.

Over the next several years of my addictions, I thought about leaving for the sake of my children and never—not once—never to save myself.

My siblings and I, who were abusing drugs and alcohol, knew we were breaking my mother's heart through the choices we made and the lifestyle we lived. She would often say to each of us something like, "I didn't raise you like that." In my case, I knew it broke her heart, especially to see me, for whom she had held out so much hope, become an addict, shooting drugs and all that. I would often hear her ask rhetorically, "What did I do wrong?"

And I would say, "It's not your fault, you did your very best. I did this to myself." But, throughout it all, not once did I think about how very badly I hurt my mother. I was only interested in being an addict. Except for my love for my children, nothing else mattered. Nothing else sustained me.

At this point, my life consisted of making terrible choices. I was an addict—I could not stop.

Big Wade And Surrendering My Children

Big Wade and I were still friends. He'd come by frequently, check on me, and we'd talk. He would also visit regularly with Tragil and Dwyane Jr. Just as my mom let our fathers visit us, I was the type of mom who didn't keep my kids from their fathers either.

Big Wade knew my lifestyle and what was happening to me. One day, in 1992, he came over and told me that he wanted to buy a house in Robbins, Illinois, and that the way he could get it was to show that his children lived with him. He showed me a document verifying that Dwyane Jr. and Tragil lived with him, asked me to sign it, and told me I would need to have it notarized.

My Mom told me, "Don't do it." She distrusted a lot of things. She said, "Don't put your name on it. It will come back and bite you."

But I was living with my cousin and didn't have a place for them to stay. I looked at it and felt that it was the best thing for my children. I did it out of pure love. So, I told Big Wade, "Yes, we'll do it,"—with the understanding that I could see my kids or get them whenever I wanted to.

This really severe life, this life with no future, no hope, lasted ten to twelve years. Out of my love for them, one by one, I *let my children go* as I wandered in the wilderness. After she came back from Big Wade's place, by the time I was thirty-nine, only Tragil still lived with me. Deanna was the first to leave when she joined a local gang at sixteen and went to live in the projects. Then, Keisha left to live with her paternal grandmother in Robbins, Illinois. Dwyane Jr. had already left with Big Wade.

In 1992, I released Dwyane Jr. to Big Wade. That's when I took a deep dive into what I now know was serious clinical depression. By 1993, I had already been in and out of jail a number of times, when it became necessary that I send Tragil away to my sister Rose in San Diego.

Then, it was just Greg and me. Some of the time we lived in various apartments, other times we were homeless, living in abandoned buildings.

I was using drugs every day, living with a man who violently abused me. I knew I had really messed up and didn't see any way out or any way back.

So, when I was separated from my children, whatever I had been doing to keep my feeble world together collapsed. I no longer felt like a failure—I *was* a failure and said, "What the heck." This capitulation, this giving up, sent me into an even deeper addiction. I was now experiencing hell on earth and carrying Satan on my back.

It would be a few more years before I could finally get *him* off my back.

Chapter 4

Prison–The First Time, Homelessness, Abuse, And My Awakening

A t this point in my life, the only thing that seemed to offer me any hope of a decent livelihood was selling drugs. In this period, while selling drugs, I was also in and out of jail, as I would occasionally get arrested right there on the street while dealing. Even though this was a precarious way to make a living, it did, at least, provide me with an adequate one.

From 1992, when I was thirty-eight, to 1994, it was a vicious cycle of arrest/jail, arrest/jail, arrest/jail. The first time, I was sent to Cook County Jail for a couple of months, followed by several of these types of episodes.

In 1993, I was caught selling drugs. When I came before the judge, because it was my first time, he placed me on probation. The next time, I was placed under house arrest. My cousin Barbara Jean, my mother's sister's only daughter, who passed in 2018, agreed to have me live in her home, which was in our same building. We called her B. J. or "Texas

Lady." B. J. was very important to me throughout my life. We were like cousin-sisters, and she was always there for me.

In 1994, when I was forty, I was arrested for the first time for both drug possession as well as selling drugs. I served two months—then, I went before a judge who put me on three years of probation. At the time of my hearing, the judge also warned me, "If I see you in my courtroom again, I will send you to prison."

I hadn't been in jail long enough before going on probation to break my drug habit. So, when I got out, I did what we all did—celebrated. I went back to the races.

I was forty when I hooked up again with my street friends who sold drugs. As I hadn't been able to obtain drugs for the couple of months I was in jail, I was suffering very painful withdrawals—I had chills, the shakes; I was sweating profusely and very nauseated. One day I went into the drug dealer's apartment to pick up rock cocaine, then went outside and began selling. I really needed a fix, but wasn't getting it. Because I hadn't been able to get a fix, I wasn't thinking straight.

This particular day, on the corner of Sixty-First Street, right off King Drive in Chicago, I saw a car parked out on the street, went up to it, and offered to sell rock cocaine to the passenger in the front seat.

It turned out the two men in the car were undercover police who had been watching me, and allowed me to sell to them, walk away, and get into my friend's car down the block. They then came over to me and said, "You're under arrest. You just sold to undercover police."

When they searched me, they found the rocks I still had on me, and got me for possession as well—then handcuffed me and took me to jail.

Not only was I feeling very sick not getting the fix I needed, I was also emotionally and physically numb; and, in that moment, I remembered the judge's words flashing through my mind, "If I see you in my courtroom again, I will send you to prison." And, as fate would have it, I was brought up before that very same judge, who was really offended because I didn't respect the fact that he had given me probation and I had abused that privilege. True to his word, he sentenced me to three years in prison.

From March through November 1994, I was incarcerated in Cook County Jail until I was finally sent to Dwight Correctional Center in Dwight, in Livingston County, Illinois.

My Spiritual Journey Begins

One day, in spite of my request not to have any of my children see me in jail, Big Wade brought Dwyane Jr. to see me. I was furious at Big Wade for bringing Dwyane Jr., who was just ten years old, to see me behind plexiglass.

I never wanted my son to see me like this. I remember leaving the visiting room and sobbing. I was crying so hard that officers came to me and asked, "What's the matter, Wade?"

And I said, "My son just saw me behind these bars. I never wanted him to see me like this." They actually tried to console me as I was going back to my cell.

I didn't have a roommate at the time, and it was time for mail call. When I returned to my cell, a postcard was waiting for me with no sender's name on it. I was surprised they even let it get sent up to me. All it said was, "Remember Job." And I'm like, "What is that?" *That's all that was on the card.*

I always had my Bible with me, and I turned to the story of Job and began to read it—and, once again, began weeping. One of the overarching messages of Job is that, despite one's challenges and suffering, Job speaks the message of great hope and reminds us that, no matter what our circumstances in life may be, we are loved faithfully and fervently by our God. Another important theme of Job is that despite all that he suffered, his faith in God never wavered, and God, of course, never abandoned him.

When I concluded the chapter and more fully understood the intent of the postcard that was sent to me, this time the tears that flowed came from my understanding—understanding that my anger at Big Wade and my overwhelming sadness that Dwyane Jr. saw me in prison were coming from my own fear and selfishness.

This recognition changed me. I was no longer angry. I thought to myself, "Perhaps God saw to it that this postcard would be sent to me this day."

As I was just beginning to be interested in God more, perhaps He knew that I was going to have to confront this moment that would lead me to deepen my understanding and my responsibility to myself.

Sometime later, Dwyane Jr. told me that he had asked his dad to see me. No one was to blame—except me for not being more patient and loving.

This was another opportunity for a profound discovery. Following my reading of Job and discovering a deeper understanding of why God wanted this meeting among Big Wade, Dwyane Jr., and me, led me to forgiveness and recognition that I'd actually never forgiven myself.

With this realization, I felt more worthy of God's love. With the beginnings of forgiveness, it was easier to love myself and embody all that I emotionally/intellectually/spiritually understood at this time to be true. Through self-love, not only did I grow in love for myself, but I actually even deepened my love for my beautiful mother, my children, and, truth be told, even God.

As I write this, I'm struck by the fact that these experiences—the confrontation with Big Wade, the miracle of the postcard—yes, even then, I had subtle inklings that miracles were possible.

The other poignant recognition for me was that this was the beginning of my wanting to grow more deeply in my connection with God. Where before I might have read occasionally from my Bible, now I began to spend more time reading it.

I wasn't always able to grasp the deeper meanings of what I was reading—that would come later. But something was beginning to percolate from within my consciousness that God did indeed love me even though, up to this moment, I did not feel deserving of love—God's or anyone else's.

For the first time, I actually felt God's unconditional love for me, which I had never experienced before. Now, twenty-two years later, I live in it every day of my life.

While in Cook County Jail, I decided one day to write to my dad. This began an ongoing written conversation that was very important for both of us. During my childhood, my dad had never lived with us and was not an everyday presence. So in my first letter, I told him that I forgave him for not always being there for us.

In this letter, I also reminded him of something he said when I was a young child that had stayed with me. I was about eleven or twelve when I overheard him tell my mother, "Mae Willie, you need to put that child away," because, as I've previously stated, he thought I was "crazy."

My dad apologized and was truly sorry that he had hurt me as deeply as he did. I asked him to forgive me as well. After that, we wrote to each other frequently, and it meant a lot for me to read his letters. Yes, he had been the father figure missing in my childhood, but now, he was willing to step up and be my dad.

While at Dwight, I met Iola Walker, who was assigned to become my roommate. She was 6'2", or maybe 6'3", and weighed over two hundred pounds—a large woman who commanded attention when she walked into a room.

While she was an intimidating presence, I came to discover a side of Iola that very few inmates knew. I found out that she was actually as sweet as she could be, but while in prison, you can never be sure who you are going to run into, so you have to keep your "face on."

She arrived about noon while I was downstairs talking to a few of the women. When they put her into my room, the guards told me, "You need to go up there and meet your roommate, Jolinda." So, I did.

As I was walking upstairs, I heard a woman shout out, "Who's in this room here?"

I told Iola, "That's me. I'm coming up there."

I then went up and introduced myself, and she said, with a bit of an edge in her voice, "I'm just letting you know I got a bottom bunk order." "Bottom bunk orders" were crucial for some people. If they had health issues, they were usually given that order. But some people had a way of getting orders—maybe for a favor. However, I liked being on the top bunk anyway. So, whenever a roommate arrived, they didn't have to worry about having a falling out over the bottom bunk.

I said, "With me, it's no problem. I like my top bunk anyway. Help yourself and, if you need me to help with anything, let me know." I was really polite with her.

She looked at me, though still not trusting, not knowing who in the heck I was. I understood that and was fine with it. I had been there for a while, and I was comfortable welcoming people because roommates always came and went.

After our first introduction, I went back downstairs so she could get settled in. I wanted her to have a feeling of privacy. As a keen observer, I had immediately sensed that she would appreciate my understanding that she needed a moment to adjust to the new environment and that she would also see that I was giving her the respect she deserved.

She noticed that I had a Bible sitting on my bed.

When I came back in and said, "Are you OK?" she said, "Yeah." She was set up nicely on the bottom bunk, reading her Bible. So, I got up on the top bunk. As I never believed in bothering anyone, I began reading my Bible and praying. I didn't know she was watching me.

About three that afternoon, she asked me, "What book are you reading?"

I told her, "My Bible."

She said, "Thank God, they put me in a room with somebody who loves Him." I don't know about "loving" Him because I didn't know Him—I just knew of Him. It brought peace—*a peaceful spirit.*

At this moment, I could both see and feel her relaxing because of what she felt from me and what she already saw in me.

She asked, "Do you understand everything you're reading?"

I said, "Not everything. I've just been reading."

She said, "If you want, can we read the Bible together?"

And, I said, "Sure." Because now I realized I had a roommate who wasn't going to cause any issues, because she clearly connected with Jesus. That's how our relationship began.

She began teaching me *the word* as she knew it, and when there was a call for church, we'd go to church together. I began spending a lot of time with Iola and learned a lot from her. Like me, she was an addict. She was in jail for forging checks and credit cards. We talked about street life as well. She only told me as much as she felt I needed to know, and I really didn't want to know that much.

That's one thing: when you're in prison, you really don't want to know everything that goes on with your roommate. That's all they are—roommates, and you know that you're really not going to see any of the inmates again once you leave prison.

We only spent three or four weeks as county jail roommates before Iola was released. Even though we were in jail, our time together was actually transformative for both of us. Following her release, I was then sent to Dwight, where I was put in quarantine for seven days before being moved again to Logan Correctional Center, a medium-security prison where I served out the remainder of my sentence.

As I entered prison for the first time, I was afraid and in awe, because I had never experienced prison before, and had no idea what to really expect. Friends had shared their experiences with me, but now I was about to undergo my own for the first time. As I was getting acclimated, I was very aware and observant.

I needed to learn what was expected of me and how the prison system worked. I needed to see what the guards, as well as the prisoners, expected of me. I was cognizant of needing to learn the "prison rules," learn about boundaries and expectations, and discover the various cliques.

In my first days in prison, I was learning to navigate my way around. I was creating an internal map that became invaluable to me and was very important in enabling me to live in this new world as safely and confidently as possible.

In crafting this memoir, one of the things I have truly loved is the opportunity to reflect and even get to know myself better. For example, writing the previous paragraphs brought me back to my childhood when I spent a lot of time observing others.

As you know, because I had contracted rheumatic fever, I could never fully participate in any group within the family or at school. It was as though I was always on the outside looking in. I couldn't run and play like other children, and because of this, I was treated differently. Because I always had this ongoing inner narrative, I felt I never quite belonged. I characterized myself as the observer, the one who was always a bit different.

Now, in those first days in prison, lifelong skills that I had been cultivating, such as being an observer, became invaluable to me.

When I arrived at Logan Correctional Center, I was housed with women from very diverse backgrounds. Even though I'd never been a "people person," in prison, there is no choice—you must adapt. The different women I had as roommates all worked out pretty well for me.

Before leaving Cook County jail, I, as a drug addict, was automatically put on a fast detox methadone program for fifteen days. It relieves the physical addiction, but mentally, you are still addicted. So, I got a rapid detox and decided I would never get drugs while I was in prison.

I told myself, "This is where I am now." Other women did pills but I never did as I wanted to be as fully present as possible—no drug or pill haze to disrupt my awareness. I was able to sustain this commitment to myself throughout my prison sentence.

Unfortunately, with addicts, it is not only the physical addiction but, equally if not more importantly, the mental and emotional addiction that is our craving. When we detox, our physical addiction may end, but I can assure you, not the mental and emotional. And, as the reader will learn, this reality became my reality upon my release from prison.

Believe it or not, there were a number of benefits to being in prison.

Perhaps the most important was learning discipline. On the streets, I never had structure or discipline as part of my life. The prison system enforced discipline on me. My mother had been a strong disciplinarian, and I was taught discipline at a young age. So, this was great! I really appreciated the structure that was provided and I flourished in it.

In this context, I want to mention a maxim that one of my mentors shared with me. He said, "Structure does not impinge; it liberates. Freedom without direction is chaos." Boy, is that true!

The structure consisted of: Number one, you have to get a job so you have something to do. Mine was to clean the women's restrooms.

We had to get up early, around six or seven, to be at our posts. The guards would come around to make sure that no one had escaped and that we were all where we were supposed to be. Then, each day, work began.

Sometimes a few of the inmates would be disrespectful, but I still did the job I was given. With the money we earned, we were allowed to go shopping in the prison commissary. I spent most of my money on stamped envelopes to write to my family and on candy, which we called "woo-woos and wham-whams."

During my first prison term in 1994, I hadn't wanted any visitors. However, while there, Deanna, my eldest daughter, who was twenty-four, had just had her first baby, my second grandchild, Michael. She really wanted me to meet Michael. So, she arranged to have someone who lived in her building and whose sister was in prison with me make an appointment for Michael and her to come visit.

I was at Logan Correctional Center at the time, and it was quite an ordeal for her to travel by bus to see me. It was so important to her that nothing was going to stop her.

When I saw them, it felt so good. Deanna was very happy to see me. We had a special bond, and she wanted me to have that same relationship with my grandson. Getting to speak with my daughter, hug her, and hold my grandson felt so good. It was a very important visit.

Throughout this book, I speak numerous times about my children's unconditional love for me. This is but one example that will help you more fully understand the depth of their love. It wasn't simply expressed through prayers or words but also unequivocally expressed through action.

Aside from this, all my other family interactions were through correspondence. Mom, Dad, all my siblings, and my other children wrote. I loved hearing from them and they loved hearing from me. They were my lifeline. Phone calls were expensive and I didn't want to put that on my mama or anyone else. So, I was good with just letters.

By this time, I had begun studying for the GED and reading the Bible regularly. In fact, I ended up leading Bible study for other inmates.

I had an inner knowing that God was guiding and protecting me in there, and when I was able to be within myself for a bit, I prayed and asked for God's help. I then began to clearly feel His presence. I *knew* He was there with me. This was 1994 to 1995, six years before my actual awakening—but this moment marks the beginning of that awareness in my life.

God had given me a great reputation while I was in prison. I was older than most of the guards, and there was actually only one guard who was disrespectful. God gave me favor with the lieutenants—the white shirts—and captains. They used to call me, "Preacher." They saw that I lived my life with God. It was nice and felt personal.

Several months into my sentence, Iola reappeared. I asked her, "What are you doing here?"

She simply said, "I got into more trouble." She was in another "house," not mine, so we'd only see each other during mealtimes.

I was not required to serve the full three years of my sentence; in November 1996, when I was released, I was credited with serving my full term and, so, was not even placed on parole. I was free—and I was drug-free. And, of course, I thought I would be able to remain drug-free forever so that I could begin a new chapter in my life.

I was given the privilege of being chosen for work release, a program designed to help former inmates transition back into society. However, because I was not required to report to a parole officer, I was also not eligible to receive any supportive services.

Even so, I didn't immediately return to the lifestyle I had been living for so many years on the streets. I did try, albeit in a somewhat robotic way, to continue the prison structure and do what I was taught in the drug rehabilitation program. I got up early, cleaned my room, and went to church with Mom. I stayed away from my old crew, but subliminally, I was still mentally and emotionally tied to the addictions and my old life.

I lived in the Westside Work Release Center in Chicago (now the Westside Health Authority's Community Re-Entry Center), not far from the old neighborhood where I used to live. I got a job as a telemarketer at night while going to school during the day to complete my GED. But my life was empty. I didn't have my children with me—not a single one—and, without them, there was no me. This, in turn, left me feeling helpless and hopeless. I could see no future.

About four or five months after being released, I decided to go visit my old neighborhood. I thought I had beaten my habit while in prison—but soon discovered I hadn't. I hadn't been buying drugs, so I had a pocketful of money, which I gave to friends who were "sick." While with them, I took a drink.

When you are living at the center, you are not allowed to drink and, of course, not use drugs. So, when I got back to the center, the supervisor smelled alcohol on my breath and said, "Now you know I could give you a violation, Jolinda, and send you back, but I'm going to give you another chance."

I said, "Thank you."

She said, "Don't ever come in here smellin' like that again." So, she gave me another chance, and the very next day, instead of getting on the train and going north to work, I went south (in more ways than one) and continued in the opposite direction, escaping from the work release center I had lived in for five months.

I returned to my old lifestyle. My thought process was that, at least in this life, I had been stuck in all those years; I knew what my present and future would be like. I knew the feeling I would get when I was high, and also knew how to behave in that world.

My addictions had been a part of me for so long that I didn't know any other way of behaving. And, because I was so empty, so bereft, and, even though I would still get to see my children, without the opportunity to be a parent to my children, I was simply lost.

One day, while hanging with some friends in my usual spot at Fifty-Ninth and Prairie, I saw Iola Walker come striding down the street. I was embarrassed because I had gone back to my old lifestyle and didn't want her to see me the way I now looked. She looked good, and I was dope sick.

She asked me about myself, and I told her the real story about my life on the street—that I was just out there. She hadn't known how devastating my life was because I hadn't shared that with her. In prison, you can be anyone you want, put up any kind of facade, but when she came into my *real life*, out on the street, living with an abuser, she saw the truth.

We wound up hanging out together and, because she was an IV drug user as well, we shared that lifestyle. I was her runner and went and got her her drugs. She had a lot of money, and I never asked where she got it. Then, I met the young man she was with, and her boyfriend met Greg. They liked each other, so as couples, we hung out together for a time.

After Iola brought me into her life, she began taking me around her neighborhood to different places where she would sell her merchandise, which included clothes and other miscellaneous items. Her customers would place orders, she would shop for them, then she'd make the deliveries.

One of her customers was the pastor of her church, and when we arrived, he showed us to his office, where she showed him the merchandise he had ordered, and he paid her. I saw all of that.

After a while, our lives diverged, and the last time I saw Iola was in Dwight Correctional Center during my second bit following my awakening, which I will discuss in a moment. She had been diagnosed with sickle cell anemia and was so thin. She said, "I'm going to die in here." And she did. She was only in her forties.

Iola was a very, very, very special individual, and I genuinely believe she was someone who was sent by God to teach me more about the Bible. That she did.

Homeless

The night after I left the work release center, I started drinking and using heroin, stayed out past curfew, and simply never went back to the center. Except for the clothes on my back and my purse, I left all of my possessions there. Afterward, the police issued two warrants for my arrest. They went into my neighborhood, talked to my sisters, my mother, my friends, but never found me.

I generally made it a point of staying away so my family and friends wouldn't be involved. The only ones who knew where I was were my sister B. B. and my late brother, Eddie.

I did not return to the center for four years, nine months, and six days, until Sunday, October 14, 2001, when the Holy Ghost said to me, "In December, you're going to turn yourself in." That miraculous story will wait until the next chapter. So, for four years, nine months, and six days I was on the run.

My time in prison was the longest time I had been drug- and alcohol-free in my entire life. The classes and support groups I attended in prison helped me for a while but, once I got out, I didn't continue with any of them. In retrospect, I certainly was not emotionally prepared, so fear very quickly began to take over, beginning with my fear of giving up my addictions. They had been such a fundamental part of my life for over twenty years, so when confronted with the reality of no longer using drugs and alcohol, I simply could not do it.

Decisions made at this moment in my life initially resulted in horrendous consequences. As you will see, I ultimately emerged victorious. Without the living hell of those four years, nine months, six days, my victory would have never been possible.

I am reminded here of the parable of Jonah, where God gave Jonah chance after chance after chance. Even though Jonah believed in himself, the people around him didn't believe in him. However, God believed in him and knew what was in his soul.

I wasn't swallowed by a great fish, but I was swallowed up by my addictions. By 1997, I was homeless. I lived from one place to the next—from a sidewalk to an abandoned building—on the run for almost five more years.

I chose to remain homeless. I could have stayed with different family members, but I chose not to, because I didn't want to *take the me that I had become* and all the problems and issues that went along with me, and bring it into their lives.

On The Run

This was literally the darkest, scariest, loneliest period of my life. The ever-present thought was that I could be caught again. It could happen any minute, any day. Something I said so often it sounded like a mantra, "The capturin' comes before the hangin'. I'm not turning myself in—they've gotta catch me." I also felt I was going crazy and, strange as it seems, this phrase kept me going.

So, I kept chasing the drugs to feed my addiction, separated myself from my mom and my family, and started living wherever I could find a space—a sofa, a sidewalk, or an abandoned building. Whenever I saw a police car, I'd dart into a building and pray that I wouldn't get caught. I was out there on my own, living wherever I could, but most often in abandoned buildings. Yes, I had abandoned myself, but as I already said, I wasn't thinking rationally and never realized that God would never abandon me.

My brother Eddie, who is no longer with us, was also caught up in the drug world. He was known as "the abandoned building landlord." Landlords asked him to take care of their empty buildings so that people wouldn't come in and take copper wires, toilets, or anything from their buildings.

With Eddie as my "landlord," I could always count on a room in one of his buildings. Even when I was so *sick*, I somehow knew that having Eddie's empty buildings to live in was God's way of taking care of me—watching over me.

During this virulent descent into the abyss, even though I was unable to raise my children or have them live with me, I still saw them and they saw me—in the rawness of my addiction. Even though I'd given up my children, I had not given up my love for my children, and that love was all I could give them at this moment in my life. As tenuous as my situation was, my love for them and their love for me continued to be my lifeline.

My son Dwyane was a teenager at this time and, every now and then, he would come to visit me. Every time before he left, I used to ask him a question. The question began when he was a little guy and continued into his teenage years. The question was, "Who is your favorite girl?" and he'd say, "You, Mom." I had nothing else.

Near the end of this period of my life, I was fortunate to also live periodically in a boardinghouse at 5925 S. Prairie. The people who ran the boardinghouse would allow me to come and stay there whenever I needed it. I was the only woman who was allowed to stay there. Once again, God was looking after me.

Panhandling

Also, at this time, just to survive, I would occasionally panhandle, although not in the literal sense of how you think about a panhandler. Rather, I would meet random people and, in our conversations, would let them know about my addictions. In response, they would often buy me a meal or give me a few dollars.

Sometimes someone from the group I was with saw me sitting on the porch and listened intently when I would speak or share scripture, then often, they would also offer to help me. I never needed to ask for it.

Occasionally, people would say they helped me because they saw something in me that I never saw. For example, one day, the owner of the store I frequented said, "You don't look like the rest of them. You're different. You shouldn't be drinking and doing the things you're doing."

The landlord of the building I often stayed in said, "There's just something different about you, and I want to help you. This doesn't seem like the life you are supposed to be living."

When people shared their observations, it confirmed what I finally came to know: I really *wasn't* this person, but I *was* living this life.

Another example of how God provided for me during this period: I had a friend named Barbara, no longer with us, who was a panhandler who would ask for money from people leaving our neighborhood store. She would then share it with me. We called ourselves "Pinky and The Brain." Whoever got the most money that day, my friend from asking for it or me from people offering it, was called "The Brain," and the other one was "Pinky."

I never had to compromise myself, so there was never any sex or funny stuff involved. This was yet another example of how God was looking out for me.

I was, of course, still going to church, and when Barbara or others would give me money, I said to myself, God was giving it to me. I had two envelopes in my coat—one of the envelopes was the "God envelope," the other was labeled, "mine." So, whatever money I had collected for that week, I would always take 10 percent and put it in the God envelope, so when I went to church on Sundays, I had something to give back to God.

At this time, I would also attend a storefront church, Revelation United Prayer Power Outreach—sometimes with my mom, sometimes by myself, and other times with my friends. When we attended church, stood near the church, or were around the elders in our community, out of respect, we never drank or did any of the other things we would usually do.

Oddly enough, throughout all these years, my love for reading and learning never ceased. While in church, this also morphed into teaching. I loved going down to the church building; I loved singing, and Pastor would always let us sing mightily. Singing in that holy place was wonderful.

I even began a small Bible study class in the boardinghouse where I would teach my friends; at the conclusion of class, I would lead everyone down to the church for services. The pastor would wait for us to arrive and, when we were seated in our pews, he'd begin the reading and sermon for the day.

I always had this love of teaching, and even in my addiction, I loved to teach the Bible from how I understood it. I didn't teach it as if I was connected to Christ because I didn't feel that.

I knew the Bible was about God and Jesus, but I didn't have any sense of the salvation that *being one with God* really meant. When I left church, when I was done teaching from the Bible, what did I do next? I went out and got high right after I left church.

But, as odd as it may seem to you, aside from my being an alcoholic, a drug addict, homeless, and whatever my personal challenges were, what was also true for me was that *I was a teacher*. I loved teaching others.

My Awakening–The Beginning

The church I attended was founded by Mother Box. My mom had been very connected with Pastor Box and often all four of my children went with me, but most of the time it was Tragil and Dwyane. Although Mother Box was not a teacher I was drawn to, I know today that God kept those church doors open wide so I'd always have a place to come to just to sit with Him.

Mother Box was somewhat sickly, and one day when I came to church, there was a new pastor in her place. I came to learn that Mother Box had brought Pastor Darrell Gibson into the church to help her and was grooming him to ultimately take over for her. Pastor Gibson, knowing Mother Box's family wasn't there for her, took her to a nursing home when she needed it, and took care of her home in her absence—in general, he was like a son to her.

Sometimes when Mama Box was praying with us, it would just be my mom and me. Now, with Pastor Gibson's arrival, there were a few more people coming through that door, and I loved the community that was being created.

That little storefront church became a haven for me. Understand, I was still on the run, still stuck in my addiction, still afraid and not knowing how to get free, but didn't want to take the steps to turn myself in to the police. At the same time, I also felt myself being drawn into the spiritual sanctity of our church on Fifty-Ninth Street and the accepting presence of Pastor Darrell.

Pastor Darrell was a short, robust young man with an air of authority about him and was always faithful about coming into the neighborhood to minister to us, to be with us, no matter what time of the day or night. He was a very caring man and, when he spoke, I intuitively knew he spoke *the truth*, and so I trusted him.

His teaching was really relatable; it was amazing, especially coming to the neighborhood where we lived. I believe that God brought him there to help minister to the people who were stuck right there, on that block, in that neighborhood—*literally stuck!*

Of course, he knew that many of us who attended church were addicts and alcoholics. For us addicts, whatever our sickness or our madness was, it never mattered to him. My sickness was heroin and alcohol. There were others who used rock cocaine or pills, some smoked hallucinogens, and some were simply out there, barely tethered to this reality—it never mattered who we were. Pastor was drawn to us because he knew he was called by God, and we were drawn to him because we, too, knew he was called by God.

I want to stress how uncanny and genuine his ability to speak to each of us was in a way that we could hear God's message through him. He never spoke down to us; rather, with unconditional love and compassion, he always spoke directly to our hearts.

Pastor Darrell never judged us and had such a playful way about him. Some of the topics he came up with were designed to speak directly to our hearts, minds, and spirits in a way that he knew we could hear him. He was brilliant!

He clearly was channeling the Holy Spirit.

Pastor Darrell took me under his wing and, often, would take me to his home, sit me in his library, and I'd watch him study. While I was studying under him, I was always in awe of how caringly and clearly he communicated with everyone.

When I teach, I too speak directly to hearts, minds, and spirits in the way that God guides me. I know now that the Spirit was teaching me through Pastor Darrell. This was God's way of keeping my mind alive and connected to Him.

I regularly watched for Pastor when I knew he would be coming into our neighborhood. When I saw his van pull up to the church, I sought him out, saying, "Pastor, I would like to speak with you. I have several questions I would like to discuss."

Of course, he would always answer, "Yes."

During Bible study, he would ask me to read that day's lessons and the accompanying scriptures. I began studying very deeply and even memorized a number of biblical passages.

I recognized that I was gaining greater confidence and understanding in my ability to interpret scripture. Through Pastor Darrell, God was awakening something in me that had been buried for many years. I believe that is part of the reason God sent Pastor to this church—to help save me.

Going to see Pastor Gibson became a daily thing. He understood that I had a habit and had an amazingly high tolerance for drugs and alcohol. At this point, I was drinking three to four liters of wine throughout the day along with the drugs. Because of my respect for Pastor, I would never allow myself to be too high in his presence in a way that would embarrass him. I also made an effort to maintain my appearance.

It occurs to me now that even though I knew my father, he never had a role in my upbringing. As Pastor Gibson continued to nurture and guide my spiritual development, he actually became that father figure for me. Without judgment, he would always tell me I could do better.

He would often say that, if I needed additional help or wanted to go to a rehab facility, he would help get me admitted. I knew I no longer wanted to live in the dark place I was in. I was fighting for my life but not yet capable of relinquishing the hold drugs and alcohol had over me, so I continued to struggle.

There were two particular sermons that had a huge impact on our community and especially on me. One was titled: "Your Body's Here with Me. But Your Mind, Where Is Your Mind?"

Oh my goodness, that hit me like an arrow in the center of a bull's-eye. I remember the title was amazing. It moved me.

At that moment, my little crew and I came in, and our bodies were there, but my mind was on, "Am I going to be able to get a fix when I leave here? Who am I going to see?" I was sitting in my chair, but my mind was just everywhere else. My body and, yes, my spirit, were there, but my mind definitely wasn't. He intuitively knew this, and his message truly resonated with me.

Another time was one of the most amazing sermons I've ever experienced anywhere, from anyone. That particular day, a Bible study day, Pastor had gone out to a local grocery store and bought about eight dozen eggs. When I walked in, I asked, "Pastor Darrell, why do you have so many eggs?"

He said, "You'll see." He then asked me to go out and round up some of the people in the neighborhood and tell them to come to Bible study that night. "It's going to be real, real interesting," he said.

I went and spoke to a few people I knew. I said, "Man, you have to come to Bible study tonight. Pastor Darrell has a way of teaching, and he has a message he wants us all to hear." I found my brother, Fast Eddie, as I called him, in the neighborhood and let him know because he hung with different people, so that he too could go out and tell some of the people he knew.

When it was time for Bible study, Pastor Darrell welcomed us. He had the eggs in cartons lined up by the lectern with a small bowl next to them. The title of this evening's sermon was "Breaking Every Yolk."

We had no idea what he meant by the term "yolk," but he simplified his message so that we were able to understand it. Once again, my goodness gracious—the impact that that sermon had on us then and still later, as we shared it with others throughout the neighborhood, was astonishing. We all spoke about how his message freed some of us that night. Even though we may not have been fully present and, perhaps mentally and spiritually exhausted, my spirit and other spirits could really hear him that night, and we felt, for a moment, true liberation.

So, what happened? Well, he asked each of us to come up to the lectern and line up and, when we got there, asked, "How many eggs do you want?" We didn't quite know what he was talking about.

He would then say, "Take a raw egg and think about yourself and how you might want to change your life. Think about whatever you want to get free from."

Each of us who came up to get an egg came with our own thoughts. We never spoke them out loud. He then taught us what he meant by "breaking every yolk." As he went on to explain to us, the word "yoke" refers to the harness that is attached to the oxen's necks and shoulders that binds the oxen to the cart they are pulling. The ox, of course, is a very heavy beast capable of carrying a very heavy load. Even though it can carry the burden, the metaphorical image is that it is taxing.

So, Pastor Darrell referred to each of us as being harnessed spiritually to this yoke. But rather than pulling carts, we were carrying the burdens of our lives around with us every day—and, unlike oxen, we are not designed to carry this load. It weighs us down; it exhausts us. It lies heavy on our hearts, on our souls, and we believe we do not know how to unleash the traces that bind us.

Continuing the metaphor, Pastor Gibson taught us that we were not only carrying this enormous burden, but we were also stuck in a primal morass and believed we could not get unstuck. In that moment, each of us actually heard the truth of what he was saying and, for a moment, even had the presence of mind to listen. I would remain stuck for many years yet, but the sermon that evening was the beginning of showing me that I could unleash the yoke that had kept me burdened all these years.

Returning to Pastor Gibson's sermon: Once we'd taken as many eggs as we wanted, he asked us to close our eyes, think about what we'd like to be free from, and break the eggs into the bowl that he had next to the crates of eggs. I remember watching my brother and my friend Juggie take their eggs and lightly drop one of their eggs into the bowl. Then, they busted another one, and the longer they stood up there and the more they went deeper within themselves, the harder they threw those eggs. Then, they began weeping; finally, they became loud and boisterous. It was beautiful to behold.

When I joined the line to get my eggs, knowing what I wanted to be free from—the yoke of drugs, of drinking, the burden of the lifestyle I had been living for so many years, I was feeling very emotional.

He continued, "Just come as many times as you need to. You don't need to break just one yolk. Come on, break some more, I've got plenty of eggs. We all have a lot of eggs to break—even me."

The first time I lightly tapped an egg on the rim of the bowl, it broke; but, the more that he taught us and the more that he encouraged us, we started cracking those eggs hard—bam!—and those yolks would spill out. Just throwing those eggs into the bowl and watching the yolk ease out became a true release for all of us.

None of us had experienced a moment like this. As I said, my brother and Juggie began crying, and others began wailing. Pastor Darrell really helped many of us that night. He taught us that, if we had the courage and a true desire to be free, we could ultimately unleash the bond that had entangled us for so long.

When we were back on the streets after service, we talked among ourselves and with our friends about what had transpired. Not one person laughed it off. When we told others who were not there, if anything, their response was, "Gosh, I wish I'd been there." Even so, looking back, it seems that perhaps I was the only one who was ultimately changed by this experience. I know now that this night was the beginning of helping me believe that I could someday truly be free.

Pastor Darrell also taught me how to respect men. Frankly, I had lost all respect for men. I had been badly abused for so many years that I, too, had become an abuser—mentally and, when necessary, physically. When I sensed a man's weakness, I would pounce on it.

Pastor taught me how to be respectful by not taking advantage of someone who was not going to do me any harm, even if I knew I could harm them.

An example: One time, I was with Mr. Anderson, an older man who looked after me. He knew I was out on the streets, and one day he told me, "You come in here, you can lie down. I'm not going to touch or mess with you—nothing like that there."

I said, "Yeah, you'd better not because, if you do, you're going to feel bad." I had become such a disrespectful person, but I still needed a place to lay my head—and he seemed like a nice guy. He allowed me to stay in his room.

Mr. Anderson always made sure I had food and ate, and gave me any spare change he had to help support my addictions. There were no strings attached. He was simply a very, very nice man who cared about me. This is another illustration of how God consistently placed people in my life who looked out for me.

He was a good guy. His daughter trusted me with him as well, because I didn't allow anyone to take advantage of him. Coincidentally, after I was released from prison the second time, his daughter asked me to officiate at his funeral. This wonderful family is still part of my life today.

Now, back to the story: On this particular occasion, Mr. Anderson and I were sitting in Pastor Darrell's van. Pastor Darrell overheard me talking down to him and took me aside. Using a look in his eye and a respectful tone in his voice, he said directly and honestly, "My sister, my sister, you don't do that."

And he went on to explain why. He understood that a man had abused me because I had shared with him that I had been subjected to "just-because whuppings." He also knew I had a son in college and grandsons.

In that instant, it all made sense. When I understood, I immediately took responsibility and apologized to Mr. Anderson and, from that moment on, I tried hard to die to that side of me—that side of me that had been abused—so that I would no longer be that abuser myself and rather, be a more loving and respectful child of God.

Abuse: My Life With Greg

The kind of abuse I had been suffering from for years went beyond a mere slap on the face. No woman, no individual, should ever experience this intense, physical, manhandling abuse, being pummeled with fists and feet, that I endured.

But throughout it all, my spirit could never be vanquished. Even in the bleakest times of my life, when I wished I could die, I still couldn't—wouldn't. No matter how damaged I was—physically, spiritually, emotionally—I never gave up.

As I write this chapter, I can see these obscene images of this abusive time in my life. However, the light that had come to be my guiding light could no longer be extinguished. And my abuser, no matter the severity of his abuse, could not vanquish me; he could not stomp me into oblivion.

However, one day I did vanquish him—*man-to-man*!

As previously noted, when I was released from prison the first time in August 1995, I returned to the streets and picked up where I had left off with most of my relationships.

Two of those relationships were life-altering: The one with Pastor Darrell Gibson, who was trying to save my life, and the other with Greg, who was trying to take my life.

Pastor Gibson's teaching enabled me to finally accept responsibility for saving my own life. This, in turn, helped me to ultimately conquer my abuser and emerge victorious. One critical point I must make is, I knew even in the moment, not just in retrospect, this newly found courage and confidence was only made possible by my complete surrender to God. I did not do this on my own. Frankly, it would have been impossible.

When Greg entered my life, my mother saw this man jumping on her child, saw how I was looking, and was livid. She was angry to the point that she actually wanted to hurt him. Yet, I wouldn't leave the abuse, and so she'd tell me, "What's wrong with you? I didn't raise you this way."

We all know the expression "a God-fearing person." This was my mother.

No matter how she personally felt, she was *always* there for me. She never closed the door to our home, her heart. She never closed her love off from me. She never stopped praying for me. She would stand before the altar in our church and pray that I wouldn't die from my abuse. Her daily prayers included asking God to deliver me from this living hell.

On the occasions when I went home to her, she would gently hold me while I cried. I felt shame that I had become this person. She had

had such high hopes for me. At the same time that I felt ashamed, I also felt like that little girl who always needed her mama to hold her.

My mother *never judged me.* She was strong for me when I couldn't be strong for myself. When embracing me, she would often reassure me, saying, "It's going to be all right." Pointing to the bedroom, she'd continue, "Go on in there and get you some rest," because she knew I needed sleep.

She would then often go speak with Mother Box or go into her room and pray for me. She protected me as she did when I was a kid. Once I was in her home, neither Greg nor anyone else could harm me.

Greg was a criminal and the cruelest, most abusive person I have ever known.

People wondered why I stayed. Well, Greg made sure that I was totally dependent on him by supplying me with drugs. I didn't have to get out there and sell my body and do things that other women had to do to get drugs. All I had to do was lie there or stand there and take the abuse.

He'd punched me multiple times throughout the years and even, at one point, knocked my head against a brick wall, knocking out my teeth.

My children were no longer with me, and he made sure that everything revolved around him. My complete dependence on him also included the fear that he would kick me out, and I'd have to find another way to get my drugs.

A friend of mine once told me about his sister. He shared very personal details about the horrific things that had happened in her life and her children's lives that would be characterized as "unspeakable." She and her children were victims of physical and sexual abuse. My friend shared her story with me because he knew what I had been through in my life, and thought I might be able to provide him with some comfort and insight.

I began by telling him that when you're involved in an abusive relationship, fear can do some bizarre things, some insidious things to you, because virtually every experience is filtered through the prism of your own fear—*your experience.*

You think that by taking all the beatings and emotional abuse upon yourself, you're protecting your children and your family. You don't see that this dark, perverted world, this "reality" that you exist within, is not of your choosing, but is a reality that has been forced upon you by the perpetrator in your life.

I first met Greg when I was in my mid-thirties. Before I met him, I never knew the devil had a face.

This particular human being, your abuser, who you have now exalted in your mind and in your life, puts a fear in you when he says, "If you do *this, this* gonna happen. If you don't do *this, this* gonna happen. And, guess what? Nobody cares about you. Nobody loves you like I love you. If I kill you now, ain't nobody gonna care."

As I continued sharing with my friend, I said, "He just kept putting this into my head." I know now that Greg had a calculated campaign to indoctrinate me into *his reality* and, boy, did he. This was the path I was on. I couldn't deviate from *his path*—I didn't stand a chance because my abuser was a master manipulator—a puppet master pulling all my strings.

I was already carrying so much guilt over the loss of my children. This, combined with the fear that Greg instilled in me, enabled him to force his version of reality on me. Man, it was like the door was shut and bolted, and he was the only one who had the key. It never occurred to me that I already had the key to unlock the door, for I firmly believed he was the only one who had that key.

I needed his permission to go anywhere. His way was the only way. It was a dark place—such a dark, dark place.

People cannot possibly understand the thoughts that come into your mind when you're locked in this prison of fear. Some of the scariest are the suicidal thoughts that continuously creep in: "I don't want to live like this. I'd rather die."

At one level, I meant this, but at a deeper level in my *knowing*, I knew I could never commit suicide because of my children. But I said it out loud anyway, which contributed to my belief that I was less than nothing. There is nothing less than nothing, and I felt even less than that.

I was so utterly desperate, so confused. I was screaming, screaming on the inside, "Help! Can somebody help me to get out of this? Can somebody find the key, hand it to me, so I can open the door and let myself out?"

However, as I continued to tell my friend, even as you consider seeking help, you realize that you've lost trust; you've lost the trust that anyone can actually help you. You also worry that, if you speak with anyone about him, your abuser may want to harm them as well.

You don't realize that people really do care. The abuser's rage permeates every single thought you have and prevents you from thinking clearly. When you consider the possibility of intervention, you end up believing it is futile even to try, because in the depths of this abusive relationship, you can no longer hear that anyone really wants to help or trust that they can.

In my case, this abuser's thoughts would pop up in the middle of the night, would disrupt my sleep, if I could even sleep at all.

He would say, "I want to have sex *now*." In spite of it all, part of me was still vainly trying to hold on to this ever-dwindling, stunted sense of self. There was no intimacy; there was no feeling; there was no "I love you." No caressing. No tingle. No kissing. Because it was *my duty*, just sex. It was just something I needed to do to keep from being beaten down on, from being beaten into a pulp, into oblivion from which I instinctively knew I would never be able to return, to stop his fists pounding into my face and hitting me upside my head as if I was not human.

Each and every time I succumbed to a beating, I just went numb. I was physically there—but not emotionally or spiritually.

I continued explaining to my friend: Words can barely express this level of fear. You may be trembling on the *inside*, but people will never see it on the outside. In this state, you are afraid to look at people because you think they may discover that something is wrong, which, of course, they already recognize. You are afraid of people thinking that you're mentally disturbed because they see the bruises and wonder why you're still in that relationship. They naively think you can just walk right out the door but they don't understand—you can't! He's got the key.

You want to scream, "I don't want to look like this. I don't want to be like this." This is the conversation that is going on inside your head. You want out!

You are banging on the bars of your emotional prison, but you are afraid to even open your mouth and ask your abuser, "Can I go see my friends?" "Can I go for a walk?" "Can I go outside?" This is inevitably followed by and not just said, but shouted, "*Only when I say so!*"

When I look back at this stage of my life, I wonder how I could have ever been attracted to such a person—a person who was so evil.

I remember one time, a woman who had been with Greg told me he had problems, and I said, "Well,"—because in my mind, I'm this cutie-pie—"that was with you. That's not me." And, when I saw the woman again, I was so ashamed to even look at her because I had been diminished down to this frail, emaciated, horrid-looking individual.

If there was any beauty left within me, I could no longer see it. I felt so ugly. I compared myself to her, her beauty, and her life—because she got away. She had warned me, but I didn't listen.

I began saying, "It's my fault. This is all my fault. It's my fault that I don't have my children. It's my fault that I became this dope fiend. It's my fault that I became an alcoholic. It's my fault that I didn't complete my education. It's my fault, it's my fault, it's my fault that I'm not who I should have been."

This tape never stopped playing in my head until one day in 1999.

The Beginning Of The End: 1999

It was a rainy, cold day in Chicago. Greg had gone out to deal and left his jacket at the apartment. I realized it and took it to him. As I was coming up the street, one of the girls who was hanging around him while he was dealing drugs said, "Here come your girl."

When I came up to him, he said aggressively, "B———, wha'chu doin' here?"

I said, "What?" I noticed how the girls were watching me. I'd even gone to school with one of them. In that moment, something in me just snapped, and I shouted at him, "No more. No more!" and began verbally going off on him.

He said, "B———, I'm gonna give you a beat down!"

I said, "You put your hands on me this time, man, I'm going to take *you* down!"

He came at me and tried to hit me with his fists, but I grabbed his arms, pushed on his chest, and stopped him in his tracks. Usually, I'd fold into a fetal position. That was the fear, but this time, there was no fear, and we fought.

The years of degradation, humiliation, and abuse that I had buried inside of me exploded like an erupting volcano. My voice felt and sounded thunderous, filled with unbridled emotion from all the years he treated me like an animal. I was screaming at the highest pitch imaginable—at the top of my lungs. The hostility in the very sound of my voice clearly stated, "*I'm going to take you out!*"

At the same time, I was crying torrents of tears. My body was quaking—but I was not afraid. Everything within me ruptured. My white-hot rage was lava spewing forth, destroying everything in its path. Greg was in my way, and I wanted him gone!

My whole life coalesced around this singular moment—the showdown. We literally fought each other the same way men would fight, with our fists, but I was able to hold on to him with a strength that came from deep within me—and it actually scared him. I remember pulling him down and saying, "Now, you've got to come on with it." And in that moment, he instantly fled and ran to my nephew, who was parked nearby.

Greg screamed, "Get your auntie! Get your auntie!"

I had run after him, heard him say this, and said, "Not this time."

Then, as Greg continued running, he asked someone else to call the police, screaming, "Get her away from me!"

After Greg fled, I didn't go looking for him. I stood there for several minutes, transfixed. Now that Greg was gone, truly gone, *my time had finally arrived.* I had found the key that released me from my bondage. I was no longer a metaphorical ox pulling the heavy load Pastor Gibson had spoken of.

My rage was spent, my burden instantly gone, and it was such an immense relief that I began sobbing once again. This time, my tears represented both joy and anguish. One thought was, "How did I let this happen to me? All those years!" Another thought: Sheer relief that the abuse had finally ended.

I then looked around and found myself standing on the corner of Sixty-First and Calumet, and I turned on my heel and, without looking back, walked toward Fifty-Ninth Street.

I looked a sight. My clothes were dirty; my hair was a mess; my face was swollen because he'd hit me with his fists. You could tell I'd been in a fight, and I had to go back to my mother's apartment looking like this.

All I thought about walking back to Fifty-Ninth and Prairie was my mama. I had no idea what she would say, but I knew without a doubt she would take me in for as long as I needed refuge. Beyond that, I didn't know where I was going to go because I never wanted to put myself and who I had become on anyone. But my body and spirit were guiding me home.

When I got to Mama's, I knew I was safe, and I stayed there in case Greg came after me. About two weeks after that, he showed up back on the block. I only knew this because someone told me, "Greg's on the block."

I went over there, took a look, shook my head—and, in that moment, I heard the Lord saying, "You can go now."

The horrific period in my life that had lasted over a decade concluded just like that. Not only had I not turned my head and looked back at Greg as I walked away, I *never* looked back—period.

It was now time to move forward. My awakening had begun.

Reflections: Returning To Life On The Streets

When I returned to life on the streets, I returned to my old lifestyle and friends. My days were still filled with violence, terror, loss, and struggle, as I remained physically and emotionally in the throes of my addictions. I was still a street person, and yet, as I continued to go to church, study with Pastor Darrell, and teach, I also had glimpses of the woman I was born to be.

Arise, shine, your Light has come.
And the Glory of the Lord has risen upon you.
Isaiah 60:1

Pastor Darrell, the church, and my Bible studies continued to be the guiding light for me. Now, my life was also becoming infused with periodic glimmers of divine light, illuminating for me what my life could be. The light and my awareness of it could now *never be extinguished*. It came into my awareness when God felt I needed to be reminded that He was there, and also came into my awareness when I would call upon Him, reminding me that God was always there.

Frankly, because of my addictions, I could not follow the path I was being guided to take. I simply wasn't ready. God knew this, and His light reminded me that He was always with me.

In addition, these next couple of years were infused with something I had never experienced. I had begun to see another light, one emanating from within me and shining out through my mind's eye, like the light on a miner's helmet.

As with my growing awareness that God's light was illuminating my worldly path, showing me new possibilities, I also became aware that this *inner light* provided *intuitive guidance*. It was like a spiritual compass orienting my mind/body/spirit awareness. Light was revealing these possibilities, but I was not yet ready to claim them. I knew I no longer wanted to live in the dark place I was in and was fighting for my life, but I was not yet capable of relinquishing the hold drugs and alcohol had over me.

Let your light so shine before men that they may see your good works and glorify your Father in heaven.
MATTHEW 5:16

Reflection: For reasons I wasn't aware of at the time, I had always attracted people into my circle who accepted me as a leader. As the reader knows, I'd been hearing God's voice for some time. Now light was also becoming very present in my life, and I recognized that this was what drew people to me and caused them to want to look out for me. Again, I realize now it was an integration of the energy that was beginning to emanate from me.

When I had something to say, both family and friends on the street would hear my heart speak and listen when I spoke. They seemed to see something in me that I didn't see. I didn't comprehend the nature of it, but it was simply: the light.

In addition, because the light had become so strong, whenever I would hear Him speak, the energy, the vibration, the sound was accompanied by a strong visual component, not an anthropomorphic one, but a pure, white energy.

Reflection: I knew God heard my heart. He knew my deepest yearnings and, even though I would never say out loud, "I'm tired of this life. I want to be free." I thought if I did, God would send the police to arrest me and send me back to jail, where I didn't want to go.

I knew what I needed to do, but was afraid to admit it. Truth be told, I recognized that God was always with me, that He knew my terror and the lie I was living, and how determined I was to leave the life I had been living.

Sometimes the light was dim, sometimes it flickered on and off. I'd been on the run for so long now that as His light began to burn brighter, I recognized that I was growing less afraid of my eventual return to prison. I also intuitively understood that prison was fundamental to my liberation.

At this point, I caught only glimpses of the light illuminating the proper path I could take. Even so, this light provided hope and gave me the courage to continue to follow it.

Awakening: Illuminating The Void—Revelations And Reflections

*"I am the light of the world. He who follows Me
shall not walk in darkness but have the light of life."*
JOHN 8:12

The divine light also revealed the void in my life. It illuminated every crevice, every hidden artifact within me. It was both painful to see and, at the same time, necessary and ultimately liberating.

Further reflecting on my life, I knew that there had always been an emptiness within me. But now, I recognized that it was more than merely emptiness; it was a deeply buried void that had been a part of me since early childhood. As you know, even in my own family, I felt an abject loneliness and deep-seated need to belong, but I had no words to express my feelings. Whether at home or school, I was always *Jolinda on the outside looking in.*

I realize now it was this emptiness fueling my desperate need to belong, to be accepted, that led me to join the middle school clique. I also understand the void led me to experiment with drugs and alcohol because when I was high, I was numb to the pain of emptiness. If it had not been for the intense, painful craving to fill the void, I might have continued to fulfill my early promise.

As I've already stated, the greatest void in my life was when my children no longer lived with me. Even though I could see them, it was such an irreparable loss. I felt such guilt and trauma that I was not the mother they deserved me to be. This led to completely losing my identity, my sense of purpose in life.

I was beyond grief-stricken, I was so bereft—that painful sorrow and sense of desolation became about more than their absence, it deprived me of my very identity and purpose in life. I was destitute—not only as a homeless drug addict, but I was spiritually destitute as well.

This yawning maw existed like a black hole consuming my life and my life force. It had been part of me for so long that it operated wordlessly inside as if intrinsic to my being. The clarity of the light enabled me to begin to separate my true self from the void, robbing the void of its power over my life choices. Little by little, day by day, following the light prevented me from becoming nothing—because that's what I felt I had become: *nothing*.

While the light illuminated all that I lacked, at the same time, it enabled me to see the positive changes that were also manifesting. I was now gradually gaining the ability to see beyond my situation and to finally begin becoming the woman God always knew I was capable of being.

I wish I could say that keeping the light on was like flipping a switch when you walk into the room—the light goes on and stays on—but it wasn't. Until I began writing this memoir, I never fully understood *why*. But, now, I've come to realize that to become the teacher, mother, and human being I am today, required that I continue to be tested and challenged, as God knew what I could withstand and was honing me so I could share from the totality of my experience.

I also had to learn this truth: *the only way out is through*. God knew that I would not only be able to survive, but that I would soar—and soar I have.

Your word is a lamp to my feet And a light to my path.
PSALMS 119: 105

In conclusion, my lesson to all of you is: Do whatever it takes to sustain your Journey day in and day out—no matter what. Never give up. When you do, your life is over. Never let the darkness overtake you.

If I never gave up, I can assure you, neither should you. As I've said before, I couldn't give up because my children, even in the evil state I had been living in, kept me alive. Also, no matter what a terrible job I may have been doing to sustain my life, deep within me, I knew I was a mother. My mother and my children were my reason for living. My mother was a lioness, and I had become one.

Chapter 5

Hearing God's Voice— And Listening
My Awakening
Sunday, October 14, 2001

"Or what woman, having ten silver coins, if she loses one coin,
does not light a lamp, sweep the house, and search carefully
until she finds it? And when she has found it,
she calls her friends and neighbors together, saying,
"Rejoice with me, for I have found the piece which I lost!"
LUKE 15:8–9

In the ensuing chapter, you will learn about the epiphanic moment when God told me to walk away. This was the beginning of the privilege provided to me to hear God's voice more frequently and consistently for the rest of my life. This is the story of how it all began.

Awakening: 10:30 a.m., Sunday, October 14, 2001

Even when we don't recognize that God is here for us, God is here for us. I am here to teach how, after my awakening, this knowledge helped me uncover this truth.

Prior to 10:30 a.m., Sunday, October 14, 2001, I had never connected the dots. One of the reasons I wanted to write this memoir is to make everyone aware that we all have transformational opportunities in our lives. Throughout this book, I candidly share my story so that you can see, both from my mistakes and moments of true courage, what the consequences or possibilities are.

It took me decades to accept the simple truth of Proverbs 18:15, "The heart of the prudent acquires knowledge, And the ear of the wise seeks knowledge." It took me half a lifetime to truly hear God's voice and then listen. What ultimately made it possible was my complete commitment to Proverbs 3:5–6, "Trust in the LORD with all your heart, And lean not on your own understanding. In all your ways acknowledge Him, And He shall direct your paths."

The essence of surrender/serve/soar is the underpinning of this chapter.

When my awakening was finally completed on Sunday, October 14, 2001, I was able to achieve victory because I fully surrendered to God and myself and no longer needed to struggle. Now that there was no longer any struggle, I could unequivocally be in service to God/ myself, and soar.

In a word, I "surrendered."

From that day forward, for the first time in my life, I believed I could do anything—even cleanse myself of all my addictions. It's not as though the Voice actually told me to stop doing drugs; *the Voice guided me and helped me discover my ability* to stop using drugs.

I absolutely knew there would be no more drugs, no more alcohol, no more cigarettes, no more self-abuse. For the first time in my life, I meant it. I knew this commitment would be totally different from the other times when I had "quit." I definitely knew there would be no going back.

This recognition did not scare or intimidate me. It was truth!

God resurrected me that day, and *His Grace* allowed me to resurrect myself. You will recall my speaking about the concept of "surrender" earlier in this book when I mentioned that a mentor taught me that it means "to yield or to give back"—in other words, to be in service. Now it's time to share the rest of what he taught me in this context—which was "serve and soar." When we surrender/serve/soar, we yield to God and are then capable of truly serving God, our vision, and our values.

It's an obvious truth, but also so elusive. If I had not been fully able to submit to Him and trust in the Lord with all my heart, the last twenty years of my life clearly would not have become what they've been. That October day definitely awakened me, allowing me to fully be in service to the Holy Spirit, my family, my community, myself, and soar—my destiny still unfolding before me.

As you've been reading, I didn't listen for many, many years, but on this day, if I hadn't listened, if I hadn't stopped when I did, I know today that I would not be here and able to share my story with you.

What made me stop? There are all kinds of different psychological, emotional, and philosophical reasons I could give you, but the principal one is—*the only one is*—God made me stop. I *heard* His words, I *heard* His voice, and it caused me to feel something I'd never experienced before.

Right then and there, God helped me change my life. He enabled me to step back from the precipice. This knowledge, this truth, instantly created a peaceful space.

Now, returning to my narrative: I woke up that morning at nine, and it was time for my daily dose of "medicine," which is what I called my fix. I was dope sick and out of money to buy that morning's fix. Church services started at eleven, and I knew I had to get my "medicine" first, and didn't have much time. So, I got dressed and hustled out.

By ten thirty, I was still standing by the side of my building, waiting for a friend who owed me ten dollars to bring it to me so I could get my hit. However, he hadn't shown up yet, and my rage was now beginning to build.

Then, I saw my mom coming down the street on her way to church. Now, I'm livid because, as I said to myself, "She's going to see me and see that I'm sick." I didn't think Mama knew I was still getting high. So, Ma did see me standing there and, in a voice as sweet as can be, she said, "Baby, church starts at eleven o'clock. Wha'chu standin' here for?"

Now, because of my rage, I raised my voice at her and said, "I know what time church starts. I'm going to be there." She didn't say another word, just walked on one more block and went to church.

Finally, my friend brought me the ten dollars he owed me, so at this point, I was further outraged because I had to wait, because Mama had seen me in my condition, and because I didn't feel as though I had any choice over whether I went to church or not. *I had to be there!*

Now, it was ten forty-five and I hurried up to Fifty-Eighth Street, "The Strip," where dealers hung out, and I knew I could purchase the dope I needed. But, as I approached Fifty-Eighth Street, I was told the police had come and arrested all the dealers and hauled them off to jail.

So, then, I saw another guy I knew who knew I was an IV drug user. He said, "They came and arrested all of them, but an old boy down the street got two-for-ten dollars."

I asked, "Who was he?" I looked at him and said, "Man, you know what I do. You know I stick myself."

He said, "I wouldn't send you on no run like that. I wouldn't do that to you. I know the guy's got what you need."

I looked him in his eyes and said, "All right."

So, I went down to the old guy and he said, "A. T. here."

"Here's ten dollars," and he gave me two dime bags for ten dollars.

Now it was five to eleven when I hurried back to Mr. Anderson's. Anderson let me into the room, and I cooked up all the dope. However, the one thing I always did before I injected it was I would taste it with the tip of my tongue. This time, when I tasted it, I instantly knew it wasn't dope.

Well, I mean to tell you, I just sat there beyond angry now, because this person had taken my last ten dollars that I had hustled for. So now, I can't go to church because everyone will know I'm sick, and I take it out on Anderson, who had always been so very kind to me. He said, "What's the matter, Baby?"

I said, "I just got beat. You got ten dollars?"

He said, "No."

Then, I said, "You go on and get up out of here. You're going to find me ten dollars," and kicked him out of his own room.

Immediately after he left, I heard a Voice say, "Get dressed and go to church."

I was sitting there. I looked around and I'm mad and said out loud, "Why do I have to go to church? Everyone else around here is lying up, but I have to go to church."

The voice didn't let me argue. Once again, the voice, calmly but commandingly, spoke, "Get dressed and go to church."

I am still livid, but I am obeying the voice, got dressed for church, grabbed my Bible and my coat, and, on my way out the door, screamed at Mr. Anderson, "Anderson, you'd better hand me ten dollars when I come back."

In a gentle voice, he said, "I'll try. I'll try."

I slammed the door behind me, leaned against it for a moment, and took a deep breath. Now, I just had to walk twenty yards to the church, when I didn't even want to be there in the first place, while thinking, "Everyone will know I'm dope sick."

I reached the church door a few minutes after eleven. No matter what I'd already been through, the hardest thing for me in that entire day was opening the door and walking in. I could have ignored the Voice, not gone to church, and instead walked up the street to find the dope I needed, *but* somehow, I knew that opening the door was both a necessity that I was commanded to do by God and, also, a metaphor. I could rage all I wanted, but I knew I had to surrender to the Voice and walk in.

Still so very angry, I took another deep breath, summoned my courage, pulled open the door, took that first step, placing my right foot over the threshold, and went in—sitting down alone in the last pew.

Our church was a small, storefront church; that morning, there were only six or seven congregants who, upon hearing a latecomer enter, all turned around and saw me. No sooner had I sat down when, out of everyone there, Pastor called on me.

"Jolinda, would you read 2nd Timothy 3:5?"

Then, as I read the scriptures, this line jumped out at me, "Having the form of Godliness, but denying the spirit thereof."

After reading this line, the Voice immediately spoke to me once again, saying, "You are going to stop denying My Spirit the power to change you." Then, everything went silent around me.

As you know, I had been hearing the Voice since I was a little girl and always ignored it. As I recall this singular moment in my life for you, I am amazed on so many levels. Very much in a rage, defiant, but I still listened and heard this Voice.

I didn't think I was crazy or that I must be hearing stuff because I needed a fix. It never crossed my mind. I simply accepted this *was* the voice of God.

And in the silence of this moment, I asked, "What is this Voice that is speaking to me?" Through a process of elimination, I *knew* it was the Lord's voice: First, I immediately recognized I wasn't merely talking to myself, as I knew what *my* voice sounded like—felt like. I knew it was not the enemy—the Devil—because the Devil would not relinquish control, send me to church, or want me to be healthy and happy.

All at once, I realized it *had* to be the Voice of a power far greater than I'd ever experienced before. It could only have been God's voice speaking to me in that holy place, and once I determined that, I gave myself over to it entirely, and it was pure love I experienced.

My defenses, my rage, my defiance instantly vanished. Nothing I had ever experienced in my entire life compared with this moment. It was a profoundly safe, loving energy that enabled me to freely and unequivocally surrender. *I knew the Lord had me in the palm of His hand.*

From that point on, I don't know what Pastor Darrell preached as I was in a trance while the Voice ministered to me. Church services usually lasted about an hour and, when I "awakened" from my trance, it was about noon when I heard the pastor pronounce, as he always did when ending his sermon, "And the book is closed."

It was in this single hour, after thirty-one years of addiction, that I was about to be delivered. My entire life was about to change. I didn't know it quite yet, but I was to be transformed!

Instead of hugging the other congregants as I usually did, I got up and hurried back to Anderson's house and, even though it was way past time for a fix, I no longer felt mean and, so, quietly said to him, "I need to use your phone."

I called my best friend, Viola, who lived about an hour and a half away in South Bend, Indiana. Viola and I grew up together in the same neighborhood and went to the same grammar school. My nickname for her is Bit-Bit. Even though I am a little older, we have always been very close.

We had both used heroin in our lives, and even though she used heroin, she was a functioning addict and didn't use it every day as I did. She might do it on the weekend because she worked during the week.

She knew my story backwards and forwards, so there was no need to attempt to hide anything from her.

When I got Bit-Bit on the phone, I said, "I need you to come and get me."

She said, "What's the matter?"

I said, "I have to go to a funeral."

When she asked, "Whose funeral? Who died?" I said, "I have to die so Christ can live."

I told her I needed to detox off the dope and alcohol, and didn't have any other place to stay. I asked her if I could stay with her for a while. As I knew she would, she didn't hesitate and said, "I'll be there."

Following my call, I walked back to Mr. Anderson's and told him not to worry about the ten dollars, anticipating that he expected me to come back and "strangle" him, which was what I would have done before I went to church, but I didn't. I spoke to him with respect. I then told him, "I'm getting ready to leave."

He asked, "Where you goin'?"

I said, "I'm going to go with Bit-Bit."

I didn't want to wait in my room because everybody in the house was getting high, and I didn't want to be around it. So, I went out and sat down on the porch to wait for Bit-Bit to come and get me. I just sat there in a blank space. Even there, I was spacing out.

While waiting for my friend, I thought about what had just transpired. Where had this notion that I needed to go to a funeral come from, followed by the recognition that, spiritually, "I had to die so that Christ could live"? A thought of both the magnitude and clarity of this truth had never occurred to me before, and I instantly understood that this extraordinary thought could only have come from God.

Over the next couple of hours while I waited for Bit-Bit, I felt calm, very safe, and protected.

While sitting there, I could see everyone across the street doing drugs. How did I manage to leave Fifty-Ninth Street without doing any drugs myself? All I would have had to do was go across the street and ask them. I could have talked somebody out of a bag or said, "Can I get this here and I'll pay you later?" I could have done all of that—but I didn't. I could have called out to A. T. because he was family—but I didn't.

I just sat there on the porch and waited for Bit-Bit. The Lord didn't let anybody come into my space. Nobody. I was just looking straight ahead for the two hours it took for Bit-Bit to stop everything she had been doing and come and get me.

When she arrived, I took nothing with me, didn't even pack a bag. All I had were the clothes on my back because I knew Bit-Bit would take care of me. I didn't say good-bye to Mr. Anderson or anyone. I just stepped off the porch, got in her car, and left—going to a city I'd never been to before.

Just like that, I was gone. My mom didn't know. The pastor didn't know. Nobody knew. My children didn't know, as we weren't in communication at that time.

On the way, I asked Bit-Bit if she had any money, and she said, "I don't have that much, Sis," and she shared what she had. She bought me two five-dollar bags of dope, two nickel bags, and then she went to the store and bought a fifth of the red wine that I drank and a pack of cigarettes, and that took all her money.

That day—October 14—we drove to her house in South Bend, where I shot it all up until I was completely out of dope and drank up all the wine. I then told her I didn't have any more drugs or alcohol. She said, "I can send you back, but I can't take you—all I have is twenty dollars."

I said, "No. I told you when I leave here, I'm not going to be doing dope, I'm not going to be drinking."

God is so amazing! Over the next three days, through His grace, I stopped drinking and using drugs.

She offered me her couch, brought some covers, and I lay down.

The Couch

The following story, "The Couch," was not in the first draft of my memoirs. Some months later, as I was rereading the manuscript (which I have done quite a lot), I realized I needed to dig deeper, needed to reveal more. I needed you, the reader, to be able to more fully grasp the magnitude of these three days by living it with me in as complete and honest a way as I can share.

Day One

I spent three days on Bit-Bit's couch, and though I didn't know it at the time, these three days were about to change my life forever. I recognize now that that experience was also preparing me for what the Lord would be asking me to do two months later, but more on this later. Suffice it to say, it would be another transformational step on my Journey.

But in this moment on that first day, October 14, 2001, I didn't know any of this because I couldn't see that far. These three days on my dear friend's sofa prevented me from relapsing, and it was the most calming and empowering experience I'd ever had, except, of course, when giving birth to my beautiful children.

One of the most amazing memories of that experience is simply how calm I was, even riding with my loving friend Bit-Bit. There is no other way to say it. I had no fear, no anxiety, no questioning of what had just transpired, beginning with hearing God's voice in Mr. Anderson's room in his boardinghouse, followed by the revelation in church. I intuitively knew I was simply in God's grace. The energy within me and around me, once again, was simply calm.

I was relieved, so relieved. I felt this powerful and loving presence enveloping me. The love was so serene, it felt like the Lord was saying to me, "I got you. You're not by yourself in this."

Even all these years later, I'm stunned remembering how still everything was. I actually knew I was closing a long, horrible chapter of the life I'd been living for so many years. I somehow knew that I would no longer do drugs or drink. It was over. However, a part of me was not sure if I could actually quit just like that. I had quit before, as you know, but this time I knew it had to be different. It wasn't just while I was pregnant or when I was incarcerated; it would be forever.

I'd never fully given myself over to the Lord the way I was being asked to do now. You see, I'd been partners with drugs, heroin, cocaine, and alcohol since the day I'd walked out of the work release center four years, nine months, and six days prior. So, there was an emptiness as well as a calmness. I initially wanted to write in this paragraph that I was changing from the moment I heard the voice in church, but a more honest assessment was I was *being changed* from that instant.

You remember I said I heard the Spirit say, "You're going to stop denying my Spirit the power to change you," and that was exactly what was happening. It was not so much that I was doing something different; it was more that I was allowing this transformation to help me manifest. I was not resisting, and the thought never even occurred to me to resist. I was simply allowing myself to be taken by God's "spiritual power" to change me.

On that first day, while I was on the couch, I was so deep in my thoughts that I didn't really even have a sense of how I was, and, shockingly, I no longer heard the Voice that brought me there. The Lord had left me alone with myself, and a new fear began to come over me.

This fear was the fear of the unknown. For many years, I knew the routine of my day—how it would begin and how it would end. Now, without my usual pattern, I didn't know what to do. I simply lay in silence in Bit-Bit's front room for hours, just listening. The lights were out, and the TV was on. It was cold in the house, so my friend thoughtfully got me more warm covers and left me alone with my thoughts and my decision.

Through the night, I watched the TV now set on the Trinity Broadcast Network (TBN), a Christian channel, which I had really gotten away from watching. I don't remember who was speaking, but whoever that speaker was, they were saying how much God loves us. I was listening, but I wasn't hearing.

I was physically there, but spiritually and emotionally, I was numb. I couldn't see or feel anything. I was still in the mindset of, "What is this all about? What am I going to do? Now that the drugs and the alcohol are not a part of my existence, *what am I going to do?*"

Bit-Bit had gone to bed hours ago, and where earlier in the day I had felt so calm, I now began to feel frightened. I didn't know where to go or what to do. The Voice was silent. I was so alone and lost.

When I was a little girl, the Lord came and reassured me that He loved me and that I was not by myself. Then, I grew up and became an adult with a "partying every day" lifestyle. "Now, look at where I am," I thought.

This shift seemed to have happened so suddenly. But a moment later, I came to realize that it actually hadn't been sudden at all. If I had been thinking more rationally, I would have understood that the Lord had been preparing me for this moment all along. He was always coming to get me, but I was never ready. So, all I knew in this moment was that I was afraid of what was going to happen next. I had been trusting His voice to guide me, but it wasn't speaking to me now, and I didn't know what to do.

You'll recall that, when we were on the way to her house, Bit-Bit bought me a pack of cigarettes. Later that evening, to take the edge off the anxiety I was experiencing, I got up off the couch and went out on the back porch to smoke. It sure was cold.

My mind was blank. And out loud, I fervently asked myself, "What's going on? What's going on with me? Why am I so blank right now?" I wasn't sure whether I was simply asking myself or asking the Lord. There were no drugs. There was no alcohol. The familiar no longer existed. My internal and external surroundings were empty. It was all blank.

What I didn't say out loud was that, within my heart, I was tired. I'd been tired for years—all that time when I walked the streets and hustled for a fix—but I'd never said it out loud. It was too terrifying.

The real reason I never said it out loud was because I believed that, if I did, the Lord would have me arrested, forcing me to give up the drugs. My mother had taught me that the Lord hears everything. So, my greatest fear was that I would be arrested and sent back to prison.

Of course, I wasn't thinking clearly. It never occurred to me that He didn't need to hear me say it out loud because He had already heard the cry, the desolation in my heart.

I was on the back porch for quite some time while finishing a couple of cigarettes, trying to figure it all out. When I put out my last cigarette, I went back into the house and lay down on the couch.

I was lying on my back, but turned over to see and listen to another pastor who came on TBN, who said the same thing that the other pastor did. Over and over again, he kept saying, "Jesus loves you and, if you are not saved, all you have to do is ask Him to come into your life. He will take you all the way through."

I was at Bit-Bit's house because of the encounter with the Lord when he told me to go to church. But now I was asking myself, "Have I been saved or haven't I been saved?" It got me thinking.

Then, the next thing I heard the pastor say was, "You can ask Him now to come into your life, come into your heart, and He will hear you and He will be your Lord and Savior."

Well, I didn't do it on day one. I just lay there now wondering, "Am I saved?"

Day Two

October 15, 2001: As day two unfolded, I was simply lying awake on the couch. I don't actually know if I ever slept that first night, as it was a very restless one. It wasn't a bad night for me because I still had some drugs in my system, but it was a restless one, and I guess I was afraid in a way because I knew I couldn't find drugs in South Bend, and I really didn't want to go searching for them. A part of me wanted to relapse and get high, while another part of me continued to keep me enveloped in a very calm state.

My friend was a teacher. Before leaving for school, she came into the room and asked if I was OK. I said, "Yeah."

She said, "I'm getting ready to go to work."

I said, "OK."

She saw that I was weak and, concerned that I didn't have access to drugs there, again offered to send me back to Chicago, repeating, "I have to go to work. If you want to go back, I can send you, but I can't take you. All I have is twenty dollars. I can put you on the train with that twenty dollars, just enough for the train fare."

I said, "No, I told you, when I leave here, I'm not going to be doing dope. I'm not going to be drinking." And I said, "No, Sis. I'm going to go all the way through with this. I came here to die."

Once again, I will pause my narrative for a moment to reflect on another reason these three days lying on the sofa in the sanctity of Bit-Bit's home were successful.

As you know, I had given up drugs and alcohol on a number of occasions, during my pregnancies and then when I was incarcerated, only to resume. The physical pain, the emotional torment, and the incessant cravings were the same as before. What was distinctly different this time was my spiritual commitment *to not give in.*

So, when I was writing this section of my memoir, I asked myself, "Why?" The answer that came to me is that I had finally begun to develop a glimmer of self-worth. I certainly didn't know this then, but I feel strongly that it's important for me to share this experience with you because I now know that I had *completely* given myself over to the Lord. I surrendered, and that is what made all the difference.

On a primal level, there wasn't even a "Jolinda," there was only a deeper Self committed to not letting myself and God down. Because of this complete letting go, decades of destructive behavioral patterns simply disappeared.

It didn't matter that my body was wracked with pain or that there were moments when I became totally lost in abysmal loneliness. All that was present was my commitment to be victorious for God. If God believed in me enough to rescue me on October 14, 2001, there were no other options than to do it for Him, and then, by the third day, also to be able to do it for myself.

I continued to lie on the couch, and now, it was just me in the house by myself. The TV was still on TBN. I just sat there, not thinking, not trying to figure anything out. I was waiting on that Voice to speak to me again, to tell me something, tell me what to do—anything. I was so very lonely. Even though I was still calm and committed, another part of me was feeling alone and lost.

Another pastor came on, and I remember his name. It was Creflo Dollar, and in that particular segment, Creflo Dollar shared his testimony.

I became so connected with it. I wouldn't even get up to go and get water. I didn't want to miss his testimony when he was sharing how he came to the Lord. I don't remember the words, but his testimony was so impactful.

I began crying, tears streaming out of my eyes and rolling down my cheeks—and I said pleadingly out loud, "I want to be free. I want to make sure that I have the Lord Jesus as my Savior."

Creflo Dollar opened up the door to Christ for me when he said, "Repeat these words after me, 'I accept you, Lord, as my Savior. Forgive me for all the decisions and all the things I did without you. Forgive me for not even recognizing you.'" Oh, it was so powerful!

When his testimony was over, I got up off the couch, got down on my knees with my head down, and simply wept and wept and wept, as I humbly asked God to come into my life.

I stayed there for quite some time, and a while later, I felt and heard God's message begin to come through me. I don't remember exactly what Creflo said in that moment—but what a moment. It solidified for me that I was, in fact, not alone.

It strengthened me. I instantly became so strong that I recognized for the first time I could actually do this. I could be drug- and alcohol-free. I ceased worrying about what was missing anymore. I now believed that the Voice was speaking to me in a different way—through His servant Creflo Dollar.

From that moment on, I would not turn that channel off. A series of pastors came on—Joyce Myers, Paula White—a litany of speakers, one after the other. At this point, it didn't matter what they were saying. It was all empowering to me and helped me empower myself.

Little by little, I was gaining confidence in my decision to accept God's choice for me to get into the car, go to South Bend, and die to myself so that Christ could live. It was an exhilarating, astonishing experience! I was still watching TBN when Bit-Bit came home. This time, I was still sitting—confidently—on her couch when she walked in.

She asked, "You all right, Sis?"

I said, "Yeah, I'm OK."

We were discussing what to eat and this and that. You have to understand, I really didn't have much of an appetite because I was dope sick. But she cooked a meal anyway and told me to eat something.

I can't remember how much I actually ate, but it wasn't much. On my second day there, my physical body was still experiencing the loss of my usual dope and alcohol fixes.

To take up the slack, I began smoking like crazy. As you know, my devoted sister already knew I would need something to fill the void, so on the way home once again, she stopped at the store and bought me another pack of cigarettes, but didn't buy alcohol because I told her I wouldn't drink anymore.

As Bit-Bit went about her afternoon and evening, I just sat on the sofa and wept. It was around five o'clock, and I began sweating and violently shaking. I wasn't cold; I was just shaking because my body had lost what it was used to for so many years.

Bit-Bit had gone to her room, leaving me alone in the living room, but would check on me every now and then, asking, "You OK, Sis?"

I'd say, "Yeah, I'm OK."

She didn't ask if I wanted her to get me some drugs or anything. That's a friend. She saw me going through detox, ridding my body of decades of addiction. She saw me shaking, sweating, and saw me running back and forth to the bathroom. I was violently ill—and it didn't faze her at all.

You see, years before this, Bit-Bit had seen me sick like this when I was still on the run. She was working as a teacher in Chicago at the time and used to visit me in the abandoned buildings I often stayed in that were managed by my brother Eddie.

On one occasion, she had shown up after school, calling out, "Sis, Sis." I was just lying in bed with the covers pulled up over me, freezing and shaking with chills even though it was summer, and I said, "I'm in here, I'm in here." When she came in, she saw that I was so sick, I couldn't move. She came over to my bed and asked, "What's the matter, Sis?" And I said, "Last night I was greedy and used up all my drugs, not saving any for today as I usually do. I am horribly sick."

When she saw the state I was in, she immediately got somebody she trusted to go and get me what I needed. Then she left, telling me to get well. After she left, I sat on the edge of the bed crying because I felt so ashamed she had seen me like this, and that she had had to help me because I couldn't help myself.

So, when Bit-Bit came to pick me up that day, she knew what to expect; she *knew* what would be required of her. I repeat, that *is* a true friend.

She heard me walking through her house, but would not say, "Come on, Sis, let me take you to get some dope to get that off of you." Not my friend. My friend was a friend.

She let me go through it all because she believed in God and the God in me. We had that type of relationship. She'd always believed in me more than I believed in myself.

I'm so glad that the Lord sent Bit-Bit to get me, because there was no one else I knew who would stand by me in the way that she did. She knew me and knew how to be there for me. Even though I didn't know how to be there for myself, God knew and Bit-Bit knew.

Had I not called Bit-Bit and chosen to stay in Chicago, I know I would have said, "Forget it," and found a bag of dope.

Don't get me wrong, folks. On that couch, I wanted to get that feeling off of me—but what I wanted more was what I was receiving from the Spirit of the Lord.

He gave me those preachers and their words, and helped me to hear them just enough to hold me as He was taking me through this painful, terrifying, transformational experience.

That night, I lay down again and managed to sleep off and on, but that TV stayed on TBN—because each person speaking was speaking to *me* and strengthening *me*.

When I share with you the ordeal of what my body went through for those three days, you have to understand that I had been doing dope every single day since escaping from the work release center in March 1997. Every single day, I did bags and bags of dope and drank Wild Irish Rose red wine. When I went out to the bars, the lounges, I would drink gin, whatever there was—just alcohol—period.

When I had walked away from the center all those years ago, I didn't know what I was going to do. I had no direction, so I simply dived deep into that numbing world of drugs, alcohol, and oblivion.

My body continued shaking because it wanted alcohol; it wanted a fix. I was able to stop both drugs and alcohol at the same time because I now knew that God would hold me. I reiterate, at the same time, not, "I'm going to stop dope now and stop alcohol later." No, it was very clear to me that this ordeal and my healing were the first steps in my recognition that God would be with me—forever.

Day Three

October 16, 2001: I woke up that morning feeling weaker than I had ever felt in my life. My friend looked at me before she left for work and, still so very concerned, again said, "Sis, if you need to go back on the train, I got the twenty dollars."

And, I looked at her and said, "No, Sis, I'm gonna do this."

She saw how weak I was. I know how it hurt her to see me look like that, but I was determined.

I had nothing in my system that second day, October 15. My body was not understanding it at all. When I woke up that third day, October 16, my body was screaming. It wanted its dope, and it wanted it now. It wanted a drink, and it wanted it now. And there I was, refusing to give in to the cravings. My friend left for work and, once again, I was alone in the house, but this time, I no longer felt alone.

Throughout my entire time on the couch, the TV stayed tuned to TBN. At that time, I didn't know God was using this channel and all the pastors who spoke to me as His surrogates. It's only in retrospect that I now realize that the Good Lord saw what I was going through, knew what was going to happen to me, and TBN was His conduit so He could reach into my heart. Praise the Lord.

At this point, I was so weak I could barely get off the couch to make it to the bathroom to regurgitate. My stomach was so empty. My body wracked with pain. I was not simply crying; I was wailing and wondering, once again, where the Voice had gone. I knew that to hear *that* Voice was so comforting to me, and I needed that comfort now. But there was only silence.

I remember getting up off the couch, making my way to the bathroom, and thinking even if Bit-Bit had given me the twenty dollars, I would not have been able to get on the train. I was simply too weak.

When I went into the bathroom, I stood over the toilet and began throwing up. Frankly, it was not as bad as I thought it would be. The DT's were far less severe than I would have anticipated. I wasn't "climbing the walls," I wasn't hallucinating, I was still aware of my environment. There were no seizures.

For someone who had been high on dope and alcohol for four years, nine months, and six days—every day, it should have been much worse. Without a doubt, the Lord had kept my suffering to a minimum.

When my vomiting ceased, I stood over the sink rinsing my mouth, washing my face, and looked in the mirror when the Voice finally returned, saying, "Look around where you are."

My friend Bit-Bit didn't have heat or hot water and had a terrible relationship with the landlord. It was then I heard the Voice say to me, "Pray for her." I was so weak that I even needed His assistance to help me pray. The Lord showed my friend's needs to me and helped me formulate the words.

What I prayed for was no longer for me, but for Bit-Bit. I prayed that she and her landlord would be able to talk, to work out their differences. I prayed that she would get hot water and that she would get heat. I prayed for her and her landlord to be able to speak with one another, and I asked God to *fix* them as soon as possible.

On the third day, October 16, the dope was completely out of my system.

The miracle of what the Lord had just done was so simple and astonishing at the same time. He had taken my mind off my troubles, enabling me to be there for my friend, who was helping me save my life.

Bit-Bit had gotten off work early that day. I don't know if it was because she was concerned about me, but she came home while I was still in the bathroom. With anxiety in her voice, she said, "I'm home. Sis, Sis, you OK?"

I said, "Yes, I'm in the bathroom." My voice was weak.

I had the door open and she came in, looked at me, and asked, "You OK, Sis?"

I said, "I just got through praying for you."

And Bit-Bit asked, "What did you pray for?"

"I prayed for the landlord to treat you with respect. I prayed for you to get hot water. I prayed for you to get your house heated."

She said, "I hope you told Him SOS."

We laughed, and I said, "Yup, I did."

Then, I went and lay back down on the couch because I was still very weak and sweaty.

That's when her landlord came to the door.

Previously, as I said, they had had a heated relationship, but this day, God allowed me to hear them talking with a sense of mutual respect for one another. I heard the landlord say, "I'm going to send the guy over and we're going to get you some hot water. Then, we're going to go down in the basement and look at that heat thing. Everything is going to be OK."

I remember lying on the couch weeping because God answered. God took my mind off whatever *I* was going through to be there for my best friend.

That night, we had hot water and we had heat.

Oh, that day was an experience. I needed Him to show me, "I got you. I got you." And He did.

Thank God for the couch.

I allowed the Spirit of the Lord to change me. Through this experience, over time, I actually became an asset to myself, my family, and the world. God showed me that there was another part of myself that He was revealing to me that I previously wasn't even aware existed.

Day Four

For three days, I had been telling myself, "No more drugs, no more alcohol."

Through God's Grace and intervention, the addictions that I had been struggling with for more than half my life took me only three days to terminate.

On the fourth day, I made the decision to give up cigarettes even though God didn't tell me to. I wanted to be completely free of any addictive substance in my body. Interestingly, it actually took another few weeks to stop smoking.

On this final day, Bit-Bit had decided she was going to take me back to Chicago and drop me off rather than send me back on the train by myself. I went back in a state of serenity—totally free in my mind. I didn't even have an urge to get high. As you know, I was still addicted to cigarettes, so the struggle continued as the Spirit of the Lord was freeing me from all things that I was a slave to.

For three days, even though it was a supreme battle with the demons trying to thwart me, I was in the security of Bit-Bit's love and home. Now I was returning to the environment where all my troubles began—where there were temptations on every corner. Even though I was spiritually serene on the drive back, emotionally, I was a bit concerned and nervous about what might happen when I got there. You see, I had been here before when I thought I had conquered my addictions—only to relapse again.

But once Bit-Bit dropped me off on Fifty-Ninth Street, a true miracle manifested. None of the usual feelings that used to overtake me were there.

I went back to the boardinghouse where I'd been staying, and the first person I saw was Mr. Anderson. He asked me if I wanted a drink. I told him, "No, I don't drink anymore," and I explained to him why I left.

When I got settled in, the first call I made was to Pastor Darrell to let him know that I was back, and he came to see me. While still at Bit-Bit's in South Bend, when I was delivered from the heroin and alcohol, Pastor Darrell was the first person I called. I was excited to speak with him and told Pastor that I had gone to attend a funeral, and he asked, "Who died?"

I said, "I had to die so that the Christ in me could live—and, I died to the heroin and the alcohol."

He was excited too and said, "I'm excited for you, my sister."

Now I saw his truck pull up, and we went into the church, and I shared my experience with him. He was so taken with my statement, "I had to die so that Christ could live," and asked, "Where did that come from?" We talked for quite a while, with me sharing where that statement came from and everything else that had transpired in those life-changing three days.

Before we parted, in his wisdom, he realized that I needed something to do to take the place of the drugs. He said to me, "Since you aren't going to be doing drugs anymore, you will be my assistant. How would you like to keep the church clean?"

I thought that was the most honorable thing I could do for what God had just done for me. I said, "Me?"

He said, "Yeah. I'll give you the keys so you can come down, open up the door, and make sure the church is clean." My first job.

There's a description in the Bible that says when you do something, do it as though you are doing it not for man, but for the Lord. When Pastor trusted me with the keys, it felt like that was what he was doing for me, and what I was doing for the Lord.

I cleaned that church with pride and humility. Every day I got up and went down to clean the church.

Pastor also told me that sometimes, if I wanted to invite someone to come in and read the Bible with me, I could do that. His trust in me gave me so much freedom and joy. In the way of the world, no one would have given me any keys. But when Pastor gave me the keys to God's house, in my heart I felt it was God Himself who trusted me. I called myself the "first fruit" that God gave Pastor Darrell on this block.

As the weeks went along, I became more of a trusted confidant. We used to sit and talk about the block and the congregation, which included drug addicts, pushers, prostitutes, and so forth. He wanted to know what we could do to reach them.

A few weeks after my return, God sent me a test. A few of the people from the church came in while I was cleaning, including Sam and Betty, who also lived in the boardinghouse. They spoke about how proud they were of me because they were watching me to see if I was going to fall—and I didn't. Then they asked me to lead them in prayer. That was an extraordinary moment.

After they left, I went into the kitchen and filled a bucket to wipe off the seats, looked on the floor, and there were five bags of rock cocaine just lying there. I said, "What is that?" and I picked them up, then looked up at the Lord.

I was holding five bags of rock cocaine in my hands. I used to smoke it, but now had absolutely no urge to use it. The question was, "What do I do with it?" I knew it was Sam's because Sam had been sitting in that spot where I was cleaning. "Do I give this to Sam or do I throw it away?" That was the question. It was worth ten dollars a bag, so he dropped fifty dollars worth.

I didn't feel I needed to give it back to him, even though it meant that he would have to pay the fifty to someone. So, I flushed it down the toilet, finished cleaning the church, locked the door, and left.

When I returned to the boardinghouse, I told Betty, who said, "You could have given it to me," and I said, "Why? To kill you?"

Sam came up to me and I told him, "You dropped some rock cocaine in the church."

Sam asked, "What did you do with it?"

I said, "I flushed it."

He said, "God probably was letting me know I shouldn't have brought it in there anyway."

I said, "You heard it."

As many times in the past as I had given up my addictions, particularly during my pregnancies, I was determined to remain clean, but the powerful cravings repeatedly drove my relapses and returns to my old lifestyle. This time, however, the cravings were completely gone, and with them my lifelong fear of the void. In place of it, I was filled with the light, the voice, and the presence of God.

As I mentioned earlier, I want you to learn from my story. An important lesson here is that, through my commitment to Source, I was better able to use the full power of my mind, my body, and my spirit to change irrevocably.

After my time at Bit-Bit's, when I returned to Chicago, as I was still on the run, I went back to live at the boardinghouse. Of course, I did not return to my old lifestyle. I had no idea of the direction I was going in—I was just following the feeling I had been introduced to on October 14.

I was doing some deep, deep listening and, because there were no longer any drugs in my system, what I was feeling and experiencing was an entirely new world to me. Also, because I was not selling drugs, I had no income. However, once again, as I began to build a new life for myself, I was provided for.

God continued to place people in my life who cared for me and wanted to help me. The people at the boardinghouse knew my plight, and everyone wondered where I had gone. I explained to Jim, the landlord, that I had given up the drugs and alcohol and was trying to straighten out my life—that I knew I needed to turn myself in. So he allowed me to stay there without paying rent. That was a blessing.

A few of the other residents knew my situation and made sure that I always had food and a little change. As before, kind people would come to me and offer me money. Also, the church distributed free clothing, which kept me decently dressed. I lived on whatever I was given and was humbled and deeply moved.

Allow me to pause my story for just a moment to speak about what I refer to as "the heart of the community"—how the people that I'd been living with on the streets, in the boardinghouse, who also had very little themselves, always provided food, clothing, a little money, a place to lay your head, for anyone who needed it. It was a lonely world we lived in. However, the "heart of our community" was also an environment where there was someone to talk to. We were close, there was no judgment, and everyone was welcome.

Jim, who owned our boardinghouse, was an extraordinary man. Sadly, he is no longer with us. He created a safe haven for addicts and, sometimes, if we couldn't afford the rent, he allowed us to stay there anyway. I was the first woman he let stay there.

Now, of course, I went back to church and volunteered to do odd jobs, which was different from before, when I didn't do anything. When I stopped doing alcohol and drugs, I felt new, regenerated, liberated, and connected to God. I felt like what the Voice had told that twelve-year-old girl when God said, "You're special." That's how I felt.

In addition, I felt like I could help others I had come to know and love who were still doing drugs and alcohol.

I continued faithfully going to Bible study. When I offered to volunteer, I asked Pastor Darrell what he thought about my bringing a Bible study class to his church one day a week. His response: He allowed me to use the keys to the church so I could go in when there were no services and, if I chose to, I could pray in private, clean the church, and prepare to teach my Bible study class. This is yet another example of God trusting me, leading me with these small steps, enabling me to believe in myself, and empowering me.

Sidebar: The Importance Of Small Steps

You don't have to see the whole staircase, just take the first step.
Dr. Martin Luther King

I share this eloquent quotation from Dr. King as a reminder to myself and to all of us that we don't necessarily have to know where we are going to end up. We merely have to trust in the path we are committed to taking to get there.

It is so easy to only think about what we want the outcome to be. However, in doing so, we no longer focus on the moment-to-moment, day-to-day, and, frankly, the discipline, the rigorous step-by-step commitment that will better assure that we accomplish what it is we set out to achieve.

Each day, I still remind myself that without my willingness and my resolve to maintain my daily physical, mental, and spiritual routine, I will never achieve my goals. In turn, I have learned that these "small steps" are not "small steps"; instead, they are the steps I take to live in the fullness of all that is possible in my life.

This period lasted about a month, from the middle of October to one Sunday in November 2001, when Tragil came to me and said, "Mom, I'm going to take you home with me." Because I wasn't receiving any kind of assistance, she reached out, wanting to make sure I was provided for, that I ate, and that I had what I needed. So, I moved out of the boardinghouse and moved in with my devoted daughter.

I didn't question this move as I knew this was where God was sending me. Once again, God gave me a place to stay, and I was under my daughter's roof. I was so very grateful. I knew being with Tragil would give me strength and help me take the fledgling steps required to become the mother I wanted to be. While there, all my children would regularly come and visit, and, as always, their love was unconditional.

It would be several more weeks before I turned myself in.

Reflections

". . . Fear not, for I am with you; Be not dismayed;
for I am your God. I will strengthen you, Yes, I will help you.
I will uphold you with my righteous right hand."
ISAIAH 41:10

Throughout my life, until the epiphany of October 14, 2001, my life had been beset by fear, trauma, and a lot of bad choices. Following my awakening, I was able to spend days, months, years rediscovering who God had designed me to be and charting a new path so that I could also fulfill the Lord's destiny for me.

One of my mentors shared with me the power of the two greatest fears.

What he said was: "There are two fears: fear of abandonment and fear of our greatness—fear of owning our power. Fear and love are our strongest emotions. Fear can propel us to success or vanquish us. The choice is ours. When adversity strikes, know that you can overcome it with self-love and emerge stronger than ever. You've all, of course, heard the expression—the 'fear of failure.' However, it is not fear of failure I'm asking you to confront. It is actually the fear of your own greatness."

My friend reminded me of what the Lord had been telling me my entire life. I have a right to be who I am. I have a right to claim my power because my power is God's power, and the more I own the fullness of my own life, everything—my wounds, my failures, every trauma, every battle—I am able to conquer it all by simply hearing God's admonition to me, "Love yourself. Reclaim my power."

Through this, I have learned how to never abandon myself again— ever—instead, to always turn to the love of self and God's love for me.

My friend continued to teach me that: *Where there is fear, there is doubt. Where there is doubt, there is no divinity.* He said, "It is arrogant to hold doubt."

Continuing, he said, "Not only are we made in the image of the Lord, but we are one with the Lord and the Lord is one with us." This is my truth as well. However, it is one thing to know this spiritually and philosophically; it is another to submit to this truth and act accordingly.

Then my friend said, "One of the principles I touched on is that whenever I'm frightened, anxious, or doubt myself, I simply allow a slow, loving, silent breath thanking God while I do so—and then say, 'I surrender and serve you, Lord.'"(He told me that the word *surrender* means to yield or give back in service to God and myself.)

He concluded by saying, "When we 'thank Source,' fear instantly vanishes because fear cannot exist in the presence of God's love. We are now able to embody our greatness and live life as the Lord designed it for us—at one with Him and ourselves, forever."

This moment in my life, at forty-six years of age, was the lowest point I had ever been in my life. I believed I'd die a dope fiend with a needle in my arm. When I viewed the landscape of my life, I saw nothing. Sometimes, when I was by myself in an abandoned building, I would envision my children's faces or, every now and then, Dwyane would pop up and come see me. As I've previously said, my connection to my children is what kept me from committing suicide or just saying, "Forget it."

God, of course, knew all this and, even though I didn't say it out loud, He also knew that I was tired of living this life. In fact, I was not simply tired; I was physically and spiritually exhausted.

I am so in awe of the God I serve. Of course, He had always been there for me, but October 14 was the day He chose to give me a new life—the life I'm living now—because I listened to the Voice.

You may think I had a choice to deny the Voice that day, but I didn't. In actuality, when the moment arrived, His voice simply took over, and I had no choice but to do what I had been told. The power of God's voice took human choice out of my hands. It was the grace of His energy that propelled me through the doors of our storefront church. Yes, it was me walking down the street and into the church, but it was God who made me do it.

In chapter 1, I mentioned that I had heard God's voice—not, of course, knowing it was God's voice—many times throughout my life. I had experienced it in my consciousness, hearing something that said, "Don't do this. Don't go there. Do this or do that," but I ignored it. It was as though when I had heard this Voice, I hung up and said, "Sorry, wrong number." And then I just continued doing things *my way*.

But this moment was the first time in my life I chose to listen.

Throughout my life, I always had trust issues with virtually everyone; however, *never* with my children, as our relationship, as you know, was always based on unconditional love, and since I *knew* this, I implicitly trusted them. I mention this here because, when I finally recognized that it was God's voice that I was listening to, there were, of course, no trust issues either, but also the feeling was similar to what I have always experienced with my children.

Hearing His voice was a virtually indescribable experience. Experiencing it made me feel as though I was nurtured and held in a cocoon, an environment that was safe, protected, and where absolutely nothing could harm me, including me harming myself.

As I write this and reflect on the life I led prior to my awakening—my rebirth, I also recall that on the day of my final confrontation with the man who had abused me for so many years, I remembered the first time I overcame fear as a ten-year-old on the school playground. It had been my own courage that I used to override my fear in order to protect someone else.

Thirty years later, on the day I confronted Greg, I did it again, but *this time I did it for me.* However, on that particular day, I first heard the Voice and heeded it, and this time it was not solely my own courage that made it possible; it was God's grace that invoked that courage. The day that I unlocked the door of all that had imprisoned me for so many years and finally left the man who had abused me, I discovered that God's voice was the key enabling me to walk free. It was not only the words I heard Him say, but it was the very vibration of His energy that liberated me.

A part of my discovery was recognizing that His Grace had always been within me.

I see it all so clearly and still feel it so deeply. Even as I write this, it is as though the liberation from Greg and the liberation from the squalor of my previous existence when God compelled me to walk into church on October 14 are all happening right now. As I relive these moments, my breath is deep and exhilarating just like it was so many years ago. I know this may not make sense, but I am crying in this moment, as I cried then. My rapturous breath and tears were so immediate, so powerful.

I've since come to understand that this emotional outpouring came from both a state of disbelief and, also, recognition that these terrifying periods of my life were finally over. In each of these moments, the decades of fear instantly vanished.

I have believed in God my entire life. However, many years while in the throes of my struggles, I rarely acted within the truth of that knowledge and, consequently, felt abandoned and terribly alone. I now realized I gave up, abandoned myself, and abandoned God, but I now knew that *God never abandoned me*.

With my *awakening*, everything—literally and instantaneously—changed. I now recognized I was not alone, had never been alone—that God had always been with me. That revelation has comforted and emboldened me ever since.

Following the life-changing, life-saving transformational moment of my awakening, each day immediately became jubilant for me. It wasn't simply a new day dawning; a new life had dawned, so it was not in any way difficult for me to leave the life I'd been living, not at all.

It was the best thing in my life and, as I write this and think back to that time almost twenty years ago, I smile as I recall that day, those few moments when God spoke to me and changed my life.

I am still astonished. The life I am blessed to live now was only possible because I answered the call.

My Awakening: My Return To Prison

The next leg of my Journey had begun.

My awakening that day was the most profound experience I have ever had in my life. Six weeks later, in December 2001, God visited me again and told me in a very commanding voice that I would have to return to prison for my redemption to be complete. I'll back up here to set the stage for that moment.

Earlier in the day, my friend Don asked me to do a Bible study with him. He lived in an apartment he shared with his sister Deborah and her family. I went to the apartment, knocked on the door, and Deborah said, "Come on in. Don went to the store; he'll be back." I went in and we sat and visited for a bit. She told me how proud she was of me, that she could see the difference in me.

Then, Don returned with a beer in his hand. He said, "Hey, Jo-Jo."

I said, "Hey, I'm ready. Are you ready?"

Don drank a lot and had the shakes. So, I told him, "Hey, if you feel like you need to take something to get the shakes off of you, God won't get mad at you."

He said, "No, I'm going to wait until we get through." God directed me to study the book of John with Don. I knew what God wanted me to read because I always sought His direction.

We read the chapter, prayed, and, as I was getting ready to start our Bible study, I heard the Voice say, "You're going to turn yourself in."

I said really loud, "What?!"

Don said, "What's the matter, Jo-Jo?"

I said, "You don't know what I just heard."

Don said, "You gotta turn yourself in."

I said, "How do you know?"

Don said that while I was sitting there, a light came over me. He saw the light over me, and he said the hair stood up on his arms. He also had a connection with the Spirit, and the Spirit had to give it to him; otherwise, how could he have known what I had heard silently in my spirit?

I started gathering up my books, getting ready to get out of there, as it was getting spooky for me, because that's the thing I had always feared the most—that one day I would have to turn myself in.

I got out of there and walked away in silence because getting rid of my addictions apparently wasn't the only issue I had to deal with. I was scared—real scared—and needed to get away. I wanted God to tell me more, but He said nothing else.

The communication I have with God today is quite different from what it was then. I certainly still hear His voice through my spirit, but also, it's sometimes a feeling I recognize, or something will pop up into my mind. But the communication that I had at that moment in Don's apartment was so precise—ever merciful yet conveyed in no uncertain terms, "You *are* going to turn yourself in."

The fear I initially felt was not one of terror, but rather disbelief, and my panic instantly subsided. I no longer walked around in fear of having to return to prison. I knew I was protected, and that helped me when I detoxed from the heroin I used and the alcohol I drank every day. I was so very tired of the drugs, the running, the streets, and was ready for it all to be over. I knew, whatever was happening at that moment, Spirit had me, and I wasn't going to fall. I actually felt genuine relief that I was returning to prison so that I could move on with my life.

At this point, the light illuminated the path before me. I knew I was going back to prison, but I didn't know when. I knew I had to tell my mother, my siblings, my children, and Pastor Darrell, but I was awaiting further direction from God. In the next few weeks, I was at peace as I simply began to prepare myself for what was about to take place.

Then, His next message was that I would be turning myself in to the police on New Year's Eve, 2001. He also told me that the time had come for me to tell my family that I would be returning to prison, so that's what I did.

Preparing myself to tell my children became the most challenging task of my life.

Chapter 6

My Renaissance–
Restitution And Redemption

enaissance means "rebirth." My rebirth, of course, had already begun. Now this renaissance would extend to my family.

Telling my children and my entire family that I would be returning to prison—that single act of courage not only changed my life, it changed the lives of everyone in my family in a positive and profound way.

The anticipation of telling my children that God actually told me to return to prison shook me to my core. Preparing to tell my children was one of the scariest moments of my life. It took me back to when I was fifteen and told my mother I was pregnant. These transformational, life-changing moments stay with us forever.

Even as I write this, it's as though it happened yesterday. I can see where I am as I prepare to speak with Dwyane, Tragil, Keisha, and Deanna. I can feel the knot in my stomach. My breath is tight. I can see what I'm wearing. I can see right where I am when I tell each of my children.

However, it is very important to be clear about the fact that the terror was in the *anticipation* of telling my children and the rest of my family; *the act of telling them was not terrifying at all—it was liberating!*

Returning to prison was going to end that exhausting, long run I had been on for four years, nine months, six days. During my escape, I merely existed. God was now giving me an opportunity to get my life back, another chance to become a better mom—the mom I deserved to be, the mom my children deserved to have—and to be the daughter my heroic mother had prayed I could once again become.

It was almost December when I told my family I was returning to prison. As I was living with Tragil, I chose to tell her first in November; then I told Deanna, Keisha, and Dwyane.

Tragil was the child who went to church all the time with Mom and was strongly connected with God. She was the child who would often come and pray with me, and if I really needed it, would provide me with food and clothing. In November, when the Holy Spirit helped me to stop doing drugs and alcohol, Tragil was the child God used to ask me, "Ma, want to come stay with me?" That's when I moved out of the boardinghouse.

One day in November, while at her home, I asked her to sit down and told her I had something important to share with her. I simply said, "It's time. I have to go back to prison. Mama is going to get her life back."

When I had finished, she wept and hugged me very tightly, telling me she was so glad I was finally doing this because she didn't like seeing her mother on the run, and was looking forward to getting her mother back.

Because my girls and I were all in one neighborhood, I then reached out to Deanna and Keisha, and we set up a day at the house that I could spend with just the girls and grandkids. We all met at Tragil's, and I told them I would be returning to prison on December 31. Once again, it was a very emotional moment because of the connection I have with my children and with the fact that I wasn't there for them for such a long time—but they truly wanted the best for me.

Deanna's son had just lost his father, who was killed in a shooting, and she was in a very challenging place with him, but I told her, "God is sending me back so I can return to you and be the strong mother that you deserve and that you need." We embraced and wept. There was no fear in the room because my girls knew God was guiding my path.

Then, in December, I told Pastor Darrell. When I found him at the church one day and shared the news with him, it affected him in a joyful way. He was proud and so happy for me. He had always seen so much potential in me and understood that I was being directed by God and that this was the right thing to do.

Later, in the middle of that same week, I returned to church, where I knew Dwyane was going to be in a meeting with Pastor Darrell.

He was the last child I told. Truth be told, preparing to tell Dwyane was one of the most intense experiences of my life. He was my baby. He was going through so many things in his life at the moment, and I was going to have to tell him what I was about to do.

When I arrived at the church, I first stood outside for some time. Then I walked back and forth from one corner to the next trying to get the words together to tell my baby that I had to go back to a place that I didn't want to go to. But when it was nearing time to go into the church to meet Dwyane, I was struggling to even open the church door and walk inside. I was not yet strong enough to go through with it.

So, I walked back to the boardinghouse, to Anderson's room where I had stayed so many times. It was just like that day in October when I didn't want to be there, but God led me be there. Even though I knew that once I opened the door and my foot passed over the threshold, everything would be fine, I was still terrified.

I was still so very fragile. It had only been two months since I lay on Bit-Bit's sofa and got sober, drug-, alcohol-, and, ultimately, cigarette-free.

So, this was the first time in my adult life where I was confronting my children with the truth of what I am about to do, experiencing energy and emotion in a way I had never felt as an adult; every other time I confronted a situation, I would require a drug, a drink, a pill, something.

In this moment, I was physically/emotionally/spiritually fragile—feeling things I had never experienced in my life and didn't quite know how to handle—which is what prompted me to walk back to the boardinghouse, sit on the bed, and ask God for help.

So, I walked back to the boardinghouse to Anderson's room, where he saw me and asked, "You all right, Jo-Jo?"

I said, "I have to tell my son that I'm getting ready to turn myself in. It's heavy; it's hard."

He said, "Just sit in here for a minute. I'll get out." He closed the door and left me in the room.

While sitting on the edge of the bed, I prayed to God to help me. I said, "God give me the words to say so that I can tell my son that I'm getting ready to turn myself in—to leave his life again. Help him to be strong, and help me to be strong. Thank you. In Jesus's name."

Being in Anderson's room enabled me get my thoughts together, helped me feel strong enough and safe enough within myself to return to the church to speak with Dwyane. Part of what I was grappling with was that Dwyane had recently told me that he was so happy to get his mom back. I, in turn, had just gotten this opportunity to be in my son's life and now I had to leave him once again to get rid of the prison sentence that had been hanging over my head.

Following my conversation with God, I certainly felt stronger. I got off the bed feeling His overwhelming presence—just like I'd felt in October and in different moments over the past two months. I now felt strong enough and knew I was ready to speak with Dwyane.

I walked back to the church and opened the door. And, as I knew it would be, the moment my right foot was over the threshold, it was as though I felt God's hand on the small of my back supporting me. I instantly physically, emotionally, and spiritually knew God had me and I walked in. The terror was miraculously gone.

I found Dwyane sitting in Pastor Darrell's office and waited for their meeting to conclude. When I saw that it was over, I went up to Dwyane and asked, "Could I see you for a moment, son?"

He said, "Yeah, Mom." He was nineteen and a freshman at Marquette University. I went into the kitchen and waited for him.

When he came in, I just started weeping. "What's wrong, Mom?"

I said, "I have something to speak with you about." I remember looking up into his beautiful eyes. The Lord's overwhelming presence was still upon me, and I knew the words I was directed to share with Dwyane would simply flow. I then took a deep, deep breath and said, "Your mom has to go back to prison."

He didn't say anything; he just kept looking at me.

I said, "I know you perhaps don't understand, but God told me I have to turn myself in."

At that moment, his eyes welled up, and the tears fell. We held each other. I explained it to him, and I said, "The Lord is leading me to do this so that I can be a better mom to you, and because you are getting ready to become a father, it will allow me to be a better grandmother to the children you will have." I told him I had to go back to get my life back.

He said he understood, but I knew he didn't. Dwyane later told me that he actually didn't understand it at the time, and, while I was in prison, he wrote me a letter that said it seemed that he had just gotten his mother back and then had to deal with having me leave him once again. It broke my heart, but I also knew that God would never give him a burden too heavy to carry.

I hugged and kissed Dwyane. When I walked out of the church, I knew that the decision I had made to come before the most important people in my life and tell them that I was getting ready to turn myself in was absolutely the right decision, absolutely the only decision I could make. I could not have made it without feeling God's power within me. It made me so strong and confident.

Following this moment, I was not merely relieved but recognized so deeply that an unbearable burden had finally been lifted from my soul. I was liberated and felt even stronger for the next phase of my Journey that was about to take place.

In the afternoon of a brisk winter day in December—December 30—the journey that had begun a month earlier, when I first sat with Tragil was completed when I told my mother.

My mother had always been the foundation of our family. Even to this day, my children and I reflect on her teachings, her strength, her principles, and her devotion to God. Mama prayed fervently for all of us every single day, both at home and at church. In spite of her prayers for my salvation, for almost two decades, I remained in a drug- and alcohol-induced downward spiral.

Now, I was standing in the kitchen at our church. I said, "Ma, I have something to tell you."

She asked, "What? What's the matter?"

I said, "Mom, I'm getting ready to turn myself in. I'm going back to prison so I can return and be a better daughter for you and a better child of God. When I return, I'm going to be who I'm supposed to be."

My mother simply looked heavenward and said, "Thank you, Jesus. You heard my prayers."

We hugged for just a moment, and I saw an expression on her face of such peace. In this very instant, for both of us, years of regret, pain, and terror vanished—just like that. This burden of flight and fear, of telling my children and my dear mother what I was about to do, had finally been lifted from my shoulders—once and for all.

One of my mother's teachings had always been that God would never give us a burden too heavy for us to carry. My mother knew this, and

I had finally come to believe it as well. As I walked out of the kitchen, having now left all my burdens by the side of the road, I was truly able to continue this miraculous Journey empowered by God.

My rebirth was about to take place.

December 31, the day God had told me I would be returning to prison, arrived. It was time to turn myself in to the local authorities.

I got up that morning, walked to the bus stop, and got on the bus to go to the police station at Twenty-Sixth and California on Chicago's east side, which I thought was the place I was supposed to go. But when I got there, they told me that I couldn't turn myself in there, that I had to go to the local Eighteenth Street police station.

I went there, but they would not take me either.

Now, confused and shaking, I was concerned that I wouldn't be able to turn myself in on that day, so I went back to my mom's because I didn't know what to do. I told Mom what was going on.

She said, "Just sit down." I sat on her couch.

My nephew, Shorty, was visiting that day, and he asked, "What's going on, Josie?"

I said, "I'm turning myself in today, Shorty. Since I was refused at Twenty-Sixth Street and Eighteenth Street, I figured I had to go to the work release center on the west side."

He said, "If you want me to take you over there. I'll drop you off, but I ain't goin' in there wit'cha."

"OK, take me over there and drop me off. I have to do this."

Shorty then drove me to the west side and dropped me off at the halfway house. Spirit strengthened me to walk up to the door and ring the bell. I took a deep breath, knowing that, once they opened the door, they would take me into custody. But when I rang the bell, no one came. I stepped back, took another deep breath, rang the bell again, and waited. Again, no one came.

I left and called Mom, telling her, "I can't get in. I don't know what's going on."

She said, "You got enough money to get back here?"

I said, "Yes, Ma'am."

She said, "Come back here to my house." So, I got on the bus, went back to Mom's house, and just sat there.

I didn't know what to do. I knew God told me to turn myself in. Mama said, "Wha'chu gonna do, Baby?"

I said, "I don't know."

I sat there for a while and thought about how calling Mom was what I always did, as Mom helped me find my way back to myself by nurturing and comforting me. Going to Mr. Anderson's house was an extension of the same thing. So, I told Mom, "I'm going to take a walk to Anderson's house."

Walking those two blocks would clear my mind so I could hear God's voice and know what to do. I left Mom's and walked down the street to Anderson's house.

Once again, Anderson asked, "What's goin' on?"—because Anderson knew I was turning myself in.

I said, "I don't know what to do. I tried to turn myself in, and I can't do it."

He said, "You need to use the phone?"

I said, "Yes, but what do I do?"

I heard Spirit tell me, "Go to the Yellow Pages." So, I started to look through them and saw the local precinct. The Voice I was hearing told me to call the local precinct, which was at Fifty-First and Wentworth.

I called and I said, "I need to ask you a question."

A woman's voice said, "Yes, Ma'am."

I asked, "When a person has been on an escape and wants to turn themselves in, what are the steps they need to take?"

She said, "Oh, they turn themselves in to their local precinct, and that's where they will be taken into custody, and it will go from there."

I remember saying to her, "OK, I'll be right there."

I hung up the phone and, once again, felt peace come over me knowing that this leg of my Journey was about to end.

I thanked Anderson and said, "I won't see you for a while," and left.

I then walked to Fifty-Ninth and State. Right there at the bus stop was a big liquor store. I had enough change to either buy a drink or get on the bus. At that time, the bus cost $1.75, and I had just enough for a bottle of wine, which, at that time, cost $1.25. If I had gone in to buy wine, I'd have had fifteen or sixteen cents in change and could have hustled with it. I knew my life would have just stayed the same, and I might have died there, so I stood there until the bus came. When I stepped up into the bus, I felt that it was over. I had made a decision not to buy any wine, but took this "bus ride to freedom" that led me to the life I'm living today.

When I finally arrived at the police station, sometime around four, I walked in without hesitation.

Looking back, it seems like it was a test. I was still so vulnerable, and like many, I could have taken any hand that was offered—in this case, it could have been to go into the liquor store or the hand of God. I think about the biblical story when the Israelites wandered in the wilderness for forty years. The lesson for me seemed to be that I had to wander to this place and that place and back again to learn that God was and is with me every step of the way.

God strengthened me, especially between the temptation of the liquor store and the bus stop. I remember the thought flashing through my mind for a fleeting moment, "Which way do I go?" When I chose to take God's hand and go the way I was being led, that's when I felt the most liberated I'd ever felt. This is why I refer to this episode as "my bus ride to freedom." Even though I was about to be incarcerated once again, I never felt so free in my entire life.

When I approached the desk sergeant, I said, "I'm the one who called and asked what steps to take when a person wants to turn themselves in, and was told to come to my local precinct. So, here I am. My name is Jolinda Wade, and I'm on escape from a sentence I was given in 1997, and I'm ready to turn myself in."

She said, "OK," and entered my name into the computer, but she couldn't find my record. She didn't want me to wait, so she said, "Baby, this is New Year's Eve. Don't you want to be with your family?"

I said, "Of course I do, but the Lord told me to do this, so this is what I must do. I will stay here until you find me in the computer."

There was another officer there who knew Jesus and overheard our conversation and told the desk sergeant, "Do what that lady tells you to do."

So, the sergeant entered my name again, and it still didn't show up. She then entered it a third time and, finally, my name came up.

Then, without handcuffing me because I had turned myself in, they escorted me to the back of the station.

Restitution: Return To Prison

My metamorphosis began on December 31, 2001. I was ultimately handcuffed and put into a van with other prisoners who had been in a holding cell, and we were all driven to the next precinct. When we arrived, I was put in a holding cell, and my handcuffs were removed. I stayed there on New Year's Eve.

I lay down on the bench in the holding cell, and the Spirit of God's voice spoke to me, told me to get up and say a prayer. Even though I couldn't see the other prisoners because we each had a separate cell, I got up and said, "We're getting ready for New Year's, and I would love to say a prayer for all of us in here." When I finished the prayer, I lay down again.

On New Year's Day 2002, they woke us up around six, gave us a sandwich, and took us straight to the county jail at 26th and California. Once there, around eight, they separated the women and men and, once again, put each group in another holding cell.

Then, the officers began calling us out one by one, and finally, they came to my name. The officer who escorted me had overheard me tell my story to the inmates about how I had turned myself in on December 31. I was fortunate to have an amazing guard who took to my spirit. Before entering the courtroom, she stopped, turned to me, and said, "When you get out there, tell the judge that you turned yourself in."

I said, "Yes, ma'am." I was confused because protocol dictated that we weren't allowed to speak. I was nervous to say anything to the judge.

She said, "I think he needs to know. You look like you're really working on something."

So, they took me before the judge. I remember walking with my hands cuffed behind my back. I was in a very peaceful, calm state, because on New Year's Eve, I had received a message from God that the desolate life I had been living was over.

When I entered the courtroom, I stood to the right of the judge. I knew I wasn't to look down, but rather, directly at him. I wasn't assigned a defense attorney because I had turned myself in, but the state's attorney was there, and his job was to bring everything that was in my record before the judge.

The judge looked at my file, which was dated 1997, and this was 2001, and there was nothing in it. Then, he asked, "What is this old case doing on my docket?"

The state's attorney said, "I don't know, Your Honor, I'm just now reading through the Jolinda Wade file, and I can't seem to find anything on her."

The judge who was assigned to me was so respectful. He looked over at me and, in a soft voice, asked, "Young lady, why are you here before me?"

You have to understand that, when you stand before the judge, you don't usually get an opportunity to speak; your attorney speaks on your behalf. Although I wasn't assigned a public defender, my defense attorney *was there*. I believe God was my defense attorney and there on my behalf to set the stage for the unusual events of that morning. I was definitely not in the courtroom alone. Every angel the Lord had brought with him was also there with me.

The judge looked at me and asked, "Can you tell me why you are here?"

As I began to respond, I wasn't nervous at all, for the judge's mild manner and his warm personality put me at ease. I calmly replied, "Your Honor, I'm here because I escaped from a sentence that I was given. I left the work release center and have been on the run for a while now."

Then the officer who escorted me into the courtroom asked, "Your Honor, may I say something?" What's so unusual about this is that the guards are not supposed to speak to the judge.

He said, "Yes."

"Your Honor, I think it's important that you know that she turned herself in on New Year's Eve." Her statement clearly made an impact on him.

I was still standing there in my calm state, looking at him, when the judge reiterated, "You turned yourself in?"

I said, "Yes, sir, Your Honor."

He asked, "Why?"

I explained, "Because I'm tired of being a liability. I want to be an asset to the world."

I had been praying to God to help me know what to say. Inwardly, I had said to the Lord, "You have always given me words to say when I needed to say them," and the Spirit provided them. The words "liability" and "asset," trust me, were not in my vocabulary at that particular time in my life. God chose them for me in that moment.

The woman who stood before the judge that New Year's Day was not a beat-down drug addict, because I was completely clean. No, the woman who stood before him was a woman who meant what she said. I was tired of being a liability to my family, my community, and myself, and wanted to become an asset. I intuitively knew once I became that, *I would be an asset to the world.*

Then he looked at me and said, "What I'm going to do is give you a $100,000 I-bond."

Even though I didn't understand what had just happened, I knew I hadn't received a harsh sentence, and it felt miraculous. I said, "Thank you, Your Honor."

The judge said, "I wish you the best."

Then, when the guard escorted me out, she said, "Wow."

I asked, "Could you please tell me what just happened?"

She said, "I have never seen this before. See, I told you that both of us speaking to the judge was going to make a difference. You really don't look like you belong here. He never gave anybody an I-bond like that—especially someone who had escaped and had been on the run."

I also echoed the guard's "Wow."

What the guard shared with me again confirmed that, once I had turned myself in, God was with me all the way on this Journey of surrender.

Then, she also wished me the best before removing the handcuffs and putting me back in the cell.

The women in the cell asked me what happened, and I told them the judge gave me a $100,000 I-bond. Everyone said that that was a big thing for him to give me an I-bond—and it meant that I could be freed on my own recognizance—but I told them I wouldn't be going home. Rather, I'd be going to Dwight Correctional Center because of my escape, and this was all a part of God's plan.

The women then asked me to pray again, so I said a prayer and sat down. A new officer called my name and took me to the next cell. She was very rude, telling me I wasn't going home.

I said, "I know, ma'am. What is my next step?"

"You goin' upstairs." So nasty and rude.

I said, "OK, ma'am." I looked back at the women in the cell and I said, "Listen, you guys be good out there. You guys don't want to come back here. I have asked God to help you go through this. Now, let Him lead you through it."

They said, "Yes, thank you. Thank you."

Then, I was sent upstairs to my room.

When I arrived, there were two other women there. Each room was supposed to be limited to two people per room, but it was overcrowded, so I was put there. One of the women began acting tough, but I knew her from the streets. She had forgotten who I was and said to me, "You stink! Go take a shower."

I looked at her and said, "I don't think you know who you're talking to, lady. Number one, I don't have to go and do anything. I've been in jail before, so I know it's not mandatory." She just wanted to show off how tough she was for the other inmate. "I understand that you are acting tough; you're in jail, but I'm not going to take anything. As a matter of fact, I'm on immediate shipment, and I will be out of here on the next shipment they call in the morning. I'm going to Dwight Correctional Center and, most likely, I'll see you there." After this, I said, "Now, lady, don't say anything else to me."

I share this because it is one example of how I knew God was with me. Without His presence, I would have handled that inmate very differently. As I said, I knew her from the streets, and here she was disrespecting me. That's one thing you never do in jail—you don't disrespect anyone.

My personality was such that I refused to be humiliated in any of my relationships. When Greg, the abuser, humiliated me publicly one day, as you know, I rebelled right then and there, ending the years of abuse.

I was no longer that same woman—not in that state of mind at all. When I heard God's voice months before telling me I could no longer deny His power, I humbly surrendered to Him and, as you, the reader, know, that Grace has remained an integral part of me ever since. So, when the incident in jail occurred, my rage and penchant for lashing out no longer had dominion over me. There was no need to lash out. God was protecting me—and I was listening.

Then, six o'clock the next morning, January 2, sure enough: "Wade!"— the door popped and I was out.

I arrived at Dwight before the other prisoner did and, as I thought, I later saw her when they brought her in with a new batch of inmates. I said, "Hey! Look who's on the new!" letting her know I remembered her. I also said, "I'm going to make you remember me from Fifty-Ninth Street, young lady,"—putting it in her mind to figure out where she knew me from.

I never saw her again in prison, but later saw her walking down Fifty-Ninth Street. I was with my brother, Fast Eddie, and a friend who had been her pimp. My brother used to give her clothes and make sure she had food to eat. They took care of her.

When she finally saw me, I asked, "Do you remember me?" She looked at me, and I then told her about the incident in jail.

She said, "I'm so sorry." The man who had been her pimp took her away, and I went about my life from then on. I heard later that she went back on drugs and was working the streets.

Returning to my narrative: On January 3, I woke up in Dwight Correctional Center to begin serving my sentence. Now I will share what transpired in the ensuing months.

When I was returned to prison, I was segregated from the general prison population. The rule is that when you "go on an escape," they "red badge" you, which means that I needed to be watched. So, they sent me to segregation from January 2002 through December 2002—one whole year.

In segregation, they allowed two inmates to share the room. We were locked up twenty-three hours a day without any privacy. The room had a window, a toilet, and a sink. There were two beds in the corner.

We came out to shower two to three times a week. They allowed us to go out for recreation, but when we went out, we were not allowed to join the general population. We had our own fenced area for those who were in segregation.

2002: One of the most profound discoveries God brought me while in prison was to *help me learn what "love" really is.*

This transcendent moment occurred one day while I was still in segregation. That day God directed me to read Romans 8:28, where He says: For God Works *all* things out for the good to those whom He Loves and those who are called according to His purpose. In my spirit, He highlighted the word "all."

This divine revelation of His love and, specifically, His love for me struck me with the force of a thunderbolt. Immediately upon reading His word, my mind/body/spirit was suffused with such a vibrant warmth and energy, and such utter joy as I had never known—could never have even imagined.

Before that moment, I had believed that speaking about love was the same as experiencing love, but now I realized that I had never truly felt love. I embodied these new feelings, which permeated my very being.

I knew I was clearly experiencing something profound and wondered at these very strange, very pleasant sensations. I was calm, relaxed, and my breathing was deep and full. It didn't matter that I was in prison, as I felt no fear or anxiety.

Further, He told me to let *everything* go and let Him in, saying, "Let Me plug in so you can really, really see Me and, then, you'll be able to truly see yourself and love yourself. It is as simple as that."

I didn't even know what it meant to "love myself." In my wonderment, I asked myself, "If this is how God's love truly feels and if God finds me worthy of His love, I must be worthy enough to love myself as well. How dare I not?" In fact, I suddenly realized that denying loving myself would have done an injustice not only to me, but to God.

The idea that my meager existence had intrinsic value led me to realize that I had never placed a value on my own life and, at the same time, I had never forgiven myself for the shattered life I had been living for over two decades. In my addiction, it was not possible to forgive myself—but now it was, and God was showing me the way. Oddly enough, in segregation, I was once again shown that I was not alone, and not only did I experience how much God loved me, but I also found I had a new best friend to spend time with—myself.

Through self-love, I not only grew in love for myself but also deepened my love for my beautiful mother, my children, and, truth be told, even God. To this day, this discovery, this knowledge, this truth has never left and will never leave me.

As you, the reader, knows, I had always heard God's voice going back to my childhood, though I did not know at the time that the Voice I heard *was* God's voice. Throughout the previous four decades of my life, I thought the Voice meant there was something wrong with me. I never imagined that God was reaching out to me, much less that I could tune in and listen to Him.

The months in isolation at Dwight Correctional Center, along with the rest of my time with the general prison population, with the revelations that were coming at me seemingly almost daily, not only did I know how to respond by doing the right thing but, since I was now connected emotionally to the understanding of "true love,"—love of

God, love of family, love of self—I was now prepared to return to my life—ready to continue the Journey.

I was now, for the first time in my life, fully in my right mind.

There is a Bible story of when Jesus crossed to the other side, and there was a man in the tombs who was cutting himself and couldn't be around family and friends. Jesus went over and visited him and, when he had his encounter with Him, they found him sitting and in his right mind.

I liken that story to me because that's what I did. I hadn't merely gotten my mind back; I got all of me back. For the first time in my life, I was the Jolinda that God intended me to be.

God's Plan

I was now fully in service to God. I had no fear. I had achieved serenity because I had surrendered. There was so much comfort in that—this state of being provided me with immense courage.

For the first time in my life, twenty-four hours a day, God had my undivided attention, and I realized that this was God's plan all along—creating this bizarre oasis for me where I could truly learn to live in a state of God consciousness.

Looking back from this vantage point, without that time at Dwight Correctional Center, my life simply would not be what it is today. God was teaching me to minister to myself. Today, I not only minister to myself, but to thousands. What a blessing!

More than twenty years later, I still cherish time in solitude. Solitude always begins my day when I can tune in to God's voice, and it prepares me for the day ahead. This time with Him is when I get my instructions.

In January 2003, I was given a green badge to show I could be trusted on the grounds and was returned to the general prison population. The time I needed to be in isolation was over. Now, I was returning to the general population as preparation for returning to life outside those prison walls.

For an entire year, God provided me with the privacy I needed and the time I needed to focus—and kept me from associating with other inmates. I knew this was the time God was introducing Himself to me. God had my undivided attention. My mind opened up, and I was receiving revelation upon revelation.

At the same time, Pastor Darrell and I became pen pals. I shared with him what the various Bible classes were, and he recommended which classes I should take while in prison, where God would provide me with the greatest help. So, I continued going to Bible study and readings, studying with others, and felt I was being used for His glory.

I only had one confrontational encounter with another inmate, a roommate. She was young, white, and very prejudiced. Her behavior was so extreme that, even though she was initially given sixty days, her sentence ultimately was extended to two or three years in segregation.

I knew that God still held and protected me, and He would bring me out of any situation unscathed—the way He did with the Hebrew boys when they were in the fiery furnace. So, I looked at this as God giving me the experience to love someone who was totally unlovable and the opportunity for me to share Him with her.

She would lie on her bed and tell stories about the big oak tree in her backyard and how she'd dream about "niggers" hanging from the tree. Because she used the word "nigger," I knew she was baiting me and expected me to react.

Again, I refused to be provoked and responded, "If you're saying 'nigger' to get me off course, you're using the wrong word because we call each other 'niggers.' So, you've got to do better than that."

She just looked at me.

I had good moments with her as well, doing Bible readings with her. She had a gift for writing, and I encouraged her—and she grew.

Another incident: My roommate got a ticket for doing something, and came into the room and opened the window. It was a February morning and cold outside. I asked her, "Could you please close the window?"

I knew it was going to be one of those days for her. This time, however, I had a full-up day as well and couldn't take it from her. Yet I still refused to be drawn into a fight. I got down off my bunk and closed the window.

She opened it again.

I said, "Jennifer, I'm asking you nicely to close the window again."

She said, "I'm not doing nuthin', nigger."

So, I pushed the button to let the guards know that she was being disruptive.

As before, I had a great reputation. They knew I wasn't a troublemaker and was close to the Lord.

When I started to ring the bell the second time, my roommate grabbed me and I grabbed her back. I told the officers that it looked like it was getting ready to go down. They ran into my room and handcuffed me so that they could move me out of the room, but they didn't handcuff her.

She hauled off and hit my face. It was not a slap; it was a full-on punch. They immediately restrained her and transferred me to another room.

They asked me if I wanted to go to the hospital, and at first I said, "No," but later, I felt pain and asked to go.

She heard me and she said, "I want to go, too."

Because I had scratched her, she knew I'd get written up, and her plan was to cause me to lose time.

However, it didn't happen that way. I did not get written up and came out all right. After a period of observation in the infirmary, I was transferred to another room. She also went to the infirmary, but there was nothing wrong with her and she was sent back to the room we had previously shared.

Later that day, I heard her at the door yelling, "I want my roommate back!"

When I awakened on the first anniversary of 9/11, God instructed me to hold a prayer circle out in the yard. I left my room, went down and told the women I met what I wanted to do, and asked them to spread the word; then, I went and sat down on the ground where I was soon joined by a circle of women.

I explained to them what I was doing and why I was doing it. I said that God directed me to honor those who died the previous year in the terrorist attacks on our nation. I then asked them to join hands and pray with me.

Even though prisoners congregating and holding hands was strictly against the rules, not one guard or prison official interfered.

The women in the circle then began sharing their feelings, and all were deeply moved, some even crying. Our prayer circle became a true healing for all of us.

Staying Connected With My Children

While in prison, I didn't want my children to visit as I wanted to stay centered on what I needed to do for myself. So, instead, we began writing to each other extensively. In these letters, we openly expressed our love for one another. We also shared important events that were happening in our lives.

One example was a letter from Deanna letting me know that she was in a relationship with a nice young man. She believed that it was a good relationship, great for her and her children.

Tragil became engaged to the man who became her first husband.

Dwyane shared his college experiences, particularly becoming a "big man on campus," and also that his son Zaire was born.

Keisha let me know that she was doing better, and her son Darin was also doing well.

In that way, they kept me up to date. In turn, I let them know that I was doing just fine—every day getting closer to God. In each letter, I also let them know how much I loved and missed them.

Along with my complete dedication to God's design for me, my children's unconditional love created the second foundational pillar supporting the woman who would emerge from this life in a few months. The fear of being alone that had initially gripped me in 1969, when I first became a mother at fifteen, evaporated like smoke dispersed by the wind. When I was freed from prison in 2003, knowing God's love, my children's love for me, and now my love for myself, I was truly prepared to be the mom my children and I deserved me to be.

As my release from prison on March 5, 2003, was rapidly approaching, the Journey I had taken for over half my life was now about to be concluded—with the bill that had come due stamped, "Paid in full."

Throughout my life, I had chosen to live the way that I lived for one reason or another, and as I mentioned earlier, I knew that I would ultimately successfully emerge from this life of suffering, despair, and poor choices. The suffering was not of God's doing; it was mine. What *was* God's doing was protecting me and helping to ultimately guide me out of the morass of my past existence. When I emerged on March 5, my entire self, physical/emotional/spiritual, had been inexorably transformed.

Released: Renaissance

March 5, 2003: Once I was released from prison the final time, my liberation brought experiences I had never dreamed of.

When I walked out of that prison and heard those enormous steel gates close behind me for the last time, I was filled with confidence. Through my communication with my family during my last days in prison, I knew I needed to get on the nearby train, which would take me to the Ninety-Ninth Street station, where Tragil would pick me up.

When she picked me up, words were not spoken. We simply looked at each other, tears welling up in our eyes, and hugged. It was such a beautiful moment.

When we arrived at her house, Dwyane came over with his first wife and their baby, Zaire. Dwyane was so thrilled to introduce me to my grandson. Dwyane, Tragil, and I hugged very tightly, so securely, and it was truly comforting and nurturing for all of us.

Later, Deanna and Keisha came over, and we all simply repeated the bountiful hugs and had a joyful time together.

The next day, I went to visit my mother. Going to see her was really overwhelming for me because my mother had never stopped praying for me, and I knew that now, finally, I would be able to make her proud of me. I no longer did drugs, drank alcohol, or smoked cigarettes. I wasn't out on the streets; I was home with my family.

My mother met me at the door and, just as in other momentous moments, when my foot crossed the threshold, all stress and concerns instantly vanished. At long last I had arrived and my mama knew she had her child back—the one she deserved to have.

She was a mother of few words, gave me a light hug, and said, "I thank God, I thank God—He heard me." She held me, and I held her. I told her I loved her, thanked her for praying for me, and said she'd see me in church.

While working on this book, I recognized how many times in this section alone I speak about my mom, always knowing I could call on her help.

It reminds me of how, when I was a little girl and was always afraid of everything—such as when my siblings watched horror movies on television and I sat with them; then, later that night, I would wake up crying and screaming from nightmares and no one, absolutely no one, could calm me down except my mother. If she was out partying, they would need to call her to come home—and, she always knew what to do, her touch, something about her that would calm me down. No one else could do it. When I lost my way on the path to turning myself in, I turned to my mother. The day I entered her home, the day after returning from prison, it was her touch and voice that finally and fully brought me home to myself and my family. In her presence, I felt peace and clarity.

I firmly believe that this was one more example of God showing me I was ready for the next stage of life's Journey.

"March Madness" 2003

March 8, just three days after walking out of Dwight Correctional Center, I was attending "March Madness," the most exciting NCAA basketball tournament of the year. This was the next-to-last round, called "the Elite Eight." For the very first time, I was going to see my son Dwyane play in a collegiate game.

Dwyane invited me to the game. Tragil urged me to go, and I really wanted to.

When I was released, I was assigned to a parole officer named Wade, who came to my home and gave me the details of where I was allowed to go.

While we were sitting there, he said, "Can I ask you something?"

I said, "Yes."

He asked, "Are you Dwyane Wade's mother?"

I replied, "Yeah!"

Dwyane was still in college, but the officer knew of him as a basketball player. Tragil was there with me and asked him if I could be released to go to the game and come right back. I believe that, because his name was Wade, he signed the release for me to attend the game.

Tragil sent me to the beauty parlor to get my hair styled. I was nervous and excited.

The crowds were huge, at least twelve thousand cheering fans. I had literally never been in such a large crowd in my life. When I walked in,

I was scared and closed into myself. I didn't know how to behave in this type of situation, and, in addition, I was carrying a lot of guilt that I hadn't been a part of the journey Dwyane took to get there.

Even though I did finally forgive myself and could actually feel self-love, it didn't remove the remnants of the experiences and old feelings I carried because of my past decisions. I hadn't known that the guilt was still within me, and I needed to face it. This experience revealed the trauma that I was still battling and also began a new period of healing for me. Dwyane had a lot to do with this as well.

When we got there, there were hundreds and hundreds of people displaying signs proclaiming "Wade!" with Dwyane's picture on them. I saw my son everywhere. All I could say was, "Wow!"

Dwyane played like a young man possessed. He was all over the place—playing defense, playing offense, seemingly scoring baskets at will. He told me later he played like that because I was in the audience. He said, "I got my mom back!"

After they cut the net down (collegiate basketball tradition when the home team wins), still sweating, he ran up the benches to where we were sitting, grabbed me, and held me. We held each other for such a long time.

No one knew that I was his mom until that moment when the murmur went up, "That's his mom. That's his mom. That's his mom."

When he finally let me go, my hair was mussed, and I was covered in his sweat. It was glorious! He had missed me so very much.

In his young life, I was seemingly always going back to jail or to prison, not being there for him. This moment after my release was the first time when we both knew I was not going anywhere.

The love and intensity of those moments showed me how much I mattered to him and how much it mattered that I was there. His joy, his unabashed expression, and his unconditional love radiating from him released me from decades of guilt over having abandoned my son.

Then, he introduced me to his head coach, Coach Tom Crean, a very important person in his life. Dwyane told me that after I told him I was going to turn myself in, he left Chicago and returned to Marquette, very angry.

This was 2001 when Dwyane was still a freshman. Coach Crean told me that he saw the change in Dwyane when he returned to Marquette, so he took him aside and asked, "What's going on?" Dwyane then shared with him that I was going back to prison, and he didn't understand why I would do it.

He was weeping and told Coach, "I just got my mom back and, now, she's gone again."

Coach Crean helped Dwyane make sense of what I was planning to do—return to prison. Coach described it in a way that Dwyane could ultimately understand. Following that conversation, Dwyane wrote me a letter that said, "I know, Ma, you always say I'm your hero—but, in all actuality, you are mine." I was so blown away. I was ready, then, to go and do my time because my son got it. And, it was because God had placed Coach Crean in his life that what I did truly made sense to my beautiful son.

I've spoken of the fact that my children had always loved me unconditionally. In spite of my aberrant behavior over the past two decades, they still simply loved me. They accepted me for who I was, and their acceptance helped save my life.

This was truly "agape"—a Christian principle that refers to this Greek word meaning "the highest form of love." In 1 Timothy 1:5: *. . . the love that comes out of a pure heart, a good conscience, and a sincere faith.* It is a profound spiritual connection with God and self. In the Bible, it is the covenant: love of God for man and man for God, and a selfless love that extends to all beings and is beyond emotion. Agape was the final awakening that manifested in this period of my life.

Chapter 7

My Unfolding

*. . . I want to unfold. I don't want to stay folded anywhere
because, where I am folded, there I am a lie.*
Rainer Maria Rilke

*The unfolding of Your words give light;
It gives understanding to the simple.*
Psalms 119:130 (New International Version)

The wonderful reconciliation with my mother and children marked the end of that harrowing, long chapter in my life. Now, for the first time in my life, I was actually looking forward to an entirely new chapter.

Where It All Began

I was released March 5, 2003. Upon my release, Tragil invited me to move into her studio apartment, as she wanted to help me transition into my new life.

One of our first outings together was to go shopping for some new clothes for me. Prior to my long period of homelessness, I used to be a very fine dresser, but once I became homeless, I began shopping at church giveaways. I still cared about my appearance but the options were limited, mostly pants in a limited color palette of basic blues and grays. Now I needed new clothes, so Tragil took me to a department store in a nearby mall. In the women's section, I saw so many bright, bold colors that it overwhelmed me. I can't explain it. I immediately ran out of the store, saying to Tragil, "I need to get out of here!"

March 6, the day after my release, I returned to the Blood, Water, and Spirit Ministry, the church that I was going to before I turned myself in, left, and went back to prison, where so many life-changing events had taken place. When Pastor Darrell saw me, he immediately recognized that I had grown so much in the Word behind the wall. He heard something in the way I spoke and observed something different in my visage, my facial expression, my eyes; something in my appearance looked transformed to him.

The pastor and I had a pretty good connection. We had developed a relationship before I went back to prison, and while there, he was a regular pen pal. I would write him about the things I was learning, about my experiences, about how God was using me to write out Bible studies and assist other women inmates who were in segregation with me by writing for them as well. He was very receptive to all that I was doing. When he saw me after I came out, he could see that I was no longer the same person.

I lived with Tragil for almost a year. Then, in 2004, I moved from Tragil's apartment into an apartment that Dwyane rented for me. My apartment, on 87th and Paxton across from CVS High School, was perfect for me at this time. It was here I learned how to care for my own home. Basically, for the last twenty years, I had been on the streets or in prison, so I literally had to relearn how to care for myself and take care of my personal property. My apartment was the place where I began to "grow up."

In addition, I needed a job. So I turned to a friend, Rev. Edward Jones Sr., who knew me from our mutual family relationships. He was an executive with a home healthcare company called Interim Healthcare, which provided assistance to people with health issues. Part of their mission was to hire former inmates who had just been released from prison and needed another chance.

After they ran a background check on us, if we passed, they would give us jobs. Rev. Ed took a chance on me and hired me to clean their clients' homes. I found this both ironic and oddly comforting, because my mother had cleaned people's homes for many years.

Decades earlier, of course, I had held part-time, short-lived jobs, but working for Interim Healthcare was the first "real job" I'd had in my life. I remember telling God that I had never gotten an income tax refund and couldn't wait to file a tax return so I could get a refund check. I also wanted an ID card. All those years on the run, I couldn't even apply for a simple ID card. I had lost so much throughout the years, and through this job, God made it all happen.

They assigned me to work part-time, four hours a day, five days a week. My favorite assignment was to take care of Miss Sarah, who lived at 78th and Green. She was a short, heavyset lady in her late sixties or early seventies. Having lost both legs to diabetes, she was wheelchair bound. She was such a joyful, spiritually insightful person.

She had a daughter who was caught up in the drug world, and she also had a son who was not, so I could talk to Miss Sarah about my own experiences. In addition, she had a very smart granddaughter who lived with her and whom she loved to death.

My duties were to bathe her, prepare her meals, clean her room, and assist her when she went to her doctor's appointments. Other times, we would simply sit together and she would read to me. She was such a loving woman, and I loved caring for her.

I continued working for Interim Healthcare for about a year, until 2004, when I was diagnosed with hepatitis C. Unfortunately, I had a reaction to the medication they gave me and was sent to the hospital. Rev. Ed was very supportive and told me to take all the time I needed to recover, but I never went back.

Once I recovered from hepatitis C and returned home from the hospital, I felt truly liberated. Within this free time that I had, I began to recognize that there was something that had been lying dormant deep within me that I had never paid attention to before. It was a longing to help others who were locked in prisons of their own making, as I was—or in actual prisons—because of the decisions they had made.

What began to emerge was the thought that I had begun to see myself as a teacher. In middle school, before my life imploded, I had thought about becoming a teacher. Now decades later, that idea reawakened within me.

Then, in May 2003, as Mother's Day was approaching, I asked Pastor Darrell if I could read a poem I had just written to express my sincere love for my mother. I told him that, if he were to allow me to read this poem as part of the Mother's Day service, it would also help other mothers in the church recognize and respect the fact that we are not all perfect. He honored my request. That Sunday was my first opportunity to stand on a pulpit and share what was coming from my heart.

My poem was entitled: "My Mom." It read: "My mom is the one God gave me, and I am glad about it. You may not be perfect in all the things you do, but I love you so much, Mother, and I thank you for praying for me through. I watched you work hard, and I didn't understand the magnitude of it all until I grew up and I saw your sacrifice wasn't small. You've come a mighty long way, Mother, and I do understand today that you can only be who you are because God made you that way. Your #3 daughter, Jolinda Wade."

When I completed my reading, Pastor Darrell asked me to explain its significance to the congregation. I explained that I wrote, "You've come a mighty long way, Mother, and I do understand today that you can only be who you are because God made you that way" to show that my siblings and I expected so much from her and, a lot of times, we were comparing her to other mothers, instead of simply accepting the extraordinary mother God gave us.

I continued, "She wasn't well educated, wasn't this, wasn't that, but she was a hard worker. She was a disciplinarian who wanted the best for her children. She showed her love that way, and she loved us unconditionally. That's why I told her, 'I understand today that you can only be who you are because God made you that way.'"

Tragil was there when I read it and, when I finished, hugged me, patted me, and said, "Thank you." Other congregants came up to me as well because, even though I was speaking directly about my mother, my poem, as I'd hoped it would, allowed them to be more unconditionally accepting of their own mothers.

After Mother's Day, I continued to go to church, becoming even more involved. Once I'd left prison, I hungered to have my spirit fed and did all I could to assuage my hunger so I stayed connected to Pastor Darrell and, at his request, I began teaching Bible study classes and Sunday school, and taking on other responsibilities as well.

It was easy for me to follow his direction as Pastor had always seen something in me, going back to the time when he observed me teaching my street friends before services. He seemed to know, although he never shared it with me, that God was always working miracles within me.

It was a peaceful time. My family was happy; my children were happy. It made me happy to see that I brought them so much joy. It pleased me to also learn something about myself. I had not been sober for so many years and "didn't know who this person was." I asked myself, "Who is she?"

Staying connected to Pastor, my family, and my teaching kept me on track and helped me grow, and I felt ready for whatever might be next on my Journey.

Pastor Petties

One day in the summer of 2004, Pastor Darrell approached me and, out of the blue, asked if I would like to enroll in a pastoral training program run by his wife's pastor, Pastor Jennie L. Petties. As you may recall, even before I went back to prison, Pastor Darrell would always allow me to teach Bible studies to my friends before services. Now that I had been out of prison for the past year, he continued to ask me to teach Bible studies and Sunday school. So, I was deeply thrilled and honored that Pastor Darrell saw that I had the qualities that would make me a good minister, but, truth be told, as I was just beginning to get my life back on track, I had no clear image of what I wanted to do with this new life. I, of course, knew that I had always loved teaching, but that's as far as it went.

I agreed—not because I felt I had a pastoral calling, but because I was interested and wanted to learn more about the Bible.

There were others who also taught at our church, but I was the only one to whom he made this recommendation. Subsequently I reflected on this and came to believe that Pastor was led by the Holy Ghost to send me to my next teacher. Pastor Darrell always saw something special in me, even when I never saw it in myself.

Pastor Darrell accompanied me to the first class, even though it was quite far away, on the west side of Chicago. He wanted to confirm for himself that this was really where he wanted me to be after all, and Pastor Petties had no problem with him sitting in on the first class.

Following that first class, Tragil would take me until I learned the bus schedules. I lived on the South Side and had to leave early, taking two buses, a ride that lasted forty-five minutes.

Pastor Petties was an exemplary teacher, and I ultimately received my pastoral certification at the end of the first year, and then remained in her program for a second year, which was required to meet licensing requirements.

When I first walked into the classroom, I saw that most of the ladies in this ministerial class were members of her congregation. I was still both uncomfortable around people as well as uneasy with people wearing colorful clothes. So, when I was around my classmates, I didn't feel comfortable in their fellowship as others seemed to—but they were friendly and outgoing toward me.

One student I met in Pastor Petties's class was Ladell Jones, who graduated with me. Upon graduation, he, too, received his ministerial license and collar and became Pastor Ladell Jones. Later, Pastor Ladell and I joined forces to create a shared ministry and together grew that ministry over a number of years.

There was one specific woman, a student, Reverend Brown, who really connected my spirit to the exact spot where it was supposed to be. This came about one day when I saw Reverend Brown and a few students discussing whose turn it was to bring coffee to Pastor Petties. Even though it was just a commonplace discussion, what was so interesting to me was that they actually seemed to be quibbling over who got to do it. To see how friendly they were with each other and to provide Pastor with anything she might need was something I had not experienced before. This was another example of unconditional love.

When Pastor Petties finally joined us that first day, I saw that she was a woman of average height, slim, with salt-and-pepper hair and beautiful brown skin that glowed with majestic energy. Her erect carriage reflected an elegant, cultured woman from the South. She even referred to herself as "the Southern Girl."

Pastor Petties was the most beautiful, gentle, yet forceful woman I had seen since coming out of what I call my "wilderness experience." She must have been in her late sixties or early seventies when I met her, yet she was so youthful you wouldn't have known it to look at her.

Then, Pastor introduced herself. Her voice was and still is, even in her late eighties, soft yet intense. Without raising her voice, she compelled you to listen. I was a student in her classroom, in awe of my teacher—another first-time, life-altering experience.

She shared her own humble beginnings, and hers were even more humbling than mine. She then told us one of her jobs was working in a chocolate factory, and she shared how God used her to begin her ministry there. She spoke with such clarity, and while she was not prideful, she was proud, for she knew the gift given by God was one she could share with all of us.

One day she said to me, "Everyone comes from something, Jolinda, and everyone has a story." This statement affected me, and I began to listen ever more deeply, paying even greater attention. She was an exemplary teacher.

It was very clear why God had wanted me to study under her. It was so that Pastor could introduce me to my "soft side," my femininity. She was what I needed coming out of prison. I had lost this aspect of myself while I was out there in the "wilderness" surviving, doing whatever I had to do to take care of my sickness while being caught up in a decades-long cycle of abuse. *The horrors of that life dictated who I needed to be at that time.* However, *I always knew it was not who I was.*

This was a new cycle in my life. I was learning to discover and convey the *emerging me.* Pastor Petties was the perfect role model, and God knew it.

This offers me an opportunity to share a teaching principle from a close friend who says, "We are not our behaviors." How we behave is how we may behave, "but," he asks, "is that who we truly are?" When I was *surviving on the streets*, I was not being who I truly was, but *circumstances dictated my behavior*. Under Pastor Petties, I was introduced to a new possibility of who I was fully capable of being and what I was truly able to contribute.

Pastor Petties shared her testimony, and, as I've already said, it wasn't always peaches and cream. Her honesty hit me with such force that, at first, I didn't quite know what had happened. I had never experienced someone share so candidly the painful truth of their Journey and also share how God helped them rescue themselves. This was the first time I ever experienced someone who could articulate the miracles that God manifested in their lives. She didn't simply teach us scripture; she also taught "life scripture." This, in turn, helped me create my own ministerial style and would eventually lead me, when I became a pastor, to candidly reveal my story and share God's miracles when teaching from my own "life scripture."

I couldn't wait to get to class—to learn from her, to listen to her teaching, to watch her mannerisms, to feel her laughter, to see not only how she ministered to women but also to men—we all trusted her. Hallelujah!

During my two years with Pastor Petties, we developed a lovely rapport. One day, she called me into her office and said, "Pastor Wade, I don't know that much about you, as you never shared your past with me. I know you elected not to because you are truly here to learn from me. But I do know that the Lord has chosen your calling to go even further than you realize right now."

I didn't see that at that time, but of course, she saw it. The fact that God spoke with her about me was immensely humbling. I had learned the knowledge that God wanted me to glean from her, while also learning another form of unconditional love, because I now also wanted, as my classmates did, to care for her and about her unconditionally, as my mother and my children had always done for me. It was an enormous opportunity and a life-changing discovery.

I later recognized that this was all part of God's plan. He was preparing me for future responsibilities and opportunities.

Eventually, Pastor Petties became Bishop Petties, which showed me that women do have an exalted place even in this particular ministry, and it has blessed me all these years to see how she keeps coming back into my life. At this writing, she still is the same beautiful soul and still Bishop-Pastor Mama, grandmama, friend, neighbor, Petties—whatever is needed.

God has blessed her to be that for all who know her.

As I've said, I remained in Pastor's program for the two years required to meet the ministry's licensing requirements. There were further steps I would need to take to achieve ordination, but they would come later. In 2005, after two years of rigorous study, I was licensed to be a minister.

In our licensing ceremony, six or seven graduated. My mom, Tragil, and my close friend Cynthia—three very important people in my life— attended the ceremony.

My friend Cynthia and I have always been very close. Her older brother, Pastor Ed Jones, who was ordained in 1989, was also like an older brother to me, and, since the moment I was ordained, he has been my advocate to this very day. We've all been through hell together on the streets, and Cynthia and I in prison as well. Cynthia and I met when I was nineteen, when she was dating my brother, Eddie, who has now passed. They had a son, my nephew, born in 1974 when my daughter Keisha was five months old. So, at the time of my licensing, we had been family and friends for more than twenty-five years. Cynthia entered prison as an addict but emerged drug- and alcohol-free and has remained so to this very day. She is such a valiant and vibrant woman with an amazingly full life.

Cynthia always believed in me, always said she knew there was something special about me, and, when we would get high together, would say to everyone, "Oh my God, that's all she wanted to talk about was Jesus, the Bible, the Bible, the Bible." For her to be there was like her graduation as well.

Seeing my mother and the look on her face made me so proud. I had finally achieved something that made my mother smile. That day lifted the burden of pain and everything she had gone through with me.

And, Tragil, my "little fighting baby," who, because of my decisions, was forced to give up her childhood to take on a very mature role for Dwyane and me, to have her there made the day even more amazing.

When the ceremony commenced, they called our names one by one. someone would hand Pastor Petties our ministerial collar. We walked up and, wearing our ministerial shirts, Pastor Petties stood before us putting our ministerial collars on each of us. When that was completed, she introduced us to all the families and friends in attendance, told the story about the class she taught, and the text she used called *Riding in the Second Chariot*. Following the ceremony, we had refreshments.

It was such a beautiful, beautiful event.

Following my first-year certification in 2004, I became "Pastor Wade." I went back to Pastor Darrell's church and continued to work on various important assignments, including teaching, organizing, and helping to maintain the church. I also taught with his wife, who supervised the women's ministry.

In addition, Pastor Darrell entrusted me with the street ministry program, where I ministered to those living on the streets ensnared by their own addictions and demons. I was experienced with street ministry because, while I was married to Big Wade, we had converted to Jehovah's Witnesses and would go door-to-door, as well as serve people on the streets, speaking with them, while also giving out books and flyers. Another important component of the street ministry program was setting up free clothing racks and food tables in the church so people could come in and get what they needed.

Since the Blood, Water, Spirit Ministry was in our neighborhood at Fifty-Ninth and Prairie, everyone on the street knew me and was happy to see me. They accepted me more freely because they knew I understood them, and knew they would be hungry for more than food. They needed special love and attention, and I trained my helpers in how to provide the love they needed.

As we walked the streets, I would ask, "How you doin'?"—not simply casually but because I really wanted to know. Sometimes, some of them didn't feel good or would be shaking because they needed a drink. I would give them one or two dollars and walk them to the store so they could buy a drink, which would help them relax. Years earlier, people had done this for me and I was simply repaying the favor. When I was on the streets, there were people who ministered to me, which is why I believed God was allowing me to do the same for others.

Often, they expressed that they wished they could do for their lives what I had done for mine, and I reassured them that they could. I would often sit with them in prayer, followed by heart-to-heart talks. These moments were poignant, meaningful, and helpful to me as well as those we ministered to.

Later, once I was an ordained pastor and had my own church, my friend Pastor Ed Jones and I often returned to my old neighborhood and ministered out of a local church that shared its facilities with us. A number of the old crowd attended that church, and as part of our sermon, Pastor Ed and I would describe our own experience as addicts living on the streets. I was now embodying the approach I learned from Pastor Petties when she candidly revealed her life to the students in her class.

I was teaching "living scripture" as well. Our time together would always end in the same type of prayer circle I had created on the grounds of Dwight Correctional Center in 2002.

Pastor Darrell And My Journey

I know I have already spoken extensively about Pastor Darrell and the impact he had on my life, but I want to share a bit more. I believe that God was calling me out and brought Pastor Darrell into my life—for he was the teacher I needed in order to become the teacher and minister I have become.

As you already know, Pastor Darrell worked under Mother Box, my mother's minister. I also attended her services with my children Tragil and Dwyane. Mother Box was a woman of keen insight, and I especially remember when Dwyane was just a young boy, she set him on her knee and said, "This boy is going to the Hall of Fame." When Mother Box became ill, Pastor Darrell stepped in for her, and that's how he became our family pastor.

Initially, when I was in his life, I was a drug addict and alcoholic, living out on the streets without a foundation or purpose. I was angry, mean, and disrespectful to men because of the abuse I experienced.

But this man came into my life and helped cut away some of my hard edges. He knew I was an addict and alcoholic, but he also knew I wasn't a criminal, and knew I was so much more than that. Pastor Darrell was the first person to see *me*, believe in me, and guide me in a way no one had ever done before.

He was warm and kind to me and saw something deep within me, which led him to do something about it. Eventually, he opened his home to me, introducing me to his mother and sister. In addition, he knew I loved to read, so he let me sit in his library and simply read his books.

In return, I had him over to my house to visit with my family and me. After I got clean, we visited even more often.

He would spend hours talking to me, counseling me, teaching me—and even trusted me to teach in his church. He knew I loved to get out into the community and speak with people about our ministry, so we'd often go out and do that together.

Pastor Darrell had the capacity to be loving and nurturing to all his spiritual children, and, through his ministry, he was a father to me. He was open and frank with me. Even when I was in prison, he was my pen pal, writing and encouraging me. He trusted God—and he trusted me—letting me know how much he appreciated me.

Occasionally, he would load us up in his van and drive us out of the neighborhood (which I loved), even spending his own money, to treat us to the movies or to see things we might never otherwise have experienced. There was one time when he took us to see the most wonderful play at a very large church in a neighboring community. It had a huge cast. To this day, I can viscerally remember the emotional impact it had on me.

Other times, his mother would personally take me out to the Loop, to Michigan Avenue. I had never seen an area such as this—so grand and beautiful. She would go there to sell jewelry and asked me to accompany her, and at the end of the day, depending on how much she sold, she would give me money for my pocket—sometimes as much as fifty dollars.

They were so loving to me. These were life-altering experiences I had never had, and that meant so very much to me—and I thank him for that.

A Fork In The Road

While I was training for my certification and licensing with Pastor Petties, Pastor Darrell came to my home one day and presented me with a book he asked me to read. I don't remember the author's name or the title, but basically, the book stated that women who preach are condemned to hell. When I read this, I looked up at him and he said, "Just keep reading, keep reading." So, I did and, as I was reading, he asked, "What do you think about it?"

I said, "Well, I have to be honest with you, Pastor, this goes against everything you and the Lord have said to me, and it condemns me to hell." The book was filled with descriptions about what women are supposed to wear, how to dress their hair, how and why women must obey men's orders, and so forth. *Everything* contradicted the truth God had been telling me all these years, as well as everything I had learned from him—and, at the very core of my being, I knew it to be wrong.

I didn't share this with Pastor Darrell at the time, but I was dismayed and profoundly conflicted by what was transpiring in this moment. However, because I had been a faithful member of his church for many years, I said, "If this is what you have come to believe, I will do my best to respect and honor that."

It was my Sunday to teach at his church, but when he left, I didn't have any peace in my mind. I clearly, indefatigably, knew what God had taught me behind those prison walls. I also knew God had already guided Pastor Darrell to place me in Pastor Petties's program.

Frankly, my mind and spirit were troubled as my ministry was called in a different direction.

Scripture: Quieting A Troubled Spirit

There are many times on our Journey when we are forced to confront a challenging situation, which can create a life-changing opportunity for personal growth. As I have recounted throughout this book, this has happened countless times in my life, but this conflict with Pastor Darrell was particularly difficult to deal with—in part, because it was so unexpected as I never saw it coming; and, too, it was delivered from a man who had been an important mentor and advocate in my life.

At this particular crossroads, I was shown by Spirit where in scripture to find the resolution that would quell my spiritual pain and confusion. Before sharing what those readings were, I first want to say, if you allow the struggle to defeat you without you fighting against your adversary, then your adversary will always vanquish you. But, if you stand up for yourself and your belief system, you will be victorious.

The reading was the story of David and Goliath.

David And Goliath

David was the youngest of Jesse's twelve sons. One day, the nation of Israel was called to fight the Philistine army that had gathered for war. While David's brothers went to fight, young David stayed back. The two armies gathered to stand on opposite sides of a deep valley. A great Philistine giant named Goliath, that stood at over nine feet tall, came to the front of the Philistine battle line each day for forty days and mocked the Israelites and their God. Goliath called to them to fight, but King Saul and the Israelites were scared and did nothing.

David was sent by his dad Jesse to visit the front lines and bring back battle news from his brothers. David heard Goliath mocking Israel and their God. David was brave and volunteered to fight Goliath. He persuaded King Saul to let him go fight and decided not to wear any of King Saul's armor. David carried his sling and gathered five smooth stones. Goliath laughed at David, but David responded that even though Goliath had a sword and spear, he came in the name of the Lord Almighty, the God of Israel. David put a rock in his sling and swung one of the rocks at Goliath's head. The rock sank into the giant's forehead, and he fell. David then picked up Goliath's sword and used it to kill Goliath and cut off his head.
1 Samuel 17:12–51

The verses I was directed to read referenced the story of a young King David being confronted by the giant Goliath, whom all the Israelite warriors and his older brothers were afraid of, intimidated by his size, ferocity, and taunts. The warriors were all stronger than David was; his brothers were stronger than he was, but they all let their fear overtake them and, instead of conquering the giant, they allowed Goliath and their fear to conquer them—until a young David refused to allow fear to overtake him. Rather, he believed that God would show him the way to conquer this giant—and, of course, we know how this story turned out.

Sidebar: One of my teachers speaks about fear as the "mind killer." He goes on to say, "When there is fear, there is doubt. Where there is doubt, there is no divinity."

Continuing: In Ephesians 6:10–20, it says:

> *Finally, my brethren, be strong in the Lord and in the power of His might. Put on the whole armor of God, that you may be able to stand against the wiles of the devil. For we do not wrestle against flesh and blood, but against principalities, against powers, against the rulers of the darkness of this age, against spiritual hosts of wickedness in the heavenly places. Therefore take up the whole armor of God, that you may be able to withstand in the evil day, and having done all, to stand.*
>
> *Stand therefore, having girded your waist with truth, having put on the breastplate of righteousness, and having shod your feet with the preparation of the gospel of peace; above all, taking the shield of faith with which you will be able to quench all the fiery darts of the wicked one. And take the helmet of salvation, and the sword of the Spirit, which is the word of God; praying always with all prayer and supplication in the Spirit, being watchful to this end with all perseverance and supplication for all the saints—and for me, that utterance may be given to me, that I may open my mouth boldly to make known the mystery of the gospel, for which I am an ambassador in chains; that in it I may speak boldly, as I ought to speak.*

It shows us here exactly what David did, as his is a lesson in courage, faith, and overcoming the seemingly impossible. When the courage in people's hearts is placed entirely in their faith in God, ultimately, victory is inevitable. David did not cower under the threats but, instead, he warned Goliath that he was fighting, not with his own hands, but with the hands of God. He rejected man's armor and shield and chose God's instead.

In summary, throughout my life, I have often had to console my troubled spirit as well as the troubled spirits of many of my congregants, and the story of David in Samuel is always paramount in my teaching. The obvious lesson is, do not let fear overtake you.

At this point in my life, whenever I seek the most effective solution, Spirit shows me where and how to find the answer—whether it be in scripture, in my own heart, or in my actions. As Spirit always resides in me, I know I can never be vanquished. My very soul is Spirit. My whole being is Spirit. Therefore, as in our interpretation of David and Goliath, we too always have the power to achieve when we are aligned with God.

That first Sunday after Pastor Darrell confronted me with the reading he presented, Spirit instructed me to go 1 Timothy 2:7–12 (New International Version), which reads:

> *And for this purpose I was appointed a herald and an apostle—I am telling the truth, I am not lying—and a true and faithful teacher of the Gentiles. Therefore I want the men everywhere to pray, lifting up holy hands without anger or disputing. I also want the women to dress modestly, with decency and propriety, adorning themselves, not with elaborate hairstyles or gold or pearls or expensive clothes, but with good deeds, appropriate for women who profess to worship God. A woman should learn in quietness and full submission. I do not permit a woman to teach or to assume authority over a man; she must be quiet.*

When Spirit directed me to read 1 Timothy after Pastor Darrell came to me, I really studied this chapter and verse very comprehensively. I went to other source material, as well as listened deeply within my soul, to understand as best I could correct interpretation of this passage, and realized that Pastor Darrell had a simplistic, literal interpretation of scripture.

In this moment, it also helped me understand that he was not the deep, wise scholar I had always believed him to be. Rather, he merely read the words in whatever translation he may have been reading, theoretically reflecting God's truth. It actually may not have been God's truth, as, for centuries, scholars have held many differing opinions regarding authorship, purpose, and interpretation based on the various translations from ancient Greek to English.

When I recognized that Pastor Darrell did not dig deeply into more broadly understanding God's teachings in these verses, I concluded that it was not in his nature to think deeply or broadly. If Spirit had not asked me to read this chapter and verse, I would not have achieved this clarity about Pastor Darrell that I needed in this moment.

Another significant teaching was that I began to recognize how Pastor Darrell ran his church. He never created an environment that allowed for questioning. He never invited dialogue; there was only his monologue. In retrospect, my impression was that, perhaps, he simply saw himself as channeling the word of God as, frankly, many ministers, myself included, do—but he never invited us to participate, only to listen and do our best to absorb the lesson.

A couple of years later, when I began my ministry, I recalled God's teaching to me from this moment and, from the very first day, I created my ministry around my philosophy. I was not here to speak from the perspective that I was the only one to hear God's truth or interpret the Lord. Rather, I began by creating an environment for discussion, for questions and answers, and thoughtful dialogue. To this day, our sermons are interactive.

What occurred between Pastor Darrell and me not only created an emotional and spiritual quagmire for me, but it also shattered Tragil. I was steadfast in my knowledge and belief that I could handle it, but one day, Tragil said to me with such raw emotion, "It was like he pulled the rug out from under me." If Tragil didn't *live with Jesus in her heart*, she really would have felt abandoned.

For years, the Blood, Water, and Spirit Ministry had been our ministry. Our whole family had attended this church, but now, Tragil and I felt that we could no longer attend services there. When we left in 2006, many others left as well.

An unexpected postscript: Three or four years later, I received a text from Pastor Darrell—calling me "Pastor."

New Mt. Nebo Missionary Baptist Church

Once I became a licensed minister in 2005, I went to Miami to visit Dwyane. I needed the space to reflect on my next steps and knew being with Dwyane would create the right environment. I knew I wanted to serve God. Before Pastor Darrell's confrontation with me, I thought his ministry, the ministry I had poured my life into for so many years, was always going to be my spiritual home. Now that we had left his church, I was unclear how to proceed.

On my return flight from Miami to Chicago, I remained in the deeper listening I had been connected with at Dwyane's. In this moment, I very clearly heard Spirit instruct me to go to my dad's church. I was so dismayed by this instruction that I even said out loud, "Dad's church?" I wasn't questioning God; I simply didn't understand.

Back in Chicago the next Sunday, I attended my dad's church, the church that God had sent me to, the New Mt. Nebo Missionary Baptist Church, which was west of Sixty-Ninth Street but still near my old community on the South Side.

At this juncture in my Journey, I was aware my family and friends were following my spiritual leadership and was subtly aware of my responsibility to lead us all to our next spiritual home.

That Sunday, my mom, my sisters, Tragil, and a few friends came with me. I had already told them that God instructed me to go to Dad's church. Though my parents had not lived together for many years, my mom and dad still had a great relationship with regard to us children.

The church did not have many members, and when we walked in the door, my dad, a deacon who sat on a bench separate from the congregation, looked up, saw us coming in, and wept, saying, "Oh no, oh no."

The other members asked him, "What's the matter, Edward?"

My father and I had not seen each other for some time, and when he saw my siblings and me, he said, "My children. I've got my children." Apparently, Dad had been praying that we'd come to his church—but never asked us because he thought we never would.

When we arrived, we looked around to see where we would sit and found seats close to him. To see the joy on Dad's face, to see my dad and mom in the same church. *Only God could do that.*

After the service, my sisters and I offered to help prepare and serve the meal, but the church members told us just to relax. Pastor also let us know that my dad, Deacon Morris, had recently been speaking about his children. Some in the congregation had even wondered whether Dad actually had children, as they had never seen any of us.

Tragil, other family members, and I began regularly attending Mt. Nebo. The ministry was led by Pastor Edward Range, who, after a while, asked me to copastor with him. I also worked by his side whenever he asked me to. One day, he came to me and said, "I'm ready to ordain you." And soon after, I became an ordained minister.

The Harvest Is Plentiful But The Laborers Are Few

Jesus went through all the towns and villages, teaching in their synagogues, proclaiming the good news of the kingdom and healing every disease and sickness. When he saw the crowds, he had compassion on them, because they were harassed and helpless, like sheep without a shepherd. Then he said to his disciples, "The harvest is plentiful but the workers are few. Ask the Lord of the harvest, therefore, to send out workers into his harvest field."
MATTHEW 9:35–38

The compelling reason I became a minister was to answer God's call to help as many people as I could.

As we know, God rescued me countless times, patiently loved me, and waited for me to fully welcome him into my heart. So, when I made the decision to become a minister, it was with the purpose of, for the rest of my life, being a magnet for the Lord, drawing as many people to Him as I could.

The scripture that Spirit directed me to what He was asking of me and what I was asking of myself, was described in the Gospels, primarily Luke 10:2 and Matthew 9:37, where Jesus said to His disciples, "The harvest is plentiful but the laborers are few."

My interpretation of that commandment was that I was to be part of the harvest, and a surprising revelation was that I emerged from the harvest also as a laborer—working with the next generation to nurture God's workforce any way I could, and a surprising revelation was that I emerged from the harvest also as a laborer—working with the next generation to nurture God's workforce anyway I could, while at the same time recruiting more laborers to support Jesus's workforce. The laborers go out among the people, spreading the word of Jesus's coming and of His miracles while praying for and with them; hold the disadvantaged; feed them; teach them.

Once I understood from this passage in Matthew that my path commanded that I become a minister, clarity and connection began to happen quickly and confidently.

During prayer time one day, I made a connection to a time in 1995 that had brought forth a revelation. I had been riding a bus down King Drive. It stopped on the corner of Fifty-Eighth Street to pick up passengers. As it did so, I looked out the window onto Fifty-Eighth Street. Fifty-Eighth Street was the same strip that I was using to drug and drink on.

Looking out the bus window, not only was I literally looking down on the people below me, but I was judging them. I said to myself, "Why are they still doing this? Don't they know better?" In this very moment, even though I myself was still using drugs and living on the street, I knew the truth of what Spirit then said to my spirit: "I brought *you* out—not them."

Even though I was still in the throes of a deep, dark life, I knew even then that I had miraculously been chosen. This truly humbled me because I was no different from them. Yet, Spirit had singled me out even before I was willing to accept His welcoming hand.

Though I could not yet love myself or raise myself up to climb out of the life I was living in, I began to have an inkling that, at some point in my life, my responsibility would be to love my fellow sojourners on Fifty-Eighth Street, embrace them, and show them through my example that there is a way out.

When I began my ministry, this story became one of the critical messages I would often teach.

Ordination And Ministry

Following this, I heard God place His commandment over my life by asking me, "Will you feed my sheep?"

My response, of course, was, "Yes!" and I immediately saw my path stretch out before me. Clearly, the time had arrived for me to complete the requirements for my ordination and begin my ministry.

Pastor Range created a curriculum for me and oversaw my studies for well over six months. One of the requirements for ordination was to sit for an oral exam administered by a panel of pastors. At that time, there was a good deal of opposition in our church to ordaining women, and Pastor Range wanted to ensure that I was thoroughly prepared so there would be no question about my qualifications. In addition, my dear friend Pastor Ed Jones was appointed to the examining panel. He and Pastor Range were two powerful advocates on my team, making sure I would be treated fairly by the examining committee.

I completed my studies with Pastor Range, passed the examination he created for me, and was ordained by him in 2007 at a church in Ford Heights, Illinois. My mother, father, my grannies, and my entire family were there. Dwyane and one of his best friends from the Miami Heat, Udonis Haslem, known as U.D., also attended. Udonis had been like one of my own children. His mother and I also experienced very similar things in life, including how we found the Lord.

A brief thought: Now that I had been ordained by Pastor Range, I realized that I never understood why Pastor Petties didn't ordain me and ask me to join her ministry. She had always been someone I could be myself with and who I felt comfortable with. So, once I'd been ordained by Pastor Range, I asked her why. She shared that she wanted to ask me to become part of her ministry, but God wouldn't allow her. She said that God told her that He wanted me to follow my own path.

In 2007, following my ordination, I was actually quaking with fear at the thought of beginning my ministry. One reason I struggled was the feeling that I didn't want to let God down. Twelve years after my bus ride and the epiphany that emerged from that, I was still in a place of trying to accept that He chose *me* to begin my ministry and to teach the disenfranchised.

Never in my life had I liked being in front of people. I always wanted to work behind the scenes, but I was now being clearly called to stand up in front of people, both as part of the harvest, as well as a laborer in God's field.

My ministerial vision became part of my mission statement: To teach the truth as I knew it to be from the Bible; always to help the abused, the misused; and to serve.

My vision was unique. It was borne from my experiences before prison, while I was still addicted and homeless. So, I knew the task and opportunity before me was to love them, embrace them, and show them, "If you choose to, there is a way out!"

In September of that year, I had the spiritual confidence to begin my ministry, but personally, I was still frightened and trembling when I thought about what was about to happen. However, I had fully surrendered to the Lord, knowing my responsibility was not to me but rather, it was clear that my calling was to serve.

Dwyane and his family offered me their home in Matteson, Illinois. Dwyane, his wife, and his son Zaire had moved to Miami when he joined the Heat, but he kept their home in Matteson.

I spoke with Pastor Range and let him know that I was told it was time to begin my own ministry, and he gave me his blessing. My family members followed me. So did a few parishioners from New Mt. Nebo, who had known me from my past life on the streets, recognized that I had changed, and subsequently became members of the church.

Pastor Ladell and I began our joint ministry in 2007 at Dwyane's home in Matteson. Bible study began on Tuesday evenings around five to accommodate all the faithful who had to travel a long way from the city, as Dwyane's home was in the suburbs.

My goal was to simply teach and focus on the youth of our congregation in order to shepherd them and help them develop faith in themselves and the Lord through my weekly teaching. While I taught the young people in one room, Pastor Ladell taught the adults in a separate room; then, at the end of every Bible study, we would bring both groups together and co-teach.

The evening concluded with a prayer circle and my simple encouragement to all in attendance, "Talk to God. Just talk to God," as many felt stigmatized that they couldn't pray, and I wanted to help remove that stigma from them—simply letting them know, "Prayer is just talking with God." Our service concluded, then we gathered for refreshments.

That first evening, I hadn't planned to initiate a prayer circle, but in the moment, in my deeper listening, I heard the Lord tell me this is how I should conclude my service. You'll recall that the first prayer circle I led was on the first anniversary of 9/11, while I was in prison, and I invited other inmates to join me in a prayer circle on prison grounds, breaking prison rules to do so. So, it was only natural for me to continue using the prayer circle as a bonding and liberating experience for all of us.

When living on the streets, various ministers would periodically come around and form prayer circles, asking, "Can I pray *for you*?" But, in our ministry, we did not pray for anyone; we prayed *with everyone*.

Sidebar: There's a through line in this portion of my story regarding prayer circles. Prayer circles have always emerged out of my deeper listening and convening with the Lord. I never worried about whether they were appropriate or inappropriate—if the Lord told me to hold them, that's all that mattered. If I broke the rules—so be it. For example, in prison, I definitely broke the rules and, in the beginning, was afraid. Still, I remained committed to God's truth coming through me and, in doing so, my fears instantly vanished—and the prayer circles became a fulfilling experience for each one of us—as God knew they would be.

To this day, my entire ministry is based on my ability to listen and hear the Lord's voice and act accordingly.

Initially, decades earlier, when I first heard God, God basically forced His way into my spirit and told me I would have to do this or that; but now, I was consciously aware at every level to the best of my ability, and definitely allowed God to always come *through me*. In doing so, my fear instantly vanished, just as years earlier the Lord commanded me to clean myself up and, in three days, I was drug- and alcohol-free. The fear and the trauma vanished at that time—and it once again vanished here.

When I stood before the children that first evening, recognizing that God had never given up on me through all the years of my giving up on myself, there is no other word for it: It was simply a miracle. God's miracles became another fundamental tenet of my teachings in my church.

As the days and weeks unfolded, I began to equate Bible stories and the teachings for the day with real-life experience. Pastor Petties's candor freed me, enabling me to tell my truth as I saw her tell hers. I was now able to do the same for these youth and other members of our church.

The children in my first congregation were my family members as well as the children of our congregants who accompanied their parents to our services. As we grew, a number of the youth who joined us had various addictions and homelessness issues. Some were runaways, some had been kicked out and lived alone on the streets, and the streets became their parents.

I, of course, first encountered street children when I too was homeless. They sold their bodies, they were on drugs, some didn't make it out, and died there. Now, these children have also become part of my ministry.

The children, who became part of and grew up in my ministry, not only listened but heard. As my life had been shattered by the temptations and trials of my preteen and teen years, I shared the stories in scripture and in my life, helping them recognize what they also might encounter as they grew.

Many confided in me how the same issues I grappled with were also happening in their lives. They often confessed to me that they never thought it would happen to them—but it did. They would relate how they often became angry with their parents, wanted to rebel, run away, wanted to just hang out with their friends, were offered drugs and alcohol, were tempted by the allures of street life, and all the other concerns that beset our youth with such horrific challenges, and were horrified and supported as I shared my childhood stories with them.

Because of the way that I shared so frankly while also connecting my stories to important lessons in the Bible, they not only heard my truth, but felt it. When I shared my stories, it helped them feel less alone, less misunderstood, and they knew I was different from many of the other "adults" in their lives. I truly believe they felt God's energy in me, but it was also the truth and honesty with which I shared God's word and made it relevant to them that helped them save their own lives. Many of these same children stayed in my ministry for years, from grammar school through high school.

Because of the success we were having, I created a program called "Steps to Success," which, when the youth graduated from high school, I would honor them with a ceremony and invite a guest speaker from the previous year's class. This created a true bond, a real camaraderie amongst us all. I still hear from many of them, some text me or I will ask their moms about them, and, from time to time, I will help out when the need arises.

As our ministry continued to grow and evolve, I realized that what we were achieving was quite unique. There was no hierarchy. I never talked down to the young people or looked down on them like that *other woman* who "looked down" on the troubled souls on Fifty-Eighth Street, not recognizing that she was one of them. I had been where these young people were. I had been where many of the adults who attended our services were. So, I believe I made a difference to the children who came up under me, especially because they knew I always spoke God's truth and recognized my truth in the stories I shared with them.

They had never met anyone else who had both lived on the street and made it out, let alone become a minister who returned to bring them the word.

I am truly humbled as I write this, for I know my ministry has saved many lives over the years, and it all began in the basement of my son's home in Matteson, Illinois.

One day in 2007, about seven or eight months into our ministry, I went to Pastor Ladell and told him that Spirit had come to inform me that it was time to move our ministry from the suburbs and closer to the city where our congregants lived. It would bring us closer to the community where we were needed and make it easier for them to attend services and Bible study.

A few days later, Pastor Ladell shared that a friend told him about a rental space that was available on Seventy-Ninth Street right off Ashland. When we looked into it, we found that it was an established church, but they were looking for an additional tenant to help defray costs. So, Pastor Ladell and I agreed that this would be a good next step, and a few weeks later, we began holding our one-day-a-week service in this new space.

Our church was named Temple of Praise: Binding and Loosening Ministries, International. I continued to copastor with Pastor Ladell Jones. The church name came from the fact that Pastor Jones heard God tell him that the church would be called "Temple of Praise," while, at the same time, I know God said to me it would be called "Binding and Loosening." So, we simply combined the names into Temple of Praise: Binding and Loosening Ministries. That same month, we incorporated and received our tax-exempt status.

Eight more months later, as our church was once again bursting at the seams, we were ready to move again.

129th Street—My First Church

When I realized that the current space we were renting at Seventy-Ninth and Ashland was no longer large enough to hold our growing congregation, I began wondering where we might move to.

So, Pastor Ladell, his wife Adelia, and I began visiting various churches at different sites in Chicago. One night, when we were about ready to give up, I spotted a building at 129th and Halsted with a "For Sale" sign out front. I pointed it out to Pastor and Adelia, and, simultaneously, we all exclaimed, "Wow!" It was the perfect building in the perfect location, and the energy that emanated from the building embraced all of us.

We pulled into the parking lot looking for contact information and found a phone number, which we called. A gentleman answered the phone and introduced himself as Pastor Cornelius. I told him that my friends and I were interested in looking at the space. He said, "I live right across the street, and I'll come over and take you through the building." Again, one of God's miracles.

When I was standing in this vast sanctuary, I heard a Voice say, "This is your church."

I turned around, looking to see who spoke, but there was no one in there with me. And I actually said out loud, "What?"

Then, I heard it again, "This is your church." At this point, I knew it was God's voice I was hearing, but I didn't tell Pastor Ladell of this conversation. The three of us just kept walking around that wonderful space. We then thanked Pastor Cornelius and left. We didn't make any commitment to him or to each other, but in my heart, it was already settled that that was the building where our Father wanted us to minister to the needs of our people.

As we drove away, all three of us sat in silence for a while. When we began to speak and share our feelings, I was clear what our decision would be, but Pastor and Adelia were less certain. So, before dropping me off at home, we agreed to meet the next day to discuss further.

When I got home, I told Tragil about it and what God told me, she immediately wanted to hop in the car and drive by—which is what we did. When Tragil saw the building and heard my description of all that the church had to offer us, and, because she trusted me implicitly, she knew this would be our next spiritual home.

A few days later, Pastor Cornelius let us know that he was holding an open house for all interested pastors to look at the building. But in my heart, it was settled. God had told me this was to be our church, and when I told Pastor Ladell what the Lord had said, he agreed.

So, following the open house, we called Pastor Cornelius and told him of our intention to purchase this building to house our church, and agreed on the price. The next step would be to go to the bank to secure a loan for the purchase.

That's when we discovered that moving into our first big beautiful building was not going to be quite so simple.

We went to Chase Bank to apply for the loan because that's where we both had accounts. When I first spoke with the loan officer, she simply said I would never qualify, even with my son's help, because my credit score was disastrous and, frankly, Pastor Ladell's wasn't any better. All I had to support my application was a list of thirty people who also had low credit scores.

When the loan officer actually said to me that I would never qualify—even with my son's help—I said in response, "Well, you watch and see, ma'am, because I heard God say that this is where I would build my first church." *That Voice again!* The date was May 4, 2008, and I also told her, "I'm going to invite you to our opening."

Around this same time, Dwyane and I attended a retreat together where he saw a vision of me having my own church. Tragil also had this same vision and, when she saw how much trouble I was having securing a loan, without my knowledge, she called Dwyane and said, "I can see Ma doing this. Mama is doing everything possible, but she needs you now." I wanted to do this on my own, but it simply was not possible. Once again, the Lord made it happen.

When Dwyane came with Tragil and me to inspect the building, he said, "You're going to do some wonderful things here, Mom." We were sitting upstairs in the banquet hall of the church. He walked around, stepped up on the pulpit, and, of course, my extraordinary son believed in me—believed enough to invest $1.5 million—and asked his business team to speak to the loan officer at the bank. This conversation enabled me to buy that church.

At this moment in time, Dwyane was arguably the greatest basketball player in the NBA. Also at this time, he was recovering from two surgeries, shoulder and knee, which required a rigorous and arduous rehabilitation program four months prior to playing on the 2008 United States Olympic Basketball Team representing our country in Beijing. At the same time, he was also going through a very contentious personal battle in his private life. In spite of *all of this*, he still made time to stand up for his mother. To quote my mentor, "A champion does it differently."

Escrow closed in May 2008, and the opening of our church was covered in *Jet* magazine.

As I said I would, I invited the loan officer to our opening. She did come, and the first thing she said to me was, "I believe there's a God." She then recounted our first conversation and recalled my steadfast belief in what the Lord had said to me. Dwyane and his son Zaire walked us in. My mother, father, and the rest of my family were also in attendance.

We actually had a ribbon-cutting ceremony that day. Dwyane spoke. "Magic" Johnson's mother attended. Shaq's mother attended. It was one of the most spectacular days of my life.

Our church was now born.

My ordination, the start of my ministry at Dwyane's home, our second ministry at Seventy-Ninth and Ashland, and the opening of our own church building all took place within the span of one year. I certainly didn't think about this at the time, but as I write my story, I am so amazed at how rapidly my path accelerated.

Side bar: You'll recall from the passage in Matthew about the harvest being plentiful but the laborers few, that His disciples were charged with getting the word out quickly. Well, God was certainly doing His best to help me do that.

I was confident that I had been led by Spirit to pastor in this perfect place. When I awakened the morning of my first sermon in our beautiful new church and began my daily prayer ritual, I was struck by the fact of what was about to occur and took a moment to reflect on the arc of my Journey that brought me to this day.

As I've said before, God had actually delivered me out of the wilderness, and in a few hours, I was about to address the congregation in a church that we owned. The fact that I could recognize and acknowledge the depth of God's love for me and mine for Him—words could not express.

I simply sat silently in prayer for some time, listening, weeping with joy, humbled by God's unconditional trust in me and belief in me. Later when I stood on the pulpit for the first time looking out at the members of our church dressed in their Sunday finery, sharing God's pure love for us and began teaching that day's scripture, my voice resounded with such power and, also, with such exquisite intimacy, as the words I was sharing were not my words alone, they were also *God's words coming through me.*

About two years into my pastoral relationship with Pastor Ladell, God came to me and said it was now time for me to stand on my own two legs. I shared with Pastor what God had told me, and he understood. When he left our joint ministry in June 2011, I changed the name of our church to New Creation: Binding and Loosening Ministries, International. Truth be told, however, to this day I have never stood alone on any pulpit I speak from or in any lessons I teach—for *God is always with me.*

A few years earlier, when I separated from Pastor Darrell, Mom told me that one of the reasons she followed me as I began building my own ministry was because she believed that, by following her child, she was following the God within me. She would always need a ride, so my sister Diann might swing by and pick her up, or someone from the church would go and get her.

Each service, seeing my mother in church, so overjoyed and proud of me, was a glorious experience. As my mother grew older, she began suffering from dementia and would occasionally shout out in church, "Jolinda! That's my daughter there—Jolinda!" While I was speaking, she would occasionally call out, "Yeah, say it! Please, child, say it! That's my daughter!" God had given her the time to see me rise out of that dark place I had lived in for so many years. In her new state of mind, she was liberated to unabashedly speak from her heart. I was touched to hear her say, "That's my kid," and, to anyone who might criticize me, she would look at them and say, "Don't you say nothin' 'bout her." The look I always I saw on her face made me want to run to the pulpit.

I had everything! God, Mama, Daddy, my children. I had never felt or been so complete in my life.

My Dad

Before I became a minister, I occasionally visited my father, but Mt. Nebo was the first time I'd ever seen him in a church. Before that, I hadn't even known my dad went to church.

You may recall that during my first incarceration in Dwight Correctional Center, I began corresponding with my dad. Even though he had continued to be an occasional presence in my life, we never had a real relationship. I never really liked him or respected him. I always felt that my never having a father figure led to the terrible choices I made in men, especially the abusive men in my life.

Of course, throughout our childhoods, he was a presence, as he lived on Sixty-Third Street and we lived on Fifty-Ninth. When we were still young kids, Mom would take us to the park to meet up with him and whatever woman he was with. We all would sit around together just being one family. From time to time, he'd say to her, "Mae Willie, can I get the kids?"

She'd say, "Yeah, you can come and get 'em."

Mom never kept us from him. She forgave him and never said anything against him. She'd say, "That's your father. Just because you didn't grow up with him, don't mean that he's not your daddy." As you know, we get our forgiveness and unconditional love from Mom. She was that person. She didn't care about the other girlfriends he may have been with. We saw forgiveness then, saw her love him from afar, and it taught us how to love him.

As I matured and went through what I went through in my life, once I'd been released from prison the last time and became a minister, I wanted my dad in my life. So, after church, I would go and visit my daddy. He was in his seventies, living in a one-bedroom basement apartment at Sixty-Fourth and Langley.

Now, I have loved books all my life, but I never knew where my love of knowledge and books came from until my dad and I connected. I knew it didn't come from Mom as she was very undereducated, and I never saw her reading books, although she did work crossword puzzles in the newspapers. I didn't know where I got that love for books from, until my dad and I connected, and I learned—it came from Dad.

We used to sit down in Dad's little sitting room, where he had bookshelves filled with books. Always drawn to books, I said, "Dad, you read these?" He said, "Yeah, I read that. Get that book right there." He could tell you what was in them.

I looked at him and asked, "Can I take them home?"

He said, "Yeah, but I want them back, Joseph." I never learned why, but all my life, he called me Joseph. He never called me Jolinda.

I said, "OK, OK." That's when I got to know my father's intellect.

We were able to sit and talk about so many different subjects. We would discuss my going into the ministry. He believed I was called by God.

He would often create a scenario designed to make me think. I remember one time he said to me, "You know, one thing about you, Daughter?"

I said, "Yeah, Dad?"

He said, "Tain't nobody can ever tell nothin' about you."

I asked, "Why do you say that?" At that time, I was on a radio broadcast every Tuesday, and he used to listen to it.

He said, "No skeletons in your trunk. You tell everything!"

I started laughing.

My dad came to live with me shortly after I opened my church, and each Sunday, I would bring him to church with me. To see my dad there meant the world to me—the first man in my life, listening to me deliver God's message. My dad was very smart and an excellent listener. He'd often say, "You did good. Mmm-mmm, I liked that. I liked that." Because he knew the Bible, sometimes he might say, "I don't know, maybe you need to go and check something out." After all the lost years, I had found my father, and my father had found me.

After my father moved in with me, I learned so much more about him, and I just got it. He was the type of man who had to have a newspaper every day, and my dad read the *whole* newspaper. He was a thinker. He loved spending time reading and thinking, but he and I loved being together, whether he was teaching me or I was sharing with him, or we were simply talking with one another. I would run a message or a sermon by him and ask him what he thought, or he might call me in and say, "Tell me what you think about this. Now, go and run and preach that." That was my dad.

Dad was direct, loving, and strong, but he wasn't the type of man or father who showed his emotions. When we were children, he would show his love with gestures such as inviting us over for a barbecue, asking our mother if he could pick us up and bring us over to his house, or taking us for an outing.

When he hugged us, they were never tight hugs, rather light hugs with a pat on the back. As adults, we experienced his love when he hugged us with the same gentle pat on the back—and, at least in my case, by occasionally seeking my company, conversation, and counsel.

My dad always respected my mom, and when he came to my ministry, my mom was going into her dementia. In her mind, she was living in a time when she and my dad were still a couple. So, he would sit in the row in front of her, and she sat behind him like she was watching over him, making sure he was OK.

I remember one time my sisters and I took her to my house to see Dad, and she said, "Where your daddy at?"

We said, "He's in the other room." We never knew what was going to come out of this woman's mouth. So, she swished her little behind into the room and sat down in a chair. We sisters were all standing off to the side, wondering what they were going to say to one another.

She said, "Edward!" and he said, "Yeah, Mae Willie?" He had always called her Mae Willie.

She said, "Tell me somethin'."

He said, "What?"

She said, "Why you do me like that?" and he said, "Do you like what?"

She said, "You mess with all them women while I was the one!" She brought it all up because that was the time she was living in, and she chose that moment to bring it to him and put it on the floor. She sure put it out there.

He said, "No, Mae Willie." He really tried to explain to her what happened that, yes, he messed around with one of her friends, this and that. You could also tell they still loved each other. It was so cute to us, because our parents were in the same room together, and she was reliving their history. Because they had known each other for so long, our dad helped us fill in the gaps in her history and their lives together.

My dad lived with me for about a year before he was diagnosed with cancer and transitioned to be with the Lord. I am eternally grateful that God granted me this opportunity to spend as much time with him as I did. As I was so grieved, I asked Pastor Range from Mt. Nebo church to officiate at Dad's funeral, which he did.

One Final Memory

Each Sunday at the conclusion of services, our tradition was to have a community meal at the church, which we prepared in the church kitchen and ate in the large dining room while we sat around and talked. Just like the students and the women in the congregation of Pastor Petties had served her, many members of my congregation stayed and helped prepare lunch. They also set a special table for me where my mother, father, children, and other family members sat. Occasionally, Mama Foster and her children also sat with us. She was a wise and wonderful woman in her late seventies, whom I met at Mt. Nebo, whose counsel I truly appreciated.

To accept the love of the congregants as they gave so openly, as we did for Pastor Petties, once again brought me full circle. It was extraordinary. Who'd ever thought this would be possible? *God—God always knew.*

We kept the church open from 2008 to 2020, when COVID-19 hit. I gave my last sermon at that church on June 28, 2020. God then sent me to Los Angeles to be near my son and his family and continue my ministry. I moved to LA on July 2, 2020.

My ministry is now more global as, online, I host weekly Bible study while also speaking around the country. Health is now also an important component of my ministry. In my weekly podcasts, *Check N' with Mama Wade*, I speak about physical, mental, and spiritual health while also occasionally including scripture in my weekly teaching.

My Journey continues to unfold.

I know how I want to conclude this chapter, but only the Lord knows the concluding chapter.

Epilogue

Unconditional Love
Stories From My Friends And Family

At this stage of my Journey, I have not merely survived—I have soared. I've shared that there were long periods of time when I felt alone, but, as you will read, unaware that I was never abandoned. Throughout the decades, trapped in my addictions, it was often hard for me to "see the forest for the trees." It is only from the vantage point that God has blessed me with to now look back and more clearly see the arc of my life.

In this memoir, I am, of course, revealing myself to you, my readers, and, also, truth be told, finally revealing myself to myself. I have tried to be rigorous, honest, and transparent, for this is the only way I now know how to live, which leads me to why I created this epilogue.

The family and friends I've invited to share their observations are here because a number of years ago I came to realize, as you've heard me say, I would not have achieved the life I've been privileged to live without the support, dedication, belief in me, positive regard, and unconditional love of this coterie of family and friends.

Here I am reminded of Mary Stevenson's moving 1939 poem, "Footprints in the Sand," which she felt divinely inspired to compose at the age of fourteen following a childhood of profound loss and hardship. It so comforted her that she began to share it as a way of comforting others who suffered. As she wrote it:

One night I dreamed I was walking
along the beach with the Lord.
Many scenes from my life flashed across the sky.
In each scene I noticed footprints in the sand.
Sometimes there were two sets of footprints,
other times there were one set of footprints.

This bothered me because I noticed that
during the low periods of my life, when I was
suffering from anguish, sorrow or defeat,
I could see only one set of footprints.

So I said to the Lord, "You promised me
Lord, that if I followed you,
You would walk with me always.
But I have noticed that during the most trying periods
of my life there have only been
one set of footprints in the sand.
Why, when I needed you most,
you have not been there for me?"

The Lord replied,
"The times when you have
seen only one set of footprints,
is when I carried you."

I share this because it is only now that I'm fully capable of looking at the entirety of my life and realizing that it was not only the Lord who carried me when I could not carry myself but, also, so many of my family and friends who have *always been with me and for me unconditionally*—literally, no matter what.

"It takes a village to raise a child" is an African proverb that exists in many African languages and reflects the emphasis placed on family and community in African culture. According to one reference I've read, it may have its source in the Bible—from Ecclesiastes 4:9–12 (New International Version):

> *Two are better than one, because they have a good return for their labor: If either of them falls down, one can help the other up. But pity anyone who falls and has no one to help them up. Also, if two lie down together, they will keep warm. But how can one keep warm alone? Though one may be overpowered, two can defend themselves. A cord of three strands is not quickly broken.*

Within my family, each of us siblings and each of our children learned unconditional love from my mother and our children's grandmother, Willie Mae Morris.

As I think about my mother's legacy and what a remarkable woman she was, perhaps her most transcendent quality was her ability to embody unconditional love and impart it to all who knew her, her children, grandchildren, and friends. Her dedication to the Lord was preeminent. Her dedication to all of us, doing whatever it took to support and raise us as best she could, is a testament to her strength—her unconditional love a testament to her integrity, to her character. To see my mother treat everyone equally, accept everyone, respect everyone, and judge no one spoke volumes. The power of her teaching resonates within each of us who are blessed to call her Mama and Grannie.

One of my friends attended my sixty-sixth birthday party a couple of years ago. Virtually my entire family was there. It was the first time he met most of my family and saw how we love and interact with one another. He is aware of all the life challenges we have faced throughout the years. He was so moved by this experience that he returned to my home the next day when my family was still in town to say to all of us, with tears in his eyes, that he had never experienced a family like ours, a family with absolutely no judgment—rather *absolute unconditional love*. He'd heard me speak of it, but now, he was experiencing it. That's the way it has always been, and that's the way it will always be—and it all began with Willie Mae.

I have concluded sharing my life story and have opened the door to others to share their stories of our mutual histories and experiences. Whether it is one of my sisters telling her truth, one of my children, or friends I've known throughout my life, either from the streets or from my ministry, the one underlying element that connects us all is unconditional love. To this day, each of us is there for one another, and that's what makes this chapter so very special for me to share with you.

Testimonials

Family

Diann Aldridge

I am Diann, the eldest daughter of Willie Mae Morris. Jolinda is my next younger sister by three years. Willie Mae had four older children by a prior relationship and raised all nine of us as a single parent, supporting us on her wages as a housekeeper.

My mom was so amazing. She had such willpower. When we were growing up, it wasn't that we had it so hard. The way my mom was, she didn't know a whole lot—so, of course, as she grew older, she learned from experience how to deal with us and our spirits. It was simply amazing how she just prayed, prayed us through—whether we knew it or wanted it or not, she was always praying for us.

Trust me, we fought, but you would not have believed that we fought. We had our little differences, but within five minutes, we would be back with each other. We never experienced any malice toward one another or anything like that. Everybody at school knew I was the eldest one, and none of the kids could do anything to my little sisters and brother because they already knew their sister Diann, and knew I would come at the drop of a hat. We were family, that's it.

As the eldest, living my own life, there were a lot of things I didn't see. However, I do remember when our mom used to take us to the annual Bud Billiken Parade and Picnic. This was a huge event in our young lives as, even now, it's the biggest African-American parade in the United States—and, in terms of parade size, it is second only to the Rose Parade. It began in 1929 to honor the newsboys who sold the *Chicago Defender*, an early successful and influential African American newspaper that is still in print to this day. In order to attract customers, the newsboys were known for doing a song and dance on the sidewalks. The newsboys band included jazz greats Nat "King" Cole and Lionel Hampton.

There were big floats and many marching bands. I remember Jolinda being afraid of the drums and, just as later when she was terrified by horror movies, she would become so scared that only Mom could calm her down and comfort her by holding Jolinda close to her.

I do remember that, even as a child, Jolinda was so into reading books, being a teacher, and teaching everyone how to read.

These days, she teaches from the pulpit and teaches in a way you can understand. She is always open. If you need help, if there's something you don't understand, she's right there—not putting you off. If you call her in the middle of the night, she wakes up, takes your call, and answers your questions. Even if you need a prayer, she is there for that, too. That's the type of teacher she was and is. It is never about her. It is *only* about the Lord's work, giving it to you just as He gives it to her.

When she had her ministry in Chicago, young people were attracted to her. There were a few who were on that edge, on the cliff, and, being who she is, she had to talk them down. What made her relationship with them so successful was that she shared her truth—unfiltered—which enabled them to relate to her and see that she had already lived what they were experiencing and became for them an example of what is possible. That was a blessing, an absolute blessing.

I am a minister as well. I go all the way back to after Jolinda was released from prison the second time, when she used to stay on Eighty-Seventh, and I was staying with her at her house. One particular day, she told me to pray. I wasn't really a churchgoer and, when my sister told me to pray, I said, "I don't know how."

She said, "The same way you talk to me, to anyone, that's the way you pray. You just talk to God."

And that's how I started on the path to the ministry—I learned how to pray. She encouraged me to join the ministry and became my teacher. She also taught her daughter Tragil and our sister B. B. When we graduated, Jolinda licensed us. She's a mother to all of us—especially once we got into the ministry.

Jolinda has such a beautiful spirit. She'll go the extra mile for anyone—I mean, anyone. Even if you are homeless, she'll still go that extra mile because she has such a caring heart.

She doesn't have enemies. When she meets someone with a bad heart, she moves around it and doesn't get caught up in the whirlwind—that's who she is. She just walks the walk—the path that God has for her. She listens to Him and does what she's supposed to do.

She's awesome already, and she gets better and better as time goes on. She is learning more insights on different things, like health issues and the different things that affect your body, like what vitamins you need to take to help support your immune system. She gathers the information and doesn't keep it to herself, but passes it along to give us the help that we normally wouldn't try to get.

Her audience learns from her wisdom. She holds nothing back but simply gives us the raw truth. When she takes steps for something she needs to go through, like going to the doctor to treat an illness, she reads up on it, finds out more, and then shares it with us on her health podcast, *Better Health, Better Me*. That's who she is today, and I wouldn't have it any other way.

My sister is just amazing, absolutely amazing.

B. B. Griffin

I am B. B., Jolinda's next younger sister. Edward Morris Sr. was our father. Willie Mae Morris, our mother, raised and supported all of us, her nine children, as a single parent. At home, Jolinda and I shared one bedroom with our other sisters and our little brother, Eddie Jr.

Unconditional love began with my mother because, in spite of it all—the life we lived and the things we were doing in our individual lives—she loved us unconditionally. That rubbed off on us because Mama used to tell us, "All you have is each other."

Being a large family, we spent a lot of time together. We knew our mother loved us and, even though she didn't express her love for us by telling us or hugging and kissing us, she made us hug and kiss each other.

In spite of the rules she taught us—the dos and don'ts, on trusting yourself and loving on each other—there were certain times when we would get rebellious with each other. At the end of the day, in spite of how we felt, she would say, "Now kiss and make up. You don't want to, but you're going to do it anyway."

We saw what she was trying to do, but it was for us to get it. We learned that unconditional love is seeing you for who you are, with all your faults, like God looks upon us. This principle was embedded in us.

And we passed it on to our children as well. Whatever we went through, we knew our kids were affected by it—but we wanted them to always know that, in spite of anything and everything, "I still love you. I'm here even if I'm gone, out of sight, out of mind, I still love you. Never forget unless you hear different."

When we were children, I used to think Jolinda was strange. She always had things going on that we couldn't understand, so we called it strange. She loved to read and used to teach herself all the time. Sometimes she would line up her shoes and talk to them while the rest of us just wanted to go outside and have fun.

Even though we went to church, we weren't grounded in it. Today I know that God was talking to Jolinda, preparing her. To see the powerful woman she has become is amazing. Everyone has a story, and her story made her the woman she is today.

As Jolinda and I grew up, even after we went our different ways and did the things we did in our lives, we always loved each other and continued to look after each other. Jolinda had and still has a good heart, but early on, she chose to go down another road. I went down the same road, but she took it a little bit farther.

In spite of everything she did back then, she was my sister. Let me chastise her; nobody else needs to say anything about her. The love and the bond we shared with each other were so strong that, sometimes, we felt each other even when we weren't around each other. We called ourselves "the sisters." "We are the sisters." We had each other to lean on. If I heard something or if something was going on in the lifestyle we were living, I used to go find my sister.

Our lifestyles took a toll on us. Jolinda went to the penitentiary, and I went to the penitentiary. Another sister went to jail. In spite of everything, we never looked down on one another because of the choices we had made in life. There was a deep affection among us, and we always looked out for each other's well-being. Our bond is strong with each other.

The road Jolinda took wasn't easy, and you could simply look at her back then and see how bad it was—but God had her. Even when she was asking for money, she was homeless. God was showing her, "I've got you, but I cannot take control unless you let go." She had to be ready to surrender. We can't pick and choose what we want to give Him. It means I decrease myself and increase Him within me.

God is the light, and she is a beacon of the light God sends us, and we know we are part of that light. Seeing her go through the storm and fire and coming out unscathed, untouched, helped us know that God is real. Now I know that she really did hear from God. When she preaches the word, it's so clear that you can't do anything else but get it. Spirit knows Spirit.

My dad was a deacon at New Mt. Nebo and knew Jolinda had a gift. People see things that you don't see. You think nobody is watching you, but people are watching you, and people came to her because they saw the light. Jolinda was on her path, and we couldn't hold her back. We had to let her go. She said, "If you love me, you will let me go." It was beautiful.

I've been with Jolinda since she began her first ministry at Dwyane's house. She truly made a difference in my life. I went into the ministry because God showed me the faces of people I was to invite into the ministry. We were already in His service through the church when she told us, "You were chosen." I knew she heard from God, so I didn't question it.

She licensed my sister Diann and me. There was no favoritism. I had my homework and I had to study. She understood and met me where I was. I had a good teacher, and I'm so proud to be her sister.

Rose Morris

I am Jolinda's youngest sister and the youngest of Willie Mae Morris's nine children. As a single parent, my mother raised us while working full-time as a housekeeper to support us. It wasn't easy, but Mama never complained. As she was gone a lot, we always looked after each other because that's the way we were raised.

First and foremost, the way my late mom, Willie Mae Morris, parented us established the course of our lives. She set rules as a parent and taught us common sense. She never tolerated disrespect or rudeness and would say to us, "You treat people nice. You open doors for people." Or "Don't say that, that's mean." She was a strong, family-oriented person and made sure we always ate together.

Because she could only do so much, even as children, individually, we decided to hold that respect for each other because it worked for us. Mama wouldn't have it any other way.

This was the beginning of the embodiment of our mother's principle of unconditional love. In addition, our mother taught us the importance of always treating each other with decency and looking at each other in a positive way, not only with respect but without judgment. This is how we were raised, and this is how we treat each other to this day. It's so amazing that one person could set that tone, and we just followed it.

My sister Jolinda followed Mama's teachings. As a sister, she automatically wanted to do the right thing. She didn't have to think about it; she simply did it. She always encouraged me. She knows me. I'm the sister who is very hard to get to know because I don't allow people in easily, but Jolinda could always get in because she always knew me, and I trusted her.

Once, when I was in second grade and I believe my sister was in fifth grade, we were getting ready for school, but I was upset because I felt like I didn't look my best. I asked her, "Can you help fix me up, make me look more attractive?" She didn't hesitate. Even though we risked being late for school, Jolinda wouldn't let me leave until she'd fixed me up. I was distraught about being late, but she looked at me and right away said, "No, I'm going to fix you."

Everybody in the house left for work and school, but she made sure I was OK, and then, and only then, did she allow us to walk out the door—happier simply because I was happy. I'm sixty-three years old now and still vividly remember that moment. That's how important it was to me.

When she was nineteen and I was still in high school, our roles changed—she had been my protector, then I became her protector. I followed her everywhere she would go—right or wrong. She would say, "No, don't go with me, and I'll be back. OK?" and I said, "No, I just want to go with you."

She said, "No! This is not the place for you." So, I'd stand back and wait. If my sister went into a store that wasn't to my liking, I'd have to wait outside while she bought what she wanted—like liquor. She would come out with the liquor, for example, but she never let me go in and witness her buying it. I used to show up and watch out for her because I couldn't afford to lose that sister, so I became her protector, but she didn't know it.

It never occurred to me to judge her. I'm like that today. None of us in the family cares if our sister is in the gutter; we're coming for you. "Put your sparkle back on." That is our kind of attitude. There is absolutely no judgment. We *never* judge one another or anyone.

We know some people go left. We don't see it. Whatever path they are on, we just ask, "Wha'chu been up to?" That's how it's going to be. That's the way it is. We take some hits because they want us to judge, but we can't. It's not in us. Again, this is our mother's teaching.

I simply didn't see what most people would see. I didn't see the drugs. I just thought that whatever my sister was going through was a change of lifestyle. My sister showed me what a sister looked like. When she married Big Wade, she became very domestic and showed me what a wife looked like and what a mother looked like. Once she left Big Wade with her four children and took her own apartment, she continued her domestic lifestyle. Jolinda would keep the house clean and would iron a week's worth of clothes for her kids. She was that type of mother. A lot of people didn't see it, but I did.

When Jolinda was released from prison the second time, I had come home to Chicago for two or three years, and we started over. I'll never forget her ordination. I was sitting there in tears. I knew her—she has always had the Lord's Spirit within her. She has always been a student and a teacher at the same time. So I wasn't surprised when she studied so hard, post-prison, to become a minister because she always loved learning.

Jolinda had always spoken from the heart, but what took me aback, coming from where she came from, was that she was able to articulate her message and the Lord's message so well. During her ordination, when it came time for the test, which we were all allowed to witness, she didn't struggle answering any of the questions the panel asked—even hard ones. She was fearless, just as she is today. She studies very hard and is confident she is ready for whatever the Lord asks of her—whether it is the exam at ordination or on the pulpit today, my sister is always prepared.

At her ordination, I said to myself, "There she goes." Inside of me, I was smiling because I said, "Don't ever give up on her. She's back. I knew it!" I was just tearing up inside. "Don't ever doubt her." That's what I would say. I was so very proud.

Her youngest daughter, Tragil, and my daughter are the same age. When they were seventeen, my daughter and I were living in San Diego. One day, I got a call from Tragil saying she needed help, and her mother had suggested she call me. When we spoke, I immediately told my niece to come to us, so moved that my sister would entrust her daughter to my care.

A couple of months later, I received another call from Tragil's older sister, Keisha, who was in a challenging relationship as well, and asked to come and stay with me, followed a year later by their eldest sister, Deanna.

Part of the reason I am sharing this is that we are family. Even if we are not living in the same city, we are still a close-knit family. To know that Jolinda would entrust her children to me speaks volumes.

As you know, our mother Willie Mae raised us to always be here for one another, raised us to take care of and look out for one another. When needed, my family took care of me and, when they need it, I will take care of them.

My sister is a shield for everyone who knows her. She is an encourager. Even when we were children, she was and still is my voice when I feel I can't be heard. She comes in many different forms. She protects us directly and indirectly. I have always seen the Spirit in her.

My sister is a person who has a heart that shares and loves. My actions for my sister Jolinda are way bigger than my words because I don't have the vocabulary—but, to this day, my actions are strong for her.

It's such a divine intervention that we are sisters. If she feels pain, I feel pain. If she laughs, I'm laughing. If she's crying, basically, I'm crying. I'm very attached to her; she's my everything!

In my experience, in my heart, and my eyes, she was and is to this day—a giant.

Deanna Morris

I am Deanna, the eldest of Jolinda's four children.

My maternal grandmother, Willie Mae Morris, raised me. My mother was sixteen and still a schoolgirl when I was born. She had all of us when she was still so young. We all, my mother included, lived with my grandmother. Willie Mae raised me, so I really took a lot from her. She would say, "You got to love your mother," and "Never go against your mother." That was something my grandmother instilled in all of us—to love our mother, no matter what—and it worked.

Willie Mae helped us understand that when your parent is weak, you don't want to make them feel weaker—break them down and make them feel like they're failing—because they already feel like that. We just knew we were a family that had to get through things together.

I want people to understand that you might paint a picture of the life my family and I lived as a rough life because we lived in the 'hood with its gangs, drugs, alcohol, and partying all around us, and as part of our lifestyle. It may sound funny to you, but we had a pretty nice upbringing. It wasn't as rough or as bad as a person might think—we had a nice life.

When I was thirteen, my mother was still young, not yet thirty, and "right in the middle of her madness." Even in her madness, she managed to let us know, and it was very important to her, that we were her first priority. She often told us how much she loved us and cared for us. She always tried to put her best foot forward. My mother loved us so much that, even when she was in the sick time of her life, she always wanted us to know how much she loved us.

It certainly wasn't always easy. Being the eldest made me aware of a lot of things that were going on around me—for example, things that my brother and sisters didn't notice, such as the drugs, the violence, and certain people around us. I noticed the stuff that I knew shouldn't have been there, but was there.

As the eldest, even as a kid, I took on a lot of responsibility I didn't always want to take on, such as having to watch the younger kids. In that context, even though I was struggling with my own issues, I understood that it was embarrassing for my mother to look at her children and still choose to use drugs as opposed to the things she should have been doing for us. That's why I say, I felt like it was just a sick time in her life. I knew it made her feel sad to look at us and still decide to use drugs. But, as her eldest child and the big sister, I would say to family and friends, "My mother's sick right now." I intuitively knew you couldn't possibly be in your right state of mind and be all right with living that lifestyle with children around.

During her illness, I occasionally would say things out of hurt or anger. I never sucked it up and, when I was about thirteen, started voicing myself and always told my mother how I felt—and we would really go at it.

When I was fourteen or fifteen, my mother introduced Greg into our home. That's when things got really hectic—and that's when I joined the gang. I didn't join because I wanted another family; I loved the family that God gave me already. I joined the gang because the gang asked me to join them. I told them the only way I would join them is if they "killed my mama's boyfriend." They agreed, and I joined, but they never killed him. They jumped him a lot of times, but nothing worse than that.

I was twenty-five, still living in the projects with my two children. I was going through a lot, trying to figure out who Deanna was, how to be a parent, when my mother told me she was going to turn herself in and go back to prison. Before she returned to prison, we all spent a week or two hanging with Mom and each other. We talked with her, played cards—getting our little family time in because, to our knowledge, she was probably going to be gone for a while. We were just trying to embrace it.

After my mother was released and returned to us, she was completely clean. I could feel God's presence in her.

As a child, I had known my mother this way before she started doing what she did, but I didn't know this person. It was irritating at first because, even though she had been clean in our early childhood, this was the first time we had known her like this as adults—and we didn't understand. We were so used to "Josie" and now, here she was, somebody else. She had come out a clean and changed person.

We all looked at her like, "What are you doing? What's going on?" Tragil understood because, unlike the rest of us, she had grown up going to church with our mother and grandmother. Even though I didn't understand, I knew it was real, and I knew I had to follow her.

After she became a minister, I went to her services, and I loved it. I had grown up knowing nothing about God, the Bible—anything. The first time I went, I went to protect my mother, watching over her, because I never wanted anybody to do or say anything harmful to my mother. Initially, that was my purpose in going. Eventually, I ended up getting the Word and got to know God in my life. She taught me a lot, and what I know today from the Bible all came from her.

I have the privilege of knowing my mother before she got sick. Even in her illness, she never skipped a beat. As I look back on her life, when she failed, she just stayed down for a minute. Once she got back up—that's who she is today. The "get back up" one. I was just there to be the one to witness it all—from age sixteen on through, I was witness to everything she went through.

As I think about her life and my life with her, I am still filled with so much emotion—because she's my mother. I love my mother. I can also say that seeing what she went through and how she came through it all has made me the strongest woman on this earth. Nothing can break me unless I allow it to. I'm a product of Jolinda, and she did a great job with me.

My mother has a beautiful soul and a beautiful heart. Thank you for giving me this opportunity to speak about my wonderful mother.

Keisha Fraley

I am Keisha, Jolinda's second daughter and the second of her four children. I always knew my mother loved us dearly because she would tell us so.

When I was a teenager, I was living with my mother in our family home. That's when she was having her life challenges, so we didn't have her there for us when we were growing up. In one respect, that was a positive for me. Because I didn't have anyone to watch over me and discipline me, I had more freedom to choose who I wanted to become and what I wanted to do with my life. However, I was never alone as I went to live with my paternal grandmother and, for a number of years, she looked after me and raised me. At the same time, I was separated from my sisters and brother, so I wasn't raised with them, but we continued to stay in touch with one another.

My family had a lot of courage that helped all of us survive, and I have to say that it was all due to our upbringing. My mother's mother, my grandmother Willie Mae Morris, was in my ear as well as my paternal grandmother. Although my mom was out there living her life, I still had her in my ear. "Keisha, no. Keisha, you know better."

While still a teenager, I became a mom. Like my sister Tragil, I too was in an abusive relationship and had to get away. During that time, Mom was incarcerated, serving her first prison sentence, and still wasn't able to be there for us. So, I confided in my Auntie Rose, who said to me, "When you're ready, just let me know."

When that time came, Tragil told me, "If you want to get away, come on." So, my son, who was four or five years old, and I made our escape when we climbed on board a Greyhound bus heading for California. Life was so much better there for us, and I was able to put my life together.

I was twenty and living in San Diego with my son when Mom began to emerge from her horrific life. That's when she began pastoring. I know she hears God's voice. When she's preaching, I can see her listening to God's voice.

When I was in my thirties and my son was a teenager, she took him in and helped me out with him. I'm so grateful for that, just the fact of her opening the door for him, because I know I wasn't able to do it. I had been so young when he was born. I still felt like I needed to live life. She means the world to him. He'll call her before he calls me. My son and I have a good relationship, but their relationship is untouchable.

My mother is a hero to me. I witnessed how, coming from the life she lived and the challenges she faced, she overcame all of them like a superhero.

Mom is someone I adore. I look up to her. What she says matters to me. Her voice, speaking, matters to me. She's loving. She's a wonderful person at heart. I love her dearly.

Tragil Wade

I am Tragil Wade, Pastor Jolinda's third child and youngest daughter. My younger brother Dwyane Wade Jr. and I are the children of Jolinda Wade and Dwyane Wade Sr. We have two older half-sisters, Deanna and Keisha. Although none of us were raised together, we have remained a close-knit family.

My mom is exceptional! In part, this is because, throughout my journey, one thing has always been foundational and true for me: she has always loved me and continues to love me, to the very best of her ability—and that unconditional love remains unquestioned to this day.

Not everyone has the ability to show love, to give love, or know how to receive love—but my mom is able to live in this state of unconditional love. When I try to help people from this space of seamless love, it has always proved more difficult for me. But one of the most exceptional things about my loving mother is her ability to interact with everybody she meets in this nonjudgmental, welcoming space.

The Lord has given her an instinctive ability, a power, to tap into an all-embracing energy when she says to someone, "I love you." When she does this, she always stops and looks you directly in your eyes. When she does this with me, whatever she's gone through in life, she makes sure I know she loves me. Again, no matter where she's been on her journey, when she says "I love you" to me, it's unquestioned that I believe it—because I feel it.

Because she was making personal choices about using drugs or choosing men who harmed her, I would often feel as though she didn't choose me but chose drugs and an abusive relationship instead.

For example, when I was about nine, she was dating a guy named Greg. I remember one time crying and saying to her, "I hate him! Why don't we leave? Why don't you put him out? He's horrible." I felt like she had the power, but she wasn't using it. I said to her, "It doesn't seem like you love me because you keep letting this man do this to us."

I watched him hurt her physically. I remember one time I came home from school and he had literally cut open all the cushions in the couches in our living room, which was also her bedroom. The stuffing was everywhere. He was so angry, he just did this. It was like a horror movie.

I asked myself, "What's next?" and I said to her, "You cannot love us and also stay in this relationship with this man. You can't!"

She looked me directly in my eyes and said, "No matter what, I love you." Immediately, in the ugliness of that moment with this abusive man, I believed her, and her words comforted me—but I felt, not just my mom when she said these words, I felt the Lord coming through her.

I remember crying one day, saying, "Come on. She does love me. I know what my eyes see, but I also know how I feel." I remember being seventeen and having conversations about my mom and my dad having been in situations and not doing their best by me. I reflected more on my mother's behavior with me than my father's because he didn't struggle with me.

When my brother Dwyane was ten, he left to live with our father. I was fifteen at the time and initially stayed there as well, but it did not work out for me, so I chose to come back and live with my mother.

We struggled together the whole way on both her journey and mine. When she was hungry, I was hungry. If she didn't have it, I didn't have it.

When she was put out on the street, I was put out on the street. Often, I would see her so sad, crying, and wanting something different, but not yet able to make it so. I believe the depth of my relationship with my amazing mother was not just a mother-daughter bond but a crisis bond. One such incident occurred in my teenage years when she fought off my abuser at the risk of her own life and her own freedom. I can never be angry with her—just the opposite.

My grandmother, Willie Mae Morris, was an example of unconditional love. That's where it all began for our family. I remember looking at my uncles and aunts and my mother, saying, "These are Grandmother's kids." I would sit with her, and she would have to watch her kids, more than one, be out there on the streets on drugs, and not being able to do anything about it. She would shake her head and say, "All I can do is pray."

Just watching her strength and how she sat with pride was astonishing. My grandmother always stood strong. I never questioned her ability to be a mother. I said to myself, "Wow! I can love, too." I remember her telling me, "That's your mother. You only got one mother. Don't ever, ever do anything against your mother. Don't speak negative about your mother. When you go to school, you don't tell that school nothing about your mother. That's your mother." That was a powerful lesson!

I know when my mother was ordained, my grandmother was very proud of her. She said to me, "Jolinda—I knew she was smart. I knew it. That's Jolinda up there. She's a preacher now, she's good. Mm-hmm, she's doin' real good. She talks good."

When my mother became a pastor, I saw her speaking the word of God, giving it to people on the street as well as those who were in her congregation, giving it to them all in the raw. They call her style of pastoring "street pastoring" or "street talk."

I know that God has a genuine relationship with her and she with the Lord. That's why my entire family began to follow her—because we don't just believe it, we see it. We call it an "anointing."

Research often says that families are the last to come around when a member of that family is on a spiritual quest—but we were the first. As a family, we have always believed in my mother. Knowing her journey and watching her transformation on the pulpit was almost magical. One of the biggest lessons for me was this recognition and this thought: "So, this is God working his amazing miracles!" Her relationship with God is something we know—without a shadow of a doubt—is true.

Having the ability to say "yes" to God and having the ability to see that there is more to life than what you see day to day is what I'm yearning to tap into all the time.

I ask myself, "What's next?" My brother Dwyane turned forty this year, and I turned forty-five. It's a new day, a new time. What am I going to do now? What are *we* going to do now?

It took me a while to get here, to tap into this space where I live in the word of God. I know for sure that my mom introduced it to me. She began to let me know when I would tell her about a feeling I just had, or ask her a question about something I just saw, heard, or felt. Then, if appropriate, she would let me know, "That is God." A lot of times I wouldn't recognize it, but she'd say, "No, no, no, that's God," or "That's from God."

Or I'd tell her, "This happened to me when I got up this morning"— and she'd ask, "What did God say?"

When she got into this very special space with God, she dove all the way in and, through this, was able to help me when it came to knowing His voice. As a young person, I was blessed. But it wasn't until she was able to more fully develop her relationship with God, and I was starting my adult journey in my late teens, that I was able to say, "Now I understand. This is how it happens." I was able to recognize it simply because I saw my mother experience it.

When I go and preach, I have my mother, who has also been my teacher, when it comes to knowing how to hear God's voice. She'd say,

"If it's late at night and you wake up, ask God what it is, and you go forward. Then, you will feel it within your spirit. He uses you." So, I go and lie down and am able to tap into it.

I'm so grateful I have that. Dwyane and I both have it. Dwyane had it as a young person and was better able to know himself than I. How does Dwyane make a decision? He prays about it, goes to sleep, and, when he wakes up, the decision is there.

Today I can search my heart, replay my story in my head, and not have one guilty feeling regarding our journey together as mother and daughter. God's restoration of my mother is unmatched. At one point, when I had the desire to have a certain type of mother and a certain type of supporter in my mother, He gave me more than I could have ever asked for.

As I said at the beginning, my mother is exceptional. I say at the end, now you know why my mother *is* exceptional.

Friends

Viola Henderson

Jolinda and I have been friends since childhood. Because I was younger and smaller, she gave me the pet name, "Bit-Bit" or, sometimes, "Little Bit"—which she still affectionately calls me. I have witnessed and often played my own part in her life journey, and so I know her story forwards and backwards.

We became playmates when my family visited my Auntie Pearlie, who lived next door to Jolinda's family, and we'd always play together. Some time later, my family moved to the same neighborhood near Auntie Pearlie, and Jolinda and I went to the same elementary school. I was a year younger and in the fourth grade. She was in the fifth grade and was like a big sister to me. On the playground at recess, the bully girls would often pick on me, so Jolinda would stand up for me and they would leave me alone. I stayed by her and she became my protector all through elementary school.

Jolinda was a very smart student. One year, the teachers chose her to star in the school play, and she knew that I wanted the part, but I simply wasn't as smart as she was, and the teachers selected her. So, by way of looking after me, she told them that she didn't want to do it, and they ended up choosing me instead.

We went our separate ways when my family moved away, but I always kept in touch through her mother because her mother never moved. Whenever I did go back to the old neighborhood, I would visit Jolinda. When she married Big Wade and he joined the military, they moved away, but we never lost touch.

After we both had had our families, Jolinda and I would hang out and go to church together—even during the time she was on the run. At that time, Jolinda was still living the street life, still addicted—but I had gotten out and moved on. Although I shared alcohol and, occasionally, drugs with her, I had been very careful not to become addicted. I'd been told that to avoid becoming a heroin addict, one should not use it three days in a row.

Although I didn't have much, I had more than Jolinda, as I had always worked. At that time, I was a fifth-grade long-term substitute teacher, had a home in the Chicago suburbs, and was supporting my newborn son and teenage daughter.

Even though it had been a few years since we'd last seen each other, she was still my best friend. Because her mother never moved, I was always able to track Jolinda wherever she moved to.

Throughout our lives, no matter how long we have been separated, we always speak with one another like it was yesterday.

Even in the throes of her addiction, God was very important to her, and she would always speak about God. One day, when we were sitting in the car visiting and drinking, she even began speaking in tongues. One time, after she'd been released from jail, I remember she told me that God had come to her and spoken to her while she was in there.

One day in the late 1990s—it may have been sometime between 1995 and 1998, I was visiting my sister in the old neighborhood when I saw Jolinda walking home from church. We were so ecstatic when we saw each other. We were both in our forties, and she was heavy into her addiction, on the run, and living in an abandoned building.

She saw me and came over, telling me she was sick and needed to get something. I never judged her. I never judge anybody, and certainly not my best friend. I know when a person is strung out on heroin, and when they don't get it, they are barely functional and can be physically sick. As I didn't have any money on this particular occasion, I borrowed ten dollars or so from my sister so that Jolinda could get her "medicine."

Whether she was an addict, an alcoholic, or whatever she did, it didn't make her who she was. Who she was was the love in her heart. That was the God in her. She has always been full of love.

After this encounter, from time to time, I would come and get her, take her to my house, take her into my life, and make a place for her as a member of my family. My son and daughter called her "Auntie Jolinda." As our friendship was so natural and rich, we always shared each other's lives.

Jolinda would often tell me how proud she was of me and the life I was living. Jolinda had always complimented me, and when a person treats you like that, you can't help but be nice to them. So, she came over in the evenings and was never high, so my children couldn't tell that she was an addict.

Jolinda always offered to help out to earn extra money. I told her it wasn't necessary and would have her help me grade papers, or we would go to the laundromat and fold clothes, wash my car, and do other household chores together.

On Sunday, October 14, 2001, Jolinda called and asked me to come and get her. She said, "OK, I'm ready. Let's do this." I was living in Indiana at that time, but I drove to Chicago to pick her up. She said she needed some money to buy "medicine" and, as I didn't have any, again I went next door to my sister's house and borrowed enough so that Jolinda could buy the drugs and alcohol she needed.

Jolinda, my son, my daughter, and I discussed if it would be all right if she stayed with me while she detoxed, and we agreed that it would. I told her I would take her home with me, but I'd have to send her back on the bus when she was ready to return to Chicago. She came home with me and stayed for a week. When we got there, she used up the drugs and alcohol we had purchased, and that was it.

During that week, she wouldn't take anything, not even a drink. If I had a drink, I wouldn't let her see it because I didn't want to influence her. She laid on my sofa for three days and, at the end of the three days, she was completely clean and sober.

After she became a pastor, I heard her speak at her father's church, Mt. Nebo. Whenever Jolinda spoke about the Lord, I could feel it in her.

A few years later, I moved to Michigan. Jolinda and I were in our fifties, were clean, and walking our path. I introduced Jolinda to my girlfriend Bertha who was also an ordained minister, but was not allowed on the pulpit as her church did not allow women to preach. Bertha was also a saved woman and very powerful, and I knew it was important for her to meet Jolinda.

When she and Jolinda spoke, Bertha could tell by her testimony that Jolinda's was a story of deliverance and strength and needed to be shared with others in our community.

Bertha worked with a particular group of women who were cancer survivors, and she invited Jolinda to speak to them. Once Jolinda shared her story of hope and survival with these courageous women, she became a regular fixture every year, speaking to both the women Bertha ministered to as well as at her church.

The church where Bertha was a member did not allow women to go up onto the pulpit. There was a stand down in the well that women spoke from and that's where Jolinda was directed to speak from when she first spoke at that church. The pastor saw her humility, her truth, and how the congregation responded to her and, thus, the second time, he asked Jolinda to come up to the pulpit. This was a big moment for the women in the ministry, liberating for Bertha and the women of the congregation as well. Because of his encounter with Jolinda, eventually, he allowed Bertha to also speak from the pulpit.

Jolinda continued to visit me in Michigan and, whenever possible, spoke at the conferences I organized there.

From childhood on, Jolinda and I have always been so very close, and remain so to this day.

Cynthia Jones-Smith

I am Cynthia, and I am here to tell my friend's story. Jolinda and I have been best friends since 1971, when we were in our teens and I was dating her brother, Eddie Morris Jr., and we had a son together, who is her nephew. His name is Antoine, but the family nicknamed him "Twilla."

I was friends with Jolinda's whole family even before Jolinda and I became friends. First, I was friends with her next-older sister, Rosalyn, and then, I became close to her next-younger sister, B.B. Then, even though we didn't attend the same high school, Jolinda and I just hooked up and started hanging out together—and we've been tight ever since.

Later, I was caught up in the street life right along with her. At the time, it didn't seem like a horrible life because we didn't know what we were doing. We were so young, both of us still in our teens. All we wanted was to hang out with our friends, party, and have fun.

That's when we began to drug together and were out on the street hustling together. However, we never turned tricks or anything like that; we only asked for money.

If it came down to it, we protected each other, for example, if one of our boyfriends jumped us, the other would intervene. I never allowed anyone to mess with her—no one, no matter what.

If I moved to another neighborhood, I always came back. I was drawn to be with Jolinda and, whenever we were together, nothing ever really changed between us. We were always there for one another.

I knew a long time ago there was something different about her. She wasn't the type you would think would get into drugs. I think it was more about the people, the men, we were with. But she was out there in a spiritual way as well, reading and teaching from the Bible and drawing an audience to her. People always gravitated to her because she was like a priest or a preacher. She probably wasn't even aware within herself that people were always drawn to her.

Even though we were caught up in the street life, Jolinda felt compelled to be our street teacher. In addition, Jolinda was always searching for something, as she always wanted to learn.

Jolinda was arrested a little more than I was. It didn't mean anything. When she came back, we just went back to where we were before. However, when I was arrested and locked up, when I came home, I was different. She was still out on the streets, and I guess she saw that I wasn't going to go back into that life again. She said I motivated her. So, the last time she went in, after she was released, she also left that life.

I was at her ordination, and it was amazing to be there.

When she was a minister here in Chicago, it was so nice to attend her services. Wherever and whenever she's preaching and teaching, she listens to God and does what God tells her to do.

My brother Ed Jones is a pastor, too, and I was with both of them because they'd often minister together and I would attend their joint services, whether in church or as part of their street ministry.

It makes me feel good, too, that we escaped the life we were living and are completely changed now. We're all different people. It's kind of hard to believe where we had been, and we are grateful for where we are now.

Everything Jolinda is doing fascinates me and makes me feel good to have a friend I can look up to. I'm still protecting her. I don't let anybody say anything against her. That's my girl; I love her. We're friends to the end.

Teachers, Mentors, Colleagues

Pastor Ed Jones

I am Pastor Ed Jones, Jolinda's lifelong friend and, now, a colleague in the ministry.

I first knew Jolinda through her brother Ed Jr., who was dating my sister, Cynthia. Also, through that relationship, Jolinda and Cynthia became the best of friends. We all came up on "the street" together. I was like the big brother, and we were kind of related because my sister also has a son by Jolinda's brother.

We were all street people, and we all did drugs and alcohol together. In 1964, when I was seventeen, I spent a year in jail. When they let me out, I told them, "I'm never coming back!"—and I never did go back.

As I look back on my life and my life with Jolinda, I realize that something that drew us together was that, even with our drug and street history, she always had a respect for God.

With our upbringing, even though the Bible says, "Train up the child in the way that they should go when they get older so they won't depart," we nonetheless departed. But we came back and always had a respect for God, especially Jolinda. Even when we were high on drugs or alcohol, she would always speak about God. God was always in our lives, though we weren't in His. Even with our street and drug history and how rough we were around the edges, Jolinda and I always had a respect for God, not only for God, but we also had a respect for people.

Jolinda's mom and dad played an integral part in her life and in Cynthia's and mine as well. We were just kids when my family first moved to Fifty-Ninth Street—so, Mother Morris and Deacon Morris would always pray for us. My sister and I always felt we were part of their family. Even when they saw us running up and down Fifty-Ninth Street, acting crazy, they would always pray for us. Mother Morris was a force in all of our lives, not as directly in mine as she was with my sister and Jolinda, who were like two peas in a pod, but all of us were always a close-knit family.

As I was older, I was a little bit out there, and there was a time when I was the street "pharmaceutical agent"—so I had certain things I could make available when they needed it, and give it away so they wouldn't have to pay for it. Jolinda, Cynthia, and I, along with others from the street, would often hang out at a lounge called the Big Apple, and we always looked out for each other. We were blessed because we survived that life, because we lost a lot of people who didn't make it out.

In 1989, I was still in and out of the church and in and out of my relationship with God. However, in 1990, I got through that part of my life and was able to begin my walk with the Lord. First, I became a deacon and then a minister-in-training. Finally, I graduated and was awarded my clergy collar.

Throughout this time, Jolinda would see me, and she just kept waiting for me to fall back into my old lifestyle, using drugs and alcohol. Of course, I never did.

Sometimes she was sick when she would see me with my wife, and my wife would ask, "What's wrong with her? Does she need anything?"

I'd simply say, "She's sick," and my wife would say, "Well, give her what she needs."

We came up with a lot of individuals who had drug histories. As I said, that was part of our lives, so we knew how to do whatever it took to be there for our friends. Even though I was no longer using, my wife and I never turned our backs on people. That's why God could use us, because we would always go and help those individuals, and Jolinda was one of those who also tried to help. If she had a line of coke and saw that you needed some, she would split it. She would always give whatever she could to whomever needed it. She's that kind of person. I grew to love her over the years for many reasons, and one important one is that once she is committed to being your friend, she is your friend.

We went through many tragic situations with my family and me—and, when everyone else turned their backs on my sister and me, Jolinda never did. She stuck by us no matter what anybody else said or did. She was always there—not only for us, but always for everyone she knew and loved. Even individuals who had done her wrong over the years, she would never turn them away. She still embraced them, supported them, and attempted to help them. That's who she is.

Jolinda had always loved to teach. Her sister told me that when Jolinda was coming up, she would always act as the teacher of the family. When she finally went into the ministry, it was at a time when certain religious doctrines didn't like women preachers. When she told me of her calling, I said, "If God called you, you do what God called you to do."

When she was ready to be ordained, I was asked to sit on the ordination committee that would test her on her qualifications. Some of the men on the committee wanted to ask her all kinds of crazy questions—so, I stepped up and asked, "Why would you ask her that? Because she's a woman? You wouldn't ask a man who is being ordained that question."

I never bought into the idea that women can't preach. I don't believe that. My grandmother was an ordained minister in the 1950s, a time when it was very uncommon for a woman to be ordained. So, when I sat on that board, I said, "God said, 'In the beginning God created male and female equal.' That's His word." And, when they tried to deviate from that principle, I said, "No."

So many times, we hear people say they are finished with drugs or alcohol. However, I realized that Jolinda was serious when she turned herself in, and the police station could not find any record of her old escape. She insisted they continue looking for her record because God told her she had to turn herself in.

At the same time, she was also having physical challenges. I told her that she had to go through this period of being cleansed for God to use her. I said, "I've known a lot of preachers, but if there's anybody I know the Lord truly speaks to, it is you."

To this day, Jolinda consults God over everything she does, and that's nothing new. Even in the midst of her insanity, she was always in touch with the Lord.

None of us, not me, not my sister, not Jolinda, went through a drug and alcohol rehab program. We did what I call "a God rehab program." Did we fall by the wayside? Sure. Sometimes we fell down, but we got back up.

She called me her mentor and her teacher. I call her the same—my mentor and my teacher, because she can preach and teach with the best of them. She still calls me to study with her and, in that way, we learned from each other and supported each other. She opened a deliverance ministry, whereas I have a faith-based ministry. We are both faith-based, and our ministries complement each other.

We never forgot about all those that we left out there. Once she said to me, "God told me to go back and told me to come and get you." So, together we would often go back to Fifty-Ninth and Prairie, which is where we came from, where we did drugs and alcohol, and we launched our ministry every Wednesday under Pastor Crawford, who owned the church we worked out of. There we stood on the street, told our stories, and preached to all who would listen.

When we ministered together, Jolinda would do giveaways and put out food—whatever we had—right out there on Fifty-Ninth Street. People would come from all over just to be with her and share in whatever she had to offer—gravitating to her like she was a "God magnet." Even to this day, Jolinda, when she is back in Chicago, goes back to the street and shares God's grace with all those she can speak to.

She is always prepared to help the people she grew up with. You have heard the expression, "Would you give up your life for a friend?" Jolinda would be the one who would give up her life for a friend. I've seen her in so many situations. When you open that door and she walks in, she walks in with unconditional love—not only for her family, but for all people, for we are all people of God. That is who Jolinda is.

Even though she has moved to Los Angeles, the connection between us is still strong and still there. We are connected as spiritual brother and spiritual sister with one another—forever.

Bishop Jennie Petties

The first time I met Jolinda was in 2003 when Pastor Darrell brought a few members of his congregation, which included her daughter Tragil, her mother, and five or six others, to an event I held at my church. As part of our program, we had a Bible contest, and I asked if anyone knew where in the Bible a particular passage was located. Jolinda later told me that she remembered studying that passage in 2002 when she was in prison and knew right where it was.

When she told Pastor Darrell she knew the answer, he said, "Raise your hand." One of my helpers took the mic to her and, when she gave the correct answer, she was overjoyed. The prize was a beautiful Bible, which I know she has with her to this very day.

I had known Pastor Darrell as his mother-in-law and father-in-law were members of my church. As a matter of fact, his wife was a member, and he married his wife out of my church, but he never became a member himself. That's how I got to know him. He came from a church where Mother Box had been the pastor, and when she died, she left the church to him. That was Jolinda's family's church, and that's how he became her pastor, and how I first came to know her.

Sometime after that event, Pastor brought her to a training I held for several women and men who also aspired to become ministers. He asked me if I would allow her to join the sessions, and, of course, I said, "Yes."

She was such an open-minded, willing person, so eager to learn, and that really excited me. She was never late, even after he stopped bringing her, and she had to get there on her own. I was on the west side of Chicago, so I would say I was a twenty-to-thirty-mile bus ride away. Even then, she was never late and never missed a single class.

Jolinda was a great scholar. She studied hard, asked questions, and followed the instructions. God just blessed her, and she started growing.

One day, I took Jolinda aside because she was growing by leaps and bounds—intellectually and spiritually—and said to her, "You've got to be careful, Jolinda."

She said, "What, Mom?"

I said, "You are going to outgrow your pastor because he's not getting the teaching that you are getting. You are going to have to be very careful with him to keep him from being jealous." I continued, "People in the ministry, they become jealous of their parishioners too, so you have to be careful,"—and we just went on from there.

Of course, she told me what he did to her—how, after I made her aware of it, he came to her door and presented her with that book that said that women do not have a right to be in the ministry and asked her to pull off her clergy collar, which she had rightfully earned. I had never known that he had issues with women ministers, and I don't know from that day to this what happened to him, because he pulled all the way away from me after that.

Even though he was bringing her to class and was 100 percent for it, he never attended himself. He only made sure that she was there, even though we had men in the class as well as members who were already pastors, both male and female.

The breach in Pastor Darrell's and Jolinda's relationship occurred at the end of the second year of our program. By that time, she had studied hard, graduated from the class, and was a fully qualified, licensed member of the ministry, and had even worked with him on the pulpit for a while.

I have been pastoring for forty-one years and have met all kinds of people—people in Jolinda's condition and some even worse. The reason I say worse is, I've met people who came out of it, studied the word, then, in their old age, have gone back to their old lifestyle, living that same kind of life, the best they can. That's why I say I've met people who have been even worse off.

Something Jolinda learned from me and embodies in her practice to this day is that she is an open book. I have always revealed myself and connected my life story to the Word, and that clearly has been one of Jolinda's signature qualities as well. The honesty with which she reveals herself contributes to the impact she has on her congregation. This clearly allows them to trust her both as their pastor and as a human being.

Jolinda hears God's voice. I recognize this because I, too, depend totally on the Lord, and He really walks and talks with me. I am so grateful. I know when it is Him doing something for me. This quality is very rare, and Jolinda has it.

Jolinda has a quiet spirit. I recognize this because I don't merely look at the outer appearance of a person; I go deeper than that. I look through their eyes, the windows to their soul. Then, I hear their voice when they are talking to me—especially if we are talking about the Lord and they are giving me a testimony of themselves. When I hear

Jolinda's voice, as with my own personal discovery, I hear and feel the Lord coming through her.

The only thing about Jolinda is that it is hard for her to turn loose and trust people. I guess she has been hurt for so long and so much until she has reservations—and I can understand that—but we are still working through that. The more she is able to share, the more she is able to get out, the freer she'll become.

Her son Dwyane Wade is my adopted godson. He became my godson later when he was already playing ball in the NBA. Jolinda was doing my training at that time, and because he loves his mom dearly and I love his mom dearly, I would say it was through her that I became his spiritual mentor. In fact, even though I didn't know it, he was calling me grandma and godma.

One day the Miami Heat came to play against the Chicago Bulls, and Dwyane invited me to the game. My seats were next to Jolinda's, right there with her family. Even though I was a Bulls fan, I had never been to a game.

At one point in the game, the Heat were losing to the Bulls, and, because I was a Bulls fan, I was sitting praying the Bulls would win— though I never told this to Jolinda. Jolinda saw me praying and asked, "Bishop?"

I said, "What?"

She said, "You watching the game?"

I said, "Yes."

"You praying?"

I said, "Yes."

She said, "Well, do you realize the Heat are losing?"

I had to say yes, and then it came to me: "The Bulls didn't invite me here. They didn't bring me here." I came to myself and just began to pray hard—for the Heat, for Dwyane—and that they would win—and the Miami Heat won the game.

As I said, I wasn't aware that he called me grandma until they interviewed him and wanted to know what happened. "You were losing and, all of a sudden, you just picked up like you had wings, and you all started winning."

Dwyane said this, "Well, when I thought about my mom out there praying and my grandma praying for me—"

"Your grandmother is here?"

He said, "Yes." So, I was looking around—you know, I didn't know Jolinda's mother was there.

Afterward, the interviewer said, "I want to meet her." So, Dwyane brought me over, and all of us laughed and talked.

Dwyane said, "This is my grandma. This is my godmom." I started laughing. It was so funny, but I didn't tell them right away what I was laughing about—that I had had my mind on the Bulls, but when Jolinda mentioned that Dwyane and his team were losing, I started praying for them.

Dwyane said, "I knew they were praying. I got light and just started playing."

Dwyane has always loved his mom—always—and takes such good care of her. Even though I hated to see her move away, I knew it was important for her to be closer to Dwyane and her family in California.

Also, when I think about what Dwyane and Tragil went through as children, to see what they have achieved and have become, it is pretty astonishing.

When Jolinda's mom passed, I adopted the whole family. Her mother was a remarkable human being. When I went to the funeral, I announced, "Your mom is only dead when everybody stops mentioning her name. As long as you call her name, then, she's alive—and, I'm here in person to do whatever I need to do, whatever I need to say to be here for you."

Jolinda has a beautiful family. Certainly, this family has had its share of challenges and still does, and yet, they express such unconditional love without judgment of one another—no judgment whatsoever.

Of course, the same is true for Jolinda—not simply Pastor Jolinda, but Jolinda the woman. Whenever you experience her, there is no judgment; there is only God speaking through her. As I said earlier, when I hear Jolinda speak, I hear and feel the Lord coming through her.

I am eighty-seven years old, a pastor for forty-one years to people from all walks of life. I can honestly say that Jolinda is one of the finest, most unique, God-conscious individuals I have ever known.

Pastor Edward Range

I am Pastor Edward Range, pastor of the New Mt. Nebo Missionary Baptist Church, and have known Jolinda as a friend and colleague for more than twenty years.

I met Jolinda through her dad, Edward Morris Sr., who was a deacon at my church. He and I used to go back and forth about inviting people to the church, and he would always tell me, "Ain't nobody goin' to come if I invite them."

I'd say, "Honestly, you never know. If you just open up your mouth and ask them, you don't know what might happen." He would never do it.

One day, after he heard that Jolinda had joined the ministry, he just summoned his courage and invited his family to the church—and they showed up.

I met her brother Eric first. Eric is Edward's youngest child from a subsequent relationship after Edward's relationship with Willie Mae ended. One day, he came to the church and played his horn for a program, and it all transpired from there.

Even Willie Mae came. That woman was so remarkable. I would joke with her and ask, "What made you marry him?"

She would laugh and say, "Rev, you so funny!"

So, Jolinda came over and we instantly clicked. She fellowshipped that Sunday, but then, following that service, she was gone for a little while. Some time later, I heard from Sister Foster, one of my members, that Jolinda wanted to come and be a part of the church. I said, "No problem. I would love to have her," and she came and joined our church.

In the following weeks, I learned that, even though she wore a collar and was licensed, she wasn't yet ordained. When she first came to me, I told her I would not hold her back. Spirit told me that she had a greater job to do, and I never wanted to stifle her ministry. The Spirit—a little voice inside of me—said that she needed to be credentialed because, especially when it comes to women in the ministry, many people don't feel that women should be in the ministry. That voice led me to let her know that the Lord had spoken to me and told me to get her ordained, so she could go out into the world to do what she was called to do and meant to do.

To prepare her, I gathered the documents and books we taught from so she could study and prepare for her ordination. When my pastor ordained me, he showed me what he wanted me to study and learn thoroughly, and I did the same for Jolinda.

In addition, I said, "As you know, some people in our ministry don't want to see a woman pastor on the pulpit." Four ordained male pastors, no women, were chosen to sit on her panel, including Pastor Ed Jones. He, like me, looked out for Jolinda to make sure that all questions were fair and unbiased.

The path to her ordination lasted about six months to one year because I didn't want to just throw her into it.

One of the things I truly loved about her was that, even though she was older than I was, she was eager to study and learn everything we were teaching. I was then in my late twenties and, oftentimes, I found that older people weren't open to listening to me. So, for her to come and fellowship with me and then study under me meant so very much.

As the time grew closer for her ordination exam and service, Tragil, Keisha, and I tried to arrange the schedule so Dwyane could be part of the ceremony. We were able to schedule the service around a game Dwyane had here in Chicago, and his coach was good enough to allow Dwyane to stay an additional day.

We tricked Jolinda, as she thought he had left. We put her in a room and, when Dwyane came, we snuck him in and hid him in another room. When she came in to sit in her chair, we brought Dwyane out. Jolinda was overwhelmed. They shared hugs and tears for the next few minutes.

After her ordination, more of her family joined our church, and once she joined the church, my pulpit was her pulpit. As I also had a regular job, when I couldn't be at the service, Jolinda would take over for me. On other occasions, when I needed to travel, she would also run the church. I felt comfortable leaving Jolinda to speak from the pulpit and communicate with our congregation as though I were there. She was a blessing to me.

One thing that was unique to Jolinda was that she never did anything without first praying. There were many occasions when she spoke with me and told me that Spirit led her to do this, do that, and, listening to her, I recognized that there was an anointing on her.

Many people who crossed paths with Jolinda seemed to recognize this as well. I remember an instance when she told me the story of when Spirit told her she had to turn herself in, as she had been on the run for several years. She told me how she went to her local police department on New Year's Eve because that's what the Lord insisted she do. However, they could find no record for her, so they told her they were letting her go home—and wished her Happy New Year! They *never* let anyone go! But Jolinda persisted until they finally located her in the system.

All this was because God had told her to return to prison to become whole again. The police were ready to let her go, but God was not. It told me that God is always going to have her back. As scripture says,

"Many are called but few are chosen." Not everyone in the ministry is *chosen*, but Jolinda is.

We pastored together for a few years, going on with Bible studies on Wednesdays, sometimes with fellowships at the church, sometimes at her house.

She extended our street ministry with giveaways and food served at the church, which attracted many people from the neighborhood. At that same time my church was sponsoring these giveaways, there was another Mt. Nebo church about a half mile away from us, and it amused me that, whenever we had giveaways, the street people would show up at their church and the pastor would say, "No, you got the wrong church! You got the wrong church!" and redirect them to our church. I share this because it is yet another example of wherever Jolinda went, whatever she did, people followed. She was the "Pied Piper" of New Mt. Nebo.

In spite of the fact that we drifted apart, I've always considered Jolinda my friend and my daughter in the ministry. Whenever I can be there for her, I'm just a phone call away. I've got her back—whatever she needs. I want her to know that I am very proud of her and have always been proud of her.

Congregants

Minister Leon Banks

I am Leon Banks, originally a congregant at the Temple of Praise and now a licensed minister who worked under Pastor Jolinda Wade at New Creation: Binding and Loosening Ministries, International.

Pastor Ladell Jones, Pastor Wade's copastor at the Temple of Praise, was a friend from my hometown. When they held the grand opening of their new church building, he invited me to come and bring my family. My wife Nicole said, "Yes, of course."

Following the grand opening ceremonies, my wife and family joined the church. I didn't join, but kept coming every Sunday to get ministered to and listen to the word of God. I'm one who, if I'm going to do something, I want to make sure that I'm moving in the right direction—no matter what it is. In this case, I needed just a little bit more time to confirm what I wanted to do.

As time went on, my family and I came out every Sunday to hear Pastor Wade speak. Just seeing how her teaching was so powerful, the knowledge that she had of the word of God, and being able to relate it to everyday life, was remarkable.

Before I ever heard Pastor Wade's story and without understanding what I was witnessing, the anointing that was upon her stood out to me—definitely a powerful woman of God. Hearing her story, seeing how she came from the lowest of the low, and seeing how she went from that and manifested into this powerful woman of God: It was undeniable. It had to be nothing but God that had His hand upon her life, and it couldn't be anything but an anointing from above that was upon her. So, that's how I knew.

We are all forever growing, but the level of life that she was experiencing at that time could not have been achieved without God taking her into His newness.

She spoke with such command, authority, and confidence. That definitely was something I had never witnessed before to that magnitude—especially from a Black woman, or any woman. As time went on, hearing her testimony, I was definitely able to relate to her story. I had never met another minister who told their personal story and connected it to scripture—not at all—and she shared it so eloquently and humbly.

When Pastor Wade was on the pulpit, I recognized that she was listening to the Lord and speaking from what she heard. I'm a sports person, so I'll use Dwyane as an example: Outside of basketball, he was quiet, liked to laugh, was down-to-earth, definitely a loving caring guy with a good heart; but, when it came time to compete on the basketball court, he switched into game mode and became the champion he is.

Relating that to Pastor Wade: Outside of the pulpit, she was zero tolerance—no foolishness, no rudeness, no disrespect, things of that nature; but, when she stood on that pulpit speaking before the people of God, as with Dwyane, her inner champion stood up for all to see.

Through her deep study and how diligent her preparation always was—which, of course, always began with prayer—when she spoke before the flock that God had given her, it was like night and day. When Pastor Wade was on the pulpit, under that anointing, everything was seamlessly integrated. As she channeled the Word and spoke with such passion, she would often begin sweating. From the way she spoke, from her mannerisms to the humanity of her teaching, once again, I knew that she was touched by something from above.

My decision to join the church came to me one day when I was at work. A coworker and I were doing our daily job when I heard a Voice say, "It's time."

When I heard that, I told my coworker, who is also a man of God, what I had heard. I told him I knew it was God because I heard it plain and clear, and my coworker said, "Man, you've been ready doing this and doing that. You've got a calling." He was encouraging me. So, that following Sunday, when the doors of the church opened, I got up, joined the church, and never looked back. The opening was in May 2008, and I didn't join until June 29—my eldest daughter's birthday.

When my family and I joined the ministry, Pastor Wade was able to speak into our lives and was a fundamental influence on our growth as a family, and definitely for me as a man of God. She told me God had shown her something within me that I never saw in myself.

I can remember one time she told me I was going to be a righteous soldier in the army of God. I guess she was able to see my faithfulness and my commitment to become a better person, learning more about

God/the Bible and how can I use that to help me become a better person, a better husband, a better father to my family, a leader, and, ultimately, become someone who is grounded in the word of God—able to speak encouragement, teach it, and walk it amongst my peers and others as a beacon of light.

As time went on, I took a more active role in church activities. For example, on Saturdays, Sister Robbye and I, along with others, joined the street ministry, went to the street corner outside the church, and prayed with and for people. Because of work I couldn't always go, but the times when I went out, our assignment was to go to the corner and, when random people walked past, with their permission, we would pray for them.

I became a minister because Pastor Wade saw it in me. This didn't occur right away but sometime later. I knew she moved according to the Spirit of God, and if that's what she said, then I saw how she was operating in the Spirit.

She had called three other people and me into her office to speak to us about training for the ministry. She relayed to us what God had spoken to her about concerning each of us and how she was instructed to help us elevate ourselves in the ministry. I would never say no to whatever she asked me to do because I knew she would never ask me to do anything that was not the will of God.

I was happy for her when she made the decision to take a new step forward in her life and move to LA.

Now she's opened a new chapter with her YouTube channel, *Better Health, Better Me*. I'm not a big social media person, but I subscribe to her channel and, as a fan, my family and I even wear her "Mama Wade" T-shirts.

Pastor Wade has come a long way, and I'm so grateful to her for being in my family's and my life. I love Pastor Wade with all my heart. She is definitely on my Mt. Rushmore of people in life. She played a big part in me becoming the man that I am today, and I have been privileged to have been able to serve the Lord under her leadership.

Nicole Banks

I am Nicole Banks. Minister Leon Banks is my husband, and my family and I were congregants at Pastor Wade's church.

I met Pastor Wade when I was working in a local school district, and a friend invited me to come to their church. I asked my husband if he wanted to go, and he said, "Yes." So, we went to the grand opening service at Pastor Wade's new church—the Temple of Praise: Binding and Loosening Ministries, International.

At the grand opening, when I heard Pastor Wade's testimony, the sharing of her story, and she was dressed in all white, I really saw an angel on that stage. When I heard her story, I was just blown away because a lot of pastors never reveal what Pastor Wade revealed that day. I had never met another minister like her. She was the first minister I ever experienced who lived her life according to the word of God when she emerged out of her darkness.

Meeting somebody who went through what Pastor Wade did, who speaks about it in such an honest and raw way and embodies it in the love and joy that she does, I realized that she was just what our community needed—because in our community there are so many individuals are trapped in the life that she was trapped in for so many years and, for her to share her story was a godsend. I saw Pastor Wade embody love—unaffected, openhearted, unconditional love. I felt the love coming from God to her, and I saw that God was love all the way around.

Pastor Wade's story is similar to my family's story.

My mom has been on drugs for many years. The things Pastor Wade said gave me hope and faith that perhaps my mom would eventually stop using drugs, stop being on the street, and so on. When I heard Pastor Wade say she didn't have to go to a drug treatment center, that she had turned her life around solely with the Lord's help, it gave me hope. She made the commitment, and the Lord walked her through it. It made me feel that my mom could do the same thing.

A while later, my mother did meet Pastor Wade. It was very graceful and so touching, as if they already knew each other. Pastor Wade spoke with my mom and said just the right things to her, and always encouraged her. At one point, looking my mom directly in her eyes, Pastor Wade said, "I know you know God in your heart."

My mom broke down, turned around, and said, "I love you," and was also able to say, "I'm sorry. I'm going to get better."

Every time Pastor Wade saw my mom, she encouraged her, "You can do it. You can believe in it. You can come out of it if you want to." It was a very touching moment every time they saw each other. I know there's a God, and that God is speaking to Pastor Wade and through Pastor Wade. I know if my mom gets to know God and hear God, one day my mom will come out of the street, come out of doing drugs.

I was raised without either my mother or my father, and was more of an abandoned child. As I said, I not only come from a mom who was on drugs, I came from people who were not even loving people. I had a rough life.

I was like Pastor Wade's daughter Tragil in the stories of our relationships with our mothers. One important difference was that Tragil knew love; I never did. Like Tragil, I helped raise a sibling—my sister. Tragil helped raise her brother, Dwyane. I always used to ask God, "God, when you send me my husband, I will make sure that he's OK." My husband and I began dating in high school. We married young and have remained together ever since—more than thirty years now.

My girls and I joined Pastor Wade's church at the grand opening. Even though my husband enjoyed the service and continued going with us every Sunday, he waited a while, then joined on the day of our daughter's birthday. He ultimately joined because he saw trueness and the Spirit of God really moving through Pastor Wade in her ministry. She would always say, "Pray, pray, pray. God answers everything."

God certainly answered our prayers, and sometime later, my husband and I both became ministers under Pastor Wade.

We all grew up in the church under Pastor Wade. We raised our kids in the church, my husband helped me raise my sister, and we grew into the loving family we are today. We are the family that Pastor Wade "birthed" under her. My kids were part of all the youth programs, and the sister we raised became the youth minister. Pastor Wade's ministry has helped us cultivate a lot of love, a lot of believing, a lot of faith. Under Pastor Wade, we discovered that when you come from love, when you recognize God's love, anything is possible.

As Pastor Wade came to know me, she chose me to be her armor-bearer. There had been other armor-bearers before me and there would be others after me but, now, she chose me out of the whole congregation. She told me she had prayed about it, had heard from God, and said, "You are the one. I want you to be close to me. I see so many gifts in you."

She just brought that out of me, and I said, "Yes. I would love to study with you and learn how you learned from the Spirit of the Lord, and learn the Bible a little bit more."

The word of God spoke about, "I knew you before you were born." I knew that under Pastor Wade, she would help me develop my gifts, so I would be able to touch others in the world, and be able to go out and reach people. That's why I became a minister.

I loved studying with her. I've been going to church off and on since I was a kid, but the way she explains the word of God is amazing. You can really pick it up. She taught us how to read the word, understand it, understand Hebrew, how to research, and how to put things together. We studied and researched; she broke it all down and made it so easy to learn. That's how she taught us.

All of us church members came with baggage, but with Pastor Wade, there was never any judgment. She loved us all unconditionally.

Through the Spirit of God loving her and how the love from her brought me in, Pastor Wade showed me how to love. She's given me all the tools and resources I need to be where I'm at now—to be with my family, to unconditionally love my family, and to love my mom, because at one time I couldn't. Without knowing God, without knowing the love of God that came through Pastor Wade to me, I probably could never have come to this moment in my life where I not only love my family and myself bountifully but am also able to love my mom and am better able to care for her.

Pastor Wade is my spiritual mom, and I look up to her for everything. If I need something spiritually, she will always be the first one I call. She always answers my calls and text messages even today, no matter what, to give me spiritual advice—everything I need to stay on track in my life. The love she shows me is phenomenal and that's why I call her my "spiritual mom."

Robbye Shepherd

I met Pastor Jolinda Wade when she opened her church, Temple of Praise: Binding and Loosening Ministries, a neighborhood church at 129th and Halsted. I attended services and became a member of her church family. Even before that, Pastor Jolinda had already meant a lot to me, as she had been ministering to my daughter, who was out on the street, and my son Nate, who has special needs. She got my daughter off the street and, through her outreach, brought them both into her church. She kept praying for my children and was full of love.

She is such a giving person and went out of her way to be there for my boy. I call Nate my "miracle baby" because he weighed only 1.5 pounds when he was born. Now he's going to be nineteen. Oh, my God! He's amazing. I always brought Nate to church. At that time, Pastor

Wade's sister Rose directed the youth ministry. Rose could deal with anybody's children, and Rose always had a special section for Nate to be involved in. Nate definitely sat up under the word with both Sister Rose and Pastor Wade.

He often said to me, "I want to talk to Pastor Wade," and Pastor Wade would always invite us into her office so that Nate could speak with her.

One day, he sat down and said, "Pastor Wade, I want to be a deacon."

She said, "You want to be a deacon?"

He said, "Yeah, I want to be a deacon."

She asked, "Why?"

He replied, "Because I want to spread the word of God. I want to talk the word of God." He was only eleven or twelve, and this is what he wanted to do.

With his special needs, he didn't behave like the other children. Sometimes he would scream, run around, or grab you. It was hard for him to sit still—he was always moving. It had to be a problem with his brain, but I just brought him on anyway, and he was treated just like any other child in the church and was involved in a lot of different activities.

Pastor Wade told him that, to become a deacon, he would have to come to church and listen to the teaching. She then assigned him to her main male minister, Minister Leon Banks, saying to Nate, "I need you to talk to Minister Leon, and he will let you know what you have to do." Both Minister Leon and Brother Bryant would often take him aside, teaching him the word and helping him understand.

One of the things that makes her a great pastor is how much she reveals of herself as a human being. Her honesty enables all of us to trust her and feel supported by her. We may not have had the same experiences, but her integrity and the stories she would tell helped us feel that we were all part of the same family, which created an extraordinary bond among us all. I remember once she spoke about the time she took a bath, relaxed in the tub, and overdosed. The way she told it was so personal, it made me feel I was there with her.

I was also drawn to her because she was so sweet. She didn't see me as slow or judge me in any way. She just saw me as God sees us all. Even though it was late in my life, she just loved me for who I was—just like Jesus loves us all.

I could feel the pain she had gone through and she could feel the pain I had gone through. When you see people hold a priest's hand, that's what I wanted to do. I wanted to reassure her, "It's OK. You see God, and it's going to be all right. So, don't be afraid. Let God and let go." That's the way my previous pastor had taught—how to be a soldier and be strong about it. Tell the truth. That's all there is. That's exactly what Jolinda does.

When I'm in Jolinda's presence, there is no judgment from her. It's important that I share this because I saw the same thing within her family. There was no judgment. They were all so close. They would never put each other down, just speak about Jesus, and just love one another.

Jolinda's church was like a family, and I became part of her church family. We, too, were all so close, loved, and respectfully related to each other without judgment. Wherever we came from, whether from another church or the streets, she immediately made us a part of her family—a family where everybody cared for one another. So, if one person is hurting, we all went and looked out for one another. When I needed somebody to pray for my pain, they would all do that. She taught each of us in her congregation how to value ourselves and taught us how not to let anyone step on us or treat us like trash.

Once I became part of Pastor Jolinda's ministry, along with other members of her church, we would often go out and do what we called "corner prayer." We would stand on the corner of 129th and Halsted, inviting all to come, to speak with us, and share a moment in prayer with us.

She taught us that God is love and peace. God is order. When we went out and ministered on the streets, she made sure we did so correctly. So, when we were from God, we were in order: We couldn't be one way and then another way.

When she was ministering on the street, you saw all of her. She never does anything halfway. She always told us that you do your very best for yourself because, when you do, you're doing your very best for Jesus.

She used to tell people about how Jesus had saved her, cleaned her up so she could go on and help other people clean themselves up. She said, "The Lord cleans us all up."

Those of us who assisted her with the street ministry depended on her leadership and guidance. Jolinda told us we were medicine, and by that she meant that by going out and ministering to the people on the streets, speaking the word, we would help heal people. However, it became clear to us that we could not let her hold our hands too long because, in a way, she had to let go of our hands so we could discover that we were strong enough within ourselves to go out and spread the word of the Lord.

Jolinda taught me how to love *my Self.* I had such poor self-esteem. One day, Pastor Jolinda had been in Chinatown and, when she came back, she asked me if I wanted to become an evangelist. "*Me?*" I asked. I never thought I was worthy enough to be anything—but God saw fit that I deserved to be somebody. So, He showed Pastor Jolinda Wade that my path was to be an evangelist.

When she asked me this, it turned my life upside down. I didn't know what to say because I never thought I deserved love or deserved to be happy. I wouldn't wish that horrible feeling on anybody. It makes you feel like you're something stuck on the bottom of a shoe. When I met Pastor Wade and accepted Jesus, they helped me turn my life all the way around—and now I am an evangelist. I never would have thought this possible.

Before Pastor Wade moved to California, I had to go out to the University of Southern California hospital for surgery. When I had my surgery at USC, she flew out and prayed for me. That's the kind of person she is.

Once she moved to California, I remained connected to her. I could feel when she wasn't feeling good, so I'd call and check on her—because she's a member of my family as well—and then I'd pray for her.

Pastor Wade has taught me that God says, "When I bless you, you bless somebody else." That's the way Pastor Wade taught us how to reach the people who needed to be reached, how to love a person who needs to be loved, how to not judge anyone, because God is the judge.

When she preaches, she preaches from God. When she moved to California, she didn't want to create a church there, and God let her know that, "You did all that you had to do in Chicago. So, this is another chapter in your life—a new chapter."

When she was leaving, I said to her, "This is your old chapter. You've got a new chapter in California. God needs you to go out there and not open a church, but go and preach to the world—and let them know about Jesus. So, you've got to go and spread the word and be a beacon of light."

When she moved to California, she never changed. Wherever she goes, Pastor Wade never changes. Even though Dwyane is so successful and showers her with his generosity, she is still unchanged, still a loving mama with a loving family.

Even though Jolinda has moved to California, I still feel that she is with us and there for us. I listen to her podcast, *Better Health, Better Me*. She's the first minister I've ever heard preach about the importance of good health and nutrition.

I have her CD as well and, when I mess up, I listen to it—especially when she's telling Bible stories like "Jesus Cleanses Ten Lepers." In this story, Jesus met ten lepers who said to him, "Jesus, Master, have mercy on us!" Jesus spoke to them, instructing them to go show themselves to the priests. After he spoke, they saw that they were cleansed. All ten left but only one returned to thank Jesus for cleansing them. I feel like those lepers, but I'm the one who returned to glorify and serve the Lord.

So, I listen to that when I'm missing her, then I feel her talking. When I'm feeling bad or I'm sad and I miss her, I play that CD and I can channel her speaking to me, saying, "It's going to be all right. Don't worry. Don't let anybody judge you." Just like when she told me, "Don't let anybody tell you you aren't an evangelist—because I've seen you with people who are feeling bad or hurting and you feel their hurt. God gave you that." That's how I feel about Pastor Wade. She doesn't need to call me and tell me how she feels; I can feel her sickness, I can feel her pain. I can feel that she's reaching out all the way from California.

When I first met Pastor Wade, there was something about her that made me feel that I had known her forever. We just clicked. I said, "I don't know why I feel this way about this lady." I feel like I'm part of her family, but I'm not. I am part of the family of Christ, not her immediate family, but I feel I'm a daughter to her.

She is a child of God and still amazing in my life. She feels great to me, and I love her.

Minister Elaine Scott

I am Minister Elaine Scott. I served under Pastor Jolinda Wade at the New Creation: Binding and Loosening Ministries, International. When I think of Pastor Wade, the first thing I recall is the grace and generosity she extended to me when I first discovered her. Even many years later, sharing this, I still get emotional.

She was the pastor at the Temple of Praise. I was not a member, but my niece had invited me to a community barbecue event that they were sponsoring at the church. My niece wanted to bring me because, at the time, I was raising my granddaughter, who was a preteen. My eldest daughter, her mother had passed, and, because I was so much older than other parents, there were not many young people for her to be around, and I wanted my granddaughter to have young people in her life.

My niece said to me, "Teetee, we have a lot of young people at our church, and we have a young people's ministry. We have teachers, and they are learning all kinds of things there—learning how to worship. They are singing and dancing. I think she'll do well there." That's why she encouraged me to go to the event.

My granddaughter had an absolutely wonderful experience, which is what prompted me to go to Temple of Praise, and that's where it all began. She literally grew up in that church and, from the very first day, she felt right at home.

She's twenty-five now and has a degree from Southern Illinois University in engineering chemistry. It was wonderful for her. Whenever one of our young people goes off to college, Pastor Wade always makes certain that we send them with a stipend, a kind of scholarship money, to help them get started. The same thing that they provided for all the young people, they provided for Ashley as well.

While at the barbecue, I had a brief conversation with Pastor Wade and she made mention of the boils and the blisters she had seen on my legs. Then, I was invited back again for a foot-washing service. Even though I wasn't a member of the congregation, I came for that service, and it was in that space I came to know Pastor Wade. We were all instructed to wash the various pastors' and ministers' feet who were there.

When I entered the church, the Spirit of the Lord was with me, and Pastor Wade took note of that. She could see and feel that the Spirit of the Lord was with me. It was both shocking and gratifying. It was such a blessed and anointed moment for me there.

She was the person whose feet I literally wanted to wash but was told to step back as there was another church member already scheduled to do this. So, I washed another minister's feet, and it was a blessed experience.

Even from the first moment of being with Pastor Wade, she was always quiet and gentle in her handling of me. She never shunned me or treated me with anything other than grace and love. I'll always remember the love with which she carried me in that space.

I came back again and continued to go until, one day, an announcement was made. We were told that Pastor Wade was establishing her own church. The new name was to be the New Creation: Binding and Loosening Ministries, International.

By now, I knew that I wanted to be part of her ministry. So, when the invitation was extended, I came up and joined the church. After I joined the church, even though I had been baptized before, I wanted Pastor Wade to baptize me this time. For me, this was my commitment to Jesus that this is where I belonged, this is what I needed, and this is where I wanted to be. When I shared this with Pastor Wade and asked her about her baptizing me, she said only one word, "Absolutely!"

Sometime later, Pastor Wade looked at me and said the Lord had spoken to her and He wanted me to become her armor-bearer. I had never in my life heard the term "armor-bearer" and didn't have any clue what that meant. She asked me to purchase a book that spoke about armor-bearers and what it meant to be one, and what the requirements were. As I began to read the book and understand, I recognized that God was blessing me by creating the opportunity to be a caring, nurturing servant to Pastor Wade.

I took care of whatever was necessary for Pastor's welfare. I looked after her, keeping her office tidy, her robes and personal garments fresh and always ready for her to wear. I made sure she had food and water and always had whatever she needed without having to ask for it.

Throughout my life, all I've ever known is how to serve. When I became her armor-bearer, God and Pastor Wade were confirming the truth of my calling.

As time went along, she even asked me to be a part of her ministry. She said she had chosen a handful of her congregants to become ministers, and I was one of them. I began taking classes from Pastor Wade—reading, studying, deepening my understanding of the word of God, and learning how to be a disciple in the ministry. I began as a deaconess, and when she later licensed me as a minister, she gave me ministerial responsibilities under her.

From the first moment I met Pastor Wade, I knew she was different. Number one, I had never been under the tutelage of a woman minister. Number two, when she spoke, I knew that she was speaking, not simply from herself, but from an inner place where God spoke to her. I felt it in how she enunciated her words. I felt it in the power and authority of the Lord coming through her. You knew it was serious business. You could see her listening. I had never seen this before—someone carrying on a conversation with the Lord.

One other point of confirmation that reflected Pastor Wade being an anointed one was affirmed when she said things to me only the Lord could know, as I had only spoken of these things to Him.

Pastor Wade always treated me with unconditional love. At this point in my life, people were saying terrible things about me, which hurt me deeply. They were treating me awfully, awfully bad, as though I was gum underneath someone's shoe. They made me feel unworthy.

When Pastor Wade learned of it, she went to them and said, "Leave her alone. Leave her be. She's all right. She's all right. Allow God to work with her. Allow Him to talk to her. Allow Him to love her."

She never once treated me like I was not worthy to be loved. She recognized and taught me that I am one of God's creatures and, because He created me, I am absolutely worthy.

Today I *know* that. Today, I know what unconditional love feels like, and no one can take that away from me.

All these years later, I still trust the God in Pastor Wade. Even today, when I am grappling with a challenging decision or confronted with a difficult moment in my life, I still call and consult with her. I know she hears from Him and know that she would not say anything to me that the Lord has not instructed her to say.

I have such deep admiration and such genuine respect for Pastor Wade, as she has profoundly affected my life.

Minister Bryant Tubbs

I met Pastor Jolinda Wade in 2009 when I attended a service at her church, called Temple of Praise.

My best friend invited me to join her for a Sunday service at her church. I attended a couple of more times and, as my mother is Roman Catholic and I was raised in the Catholic faith, Pastor Wade's church was a new and very different experience for me. I actually enjoyed myself, just listening to the word and observing people praising God. Pastor Wade's preaching style was completely different, and I was blown away by it.

When they say, "You can see the anointing on that person," it means to me that you can see the connection that person has with God. Although in the beginning I didn't understand, I could see it in Pastor Wade, and when she was preaching, it was like a movie. When she was done, I wanted to say, "Wait, wait. There must be more. So, OK, I need to come back and see what she's going to do next." Every time I heard her, I said to myself, "I want to hear this next piece. I want to see the next part of this movie." Really, she just teaches, but the style that she uses is visceral, visual, and compelling—and it kept me coming back for more.

After that first visit, I would go to her church service every Sunday and continued to enjoy it, but because I grew up going to a Catholic school where a required subject was religion, my understanding of what religion meant was completely different. When I asked my friend about this, she said, "If you're not understanding everything, come to Bible study, and Bible study will teach you more because you can ask questions."

So, I started going to Pastor Wade's Bible study class, and the Bible studies were even better because I had the opportunity to ask questions. Because it was a smaller setting, afterward, when class was over, I had the chance to meet Pastor Wade. At that time, I was in my thirties, but I was still like a kid talking to his mom—that's how it felt.

She was just so humble and grateful that I wanted to come and listen. She wanted me to ask questions, and she, in turn, asked questions, wanting to know, "What made you come here? Who invited you?"

I knew to be quiet when Pastor Wade was talking, and when she spoke, I knew I was getting a life lesson.

At the time I became one of her congregants, I did not know her story until one time I heard her talk about it in one of her sermons—then, I also invited my parents. My mother heard her sermon, listened to her story, and said, "Man, she's got a powerful story. You know what? If she's got a book, I'm going to get you that book because this is a special lady here."

It was so strange. Even though my mother was Roman Catholic, she was blown away by Pastor Wade and instantly fell in love with her—my whole family just loved her.

In 2010 to 2011, the church shifted from two pastors to just one, Pastor Wade. I continued to worship with Pastor Wade, learning the word from her and applying it to my life.

One day, Pastor Wade asked Minister Leon to come and talk to me after the service. He said, "Hey, Pastor Wade wants to have a conversation with you. She'll talk to you now."

When I went round to her office, she invited me in. I told her I wanted to be more a part of the church, but I didn't know how. She said, "What I can let you do is help Him do things. Do you have a black suit?"

I said, "Yes."

She said, "Wear a black suit. That way I can identify you when you're there."

I just went from there to becoming her armor-bearer—going to church, Bible study, learning more, and getting closer to God. The closer I got to God, the next thing I knew, I was coming to church every day, opening up the church at eight on Sunday mornings, opening and closing it on Tuesdays for Bible study. Pastor Wade told me, "You're showing yourself faithful to God."

I said, "I'm not a faithful member."

She said, "When you're tired, you still come to church. You are a faithful member." It wasn't long after that that Pastor Wade asked me if I would be interested in studying for the ministry.

I knew Pastor Wade and her church were something special, but I didn't understand how special they were. A lot of times, you'll hear people tell you, "Oh, man, if you go to church, all they want you to do is give them money."

Pastor Wade's church was never about money. It was, "Come get the word. I don't care how you look, just come. You don't have to change or anything. Nobody needs to tell you to change anything; just come, see it, and enjoy. Go and, if something happens along the way, let's talk about it."

That's what happened for me. I went, I saw, and enjoyed it, and then, something changed along the way—not what I expected—but it changed my life.

Afterword

A Message Of Hope

At this moment of my writing, I am weeping. I am weeping for joy, remembering what it was like to glimpse the light that would ultimately lead me up out of a place I was not born to be in. The reality of that moment was both terrifying and exhilarating as I was being shown the possibility that my life could be different—my life would be different.

Writing this memoir of my Journey itself has been a journey—a journey accompanied by you, my dear reader, who may also have travelled your own Journey of exile and darkness. A lonely and fearful passage at times, perhaps haunted by your own demons and/or in the throes of addictions. I know there are those reading this memoir who seek to understand, aid, and even comfort family and/or friends who may be afflicted by life challenges and/or drug-driven disease.

This has been a selfless, humble endeavor. I wrote this book to give back.

If I can help even one person, then it's been worth it.

The journey of writing my memoir has been liberating. It gave me insight into how I conquered things I couldn't see while I was going through them, and from it, I got to know and understand Jolinda a lot better, and I grew from it. It is so important to *know ourselves* so we can't get lost *in ourselves*. When we don't see it, we may remain stuck and imprisoned by our fears in a place that feels like a place of failure, but, in reality, it can become a place of powerful liberation and freedom.

Writing has helped me see that. I discovered as I wrote that, when sharing my life's Journey, I actually slowly began to recognize how heroic my Journey was.

"Conquering me" was not only the best thing I could have ever done—it was the *only* thing I could have done. It was I who owned a fear that wasn't given to me by my Creator. He said, "I didn't give you a spirit of fear. I gave you a spirit of power, of love, and a sound mind." Fear dilutes our power. When we are in fear, we can't operate in a sound mind.

Through my writing, I clearly saw that the strongest defining element in my story, in its many chapters, is *love*. Love brought me through all the way—even when I didn't understand, it brought me all the way through. What I had to do was to learn to love myself.

As I've said at various times, in different ways, I saw death coming for me when I was homeless, living in abandoned buildings, or sleeping in cars. When the men I was with beat me, it was my children, who were also my protectors, who kept me wanting to live. Every time I saw death, I saw my four children's faces—Deanna, Keisha, Tragil, Dwyane—my biggest cheerleaders—who just wanted their mom to survive, who just wanted their mama back. They were my lifeline that kept me in the game. I love them, with every fiber of my being. Their love for me when I was at my lowest was what raised me up every step of the way. So, I thank God for protecting the children He blessed me with.

This book has changed my way of thinking toward my family and my ministry today. It has taught me to love myself even more. I have become my own best friend because I now have a better understanding of myself. It has reintegrated the very fragments of my life, enabling me to see the entire picture of my life's Journey. I am no longer a broken picture lying on the ground that you step around for fear of being cut. I am beautifully framed—my life experience helping me glow evermore.

Now I can stand in front of any challenge when it comes and let it know, "I will win. Each and every time, I will win." No matter how many times I might continue to fall down, I will always get up. I no longer take this Journey alone. I know I can valiantly say, "I can win," because I know that God lives within me and I strive every day to feel His presence and hear His perfect voice guide my life.

I do believe that my story will inspire you to reflect on your own life, to recognize not merely that you have survived, but that you are also capable of soaring, and to discover that you, too, have it within you to discard all that is harmful, with it no longer preventing you from fulfilling your life's vision.

Right from the outset it was important to me to share my life story as fully and honestly as possible and, by telling you my truth with clarity and compassion, I firmly believe it can help others to find reassurance and strength, which would then help whomever reads this book to step up and claim more confidently who you are capable of being.

I want people to know that we have the ability to be conquerors of ourselves. We have the capacity to conquer all fears and overcome all life's challenges.

I have been where you may be or have been. Even if you have not lived a life as severe as mine, there are still things that may hold you back in your life. By revealing my truth, I have created a context for you to trust someone while also providing you with real tools that, in turn, can show you how to live *your* life journey as fruitfully and in as empowered a way as possible. I believe you will feel emboldened through the courage of my example and it will help you also recognize the power of God's voice in all of us.

This writing journey has been awe-inspiring for me as it drew me closer to all those who have always been there for me unconditionally, loving me throughout my life—no matter what. Where I put myself in a box or built a wall around me to keep people out, they created a door in that wall, opened it, peered in, accepted me, and shared their love with me. I find that, where in the past they would have had to pry the lid off my box or pull the door open—as I was holding the doorknob on the other end resisting their entreaties—now, there is no door being held shut by me from within. It is wide open.

As I wrote this book, it was fascinating for me to explore the arc of my life. I got to look back at my young self and to view the beginning of my life from the perspective of time, which enabled me to grasp and understand how it all began.

Then continuing from my young self, through my teenage years, to the birth of my beautiful children, every step of the way, from the unseemly and terrifying to the joys of conquest into my mature self, I believe I've done the very best I could not to shield myself from the mistakes and the harshness of so much of my life. I would often fall off the tightrope, but I would always pull myself back up.

Of course, it was God who enabled me not just to survive, but to soar. On a more personal level, it was also my endurance—my indefatigable ability to persevere because I could never give up and allow my children to see me give up. In turn, I could not give up because I couldn't quit on God, and God wouldn't let me give up.

First of all, God expects me to tell the truth, and second, a loving mentor once told me that, "When you close down to keep out the pain, you also keep out the joy." And, yes, there is exultant joy to celebrate throughout my life.

I didn't realize until I read their testimonies that there was always a core group of people who had rooted and prayed for me, who shouted, "You can do it, Jolinda! You can come out of this. You can reign. You can live. You can be." The team: my mom, my dad, my siblings, my children, and others.

This is yet another example of the purity of unconditional love. This is also another example that it was God, through the love of others, making sure that I was covered even when I had lost faith in myself.

A lot of the experiences I had came from *my* choices, *my* decision-making, not thinking about or knowing what was on the other side of those choices. I opened doors that you might call "forbidden doors." I went in, and it was so very dark in some of those places, but I bless God for the little light that continued to shine, that always led me out of the darkness and back into the light.

My purpose in sharing my life scriptures with you is to communicate that no matter how bleak our Journey may seem or the path may appear to be, God is always with us and His light will help us see more clearly than we could ever imagine and help us recognize there is a way out of any situation.

If we take a moment to look even right now and say to God, "I love you. Please show me the way," light will appear. The light or the joy might only be temporary, it might just be a glimpse—but it proves to us that it exists.

Hold on to this for dear life and watch how your story will more commandingly evolve each and every day as you breathe these words into your life. Ultimately, your life can be and deserves to be as abundant as mine has become and continues to be. It is never beyond our reach.

The scripture that opens my memoir came from Romans 12:2. As I near the end of my memoir, I want to once again offer a scripture from Romans 12, but this time both verses 1 and 2. The Spirit of God spoke these words to me when I was in the darkest part of my Journey:

Offer your body as a living sacrifice—holy and acceptable unto me—which is your reasonable service. To be not conformed to this world but be transformed by the renewing of your mind.

His word gave me instruction, direction, and gave me hope.

I knew then that the only way out of this, the only way I would be able to conquer myself and achieve the transformation God saw for me, was by renewing my mind. When I studied and reflected on the verses above, I realized that I would have to rethink my every thought and design an entirely new thought process. Not only would I have to undo decades of impoverished thinking, but to take the place of the negative thought patterns I was discarding, I would have to replace them with something new and untested.

When I realized my task, I also recognized the only way I could achieve this was in partnership with the Lord. Once I was able to do this, life opened up for me like a glorious sunrise after a terrifying storm had subsided.

So, I say to you what I said earlier in my memoir: *We are not our behaviors.* We can, by tuning in to the Lord and changing our very thinking, actually write a whole new chapter for our lives—a chapter that can be joyful and fulfilling. Not only can you dream again, but your dream can become a new reality.

Now, your awakening may not come to you in the same way it came to me. While I share with you that God has always supported me on my Journey, you may have another faith, another belief system, or other sources of support, somebody or something, that you can hold on to. Perhaps my book is leading you to want to know more. Perhaps you are saying to yourself, "Well, let me get to know this God."

There is only one part of you that is imprisoned. Even if, because you are merely a human being, you fell off the path, even if you live in a dark place, as I did, even if you have not been able to change your circumstances to this day, you still have the qualities within you, in spite of your fears or whatever holds you back, to summon your courage and confidence—putting one foot in front of the other, to get to the place where you can define for yourself what is holding you back.

It all has to do with life choices. *Everything* that we do is wrapped up in the choices we make—*everything*. I can't reassure you that it's easy, but if you take action, if you are committed to doing the necessary work, then *you too will become your own hero*.

Surrender/serve/soar expresses so perfectly what really happened with me, and I do believe that it can happen also with whoever is drawn to read this book. A lot of times, we don't want to surrender to ourselves because that means, "Now, I have to look at me," and, many times, we don't want to feel the fear or see the abuse—but, when we surrender, we are compelled to look inward. When we surrender automatically and without thinking about it, we simply give it all up and no longer need to hold ourselves back.

God is love. God has a plan, and I'm glad I have a part to play—to even touch the lives of the people that I touch just being me—being Him through me.

When you join forces with God, you can accomplish anything.

If, when reading my story, you identified elements of your own journey, if you found words for your feelings, if you felt seen, heard, and understood for the first time in your life, then I have done my job.

If you have discovered God's loving presence in your life, renewed your faith, found comfort, forgiveness, and love, then I have succeeded in my ministry.

If you are inspired to make the necessary changes that will alter your life path, then you too will become your own hero—and I will have achieved my goal.

All it really takes, to paraphrase my spiritual son, Minister Bryant Tubbs, is an openness to what comes, to do whatever is required, and to make the commitment to stay and see what happens. Then, something may change along the way, perhaps not what you might have expected—but it *can* change your life.

This is a book of liberation. It has liberated me in ways I could never have foreseen, and I'm hoping that, if you are seeking liberation in your own life or seeking liberation for others, I have been helpful. I feel peace in closing out this book and releasing a treasure that's more important than silver and gold.

To My Fantastic Four:
Deanna, Keisha, Tragil, Dwyane
An Open Letter To My Children

other loves you beyond words! I can only show you the truth of this through my actions and emotions, and the feelings I reveal to you when we speak or are together. One of the purposes of this letter is to share with you my truth about who you are and the bountiful treasures I recognize that lie within each of you.

Your struggles are your strength. When there is abrasion of sand against the interior of an oyster shell when it is forming, what emerges is a beautiful pearl. Therefore, I want you to see that your pain can be your gain. All of you are perfect pearls. You are originals who come from an *exceptional* stock.

You don't always have to understand the path you are on; simply go with it. And remember: Your path is designed by God. The stronger God is on the inside of you, the more He can do with the outside. So, please, take bold steps on your Journey and feel God's hand ever present on the small of your back, both supporting you and pushing you forward.

My babies, you can do all things through Christ. You *can* become whatever you desire to be. There's a *fight* in you. There's toughness in you, and you can call upon this at any time. You are not meant to be doormats. You are not meant to be slaves. You are not meant to be *man-* and *maidservants*. You are *queens and a king*—so, please wear the mantle proudly. When someone or something bothers you, don't let them or the situation determine your day. *You* determine your day.

Look up, my children. Continue to rise, to soar. Let no one or anything take your peace or joy from you. Your ability to hold true to who you are and feel the Lord's presence in your life is where your strength lies.

I certainly have not always been there for you to place these values within you. But, through your mother's experience, through your mother's path, through your mother's Journey, I see each of you as you truly are.

Each of you, my precious pearls, was raised with me in different seasons of my life. Some of you saw my strength. Others saw more of my suffering and pain, but all of you experienced my love.

I don't claim to be the best mom, but by God's grace, I was *chosen* to be *your mom*. And, as your mom, I will not allow you to ever settle in this life for anything less than what you truly deserve.

Pass on *your* knowledge, *your* experience, *your* struggles, and *your* pain to your children. Share with your dear children the value of your Journey as I share the value of mine with you. Share your life in all its richness, triumphs, failures, pain, and joy. This will help your children become better attuned to what they are destined to encounter on their own journeys.

Be thoughtful about making your choices and decisions. If you discover they don't serve you, please *know* you can always make new choices, new decisions. Never let fear shut you down. Be aware of your surroundings. Be mindful of whom you allow into your inner circle. Please remember, there *are* Judases who will betray you. Be astute. Use your insight, and please trust your intuition. These qualities are God speaking to you.

My children, I have always said, "An apple is an apple. A banana is a banana. An orange is an orange." Don't make people what you want them to be. Be aware of who they are. Give them time, and they will show you their true selves. Don't try to change them because "an apple is an apple; an orange is an orange; a banana is a banana." You cannot make an orange into a banana. Please know, dear children, you always have the choice to choose those you want and who deserve to be in your inner circle. When you make this empowering choice, this bond is then unbreakable.

You are givers. It is innate within each of you to be generous and to give selflessly. But you are not fools. That's innate within you also. As it says in Ecclesiastes 3:11, "To everything there is a season." There is a time to give, a time to take a stand, and there is a time to move on.

Remember, you *are* Willie Mae's offspring. You are *survivors*. You are *protectors*. You *are* children of faith. When it comes to risking, growing, and progressing in your life, the words *I can't* are not in your vocabulary. If anything, if someone is harmfully or inappropriately interfering with your life, you can say, "*I will not allow your foolishness*," or, "*I can't allow your behavior to interfere with my life*."

Life is precious. Please value, not simply each day of your life, but each moment of your life. This will help you more fully live who you are. Embody your brand. Your brand is—success.

Your mother loves you. I said that before, and I will say it over and over again until my last days on this earth. I am your protector. I am your watcher. I am your listener—and I will *always* back you up. I will tell you when I see a train coming down the track, and I see you standing there while the warning bell is going off. *I will tell you, "Get off that track!"* I will also help you identify the correct train to take you to your destination. You are children of destiny, and as your mother, part of my responsibility is to help you fulfill your destiny.

We have a limited number of blessed years to live within these bodies. Do well with yours. Do not compare yourself with others. You have your own distinct role and purpose in this life. Your voices lift people up. You have been chosen by God to make a difference, a contribution in this life that only you can make. You are wealth, my children. Wealth is not simply money. Wealth is not merely material. Wealth is the power that you hold within you. Be who you are.

In my memoir, *Conquering Me*, I have shared who I am, who you are in my life, with the world. But here, my beautiful children, Deanna, Keisha, Tragil, and Dwyane, I say directly to you, you are conquerors. *Conquer your fears. Conquer your doubts. Claim* your power. *Claim and live the life God has chosen for you* as magnificently as possible. Live an abundant life. Feel God's presence each and every day.

Kisses and hugs to my *fantastic, fabulous four!* I love you.

Before I close the most personal letter I've ever written in my life, I want to share an exquisite poem that summarizes all that I believe. It was written by the American poet Max Ehrmann and is called "Desiderata." I'd like you to see my letter to you and the "Desiderata" as your true north. Whenever you are troubled or lost, simply read my tribute to you and/or the "Desiderata," and you will successfully get back on your path.

Desiderata

Go placidly amid the noise and the haste, and remember what peace there may be in silence. As far as possible, without surrender, be on good terms with all persons.

Speak your truth quietly and clearly; and listen to others, even to the dull and the ignorant; they too have their story.

Avoid loud and aggressive persons; they are vexatious to the spirit. If you compare yourself with others, you may become vain or bitter, for always there will be greater and lesser persons than yourself.

Enjoy your achievements as well as your plans. Keep interested in your own career, however humble; it is a real possession in the changing fortunes of time.

Exercise caution in your business affairs, for the world is full of trickery. But let this not blind you to what virtue there is; many persons strive for high ideals, and everywhere life is full of heroism.

Be yourself. Especially do not feign affection. Neither be cynical about love; for in the face of all aridity and disenchantment, it is as perennial as the grass.

Take kindly the counsel of the years, gracefully surrendering the things of youth.

Nurture strength of spirit to shield you in sudden misfortune. But do not distress yourself with dark imaginings. Many fears are born of fatigue and loneliness.

Beyond a wholesome discipline, be gentle with yourself. You are a child of the universe no less than the trees and the stars; you have a right to be here.

And whether or not it is clear to you, no doubt the universe is unfolding as it should. Therefore, be at peace with God, whatever you conceive Him to be. And whatever your labors and aspirations, in the noisy confusion of life, keep peace in your soul. With all its sham, drudgery and broken dreams, it is still a beautiful world. Be cheerful. Strive to be happy.

Once again, *I love you,*
Your mother

The Hero's Journey

A Commentary
By Arthur Samuel Joseph, MA

The cave you fear to enter holds the treasure you seek . . .
The privilege of a lifetime is being who you are.
JOSEPH CAMPBELL

efore I begin my commentary, my tribute to a miraculous woman, Jolinda Wade, I want first to introduce myself. I am a communications strategist and the creator of the Vocal Awareness Method and have been teaching my work for over six decades. I first met Jolinda over three years ago and, from the first moment we sat down together, she truly allowed me to teach—her trust was immediate and the journey which has culminated in this book began.

I say to everyone I teach, "When you give me your voice, you give me who you are," and that relationship is sacrosanct. So, to you, dear Jolinda, thank you for your love, and please feel mine for you.

It has been such a privilege to know, teach, and collaborate with Jolinda over the last three years, crafting this memoir. Her sharing the breadth and depth of her life through transformational stories is an experience I have had only one other time in my life. A number of years ago, I had the distinct honor of working with significant numbers of Holocaust survivors from World War II. Of course, what they lived through defies our contemporary understanding—but live through it they did.

Fast forward a number of years to when I first began working with this valiant and courageous woman. I discovered she is the only person I've ever known whose life was as harrowing as theirs and recovery as remarkable. During the writing of this memoir, there were numerous occasions when I said to her, "When you began your torturous Journey over five decades ago, in the deepest part of who you are, you knew you *would* survive it. However, God *knew* that you would not only survive— you would *soar* from it. Even when you didn't consciously know God was with you, in your soul, you *knew* God was with you." God always kept you in the palm of His hand. No matter how dark, how terrifying, how many near-death experiences you had, you were never vanquished.

Jolinda, you said to me one day that you had the Journey you had so you would be able to minister to the people you have ministered to for almost three decades. You said you knew how to speak their language, to feel intimately what they were going through, enabling you to touch what they needed. You went on to say, "I believe I was appointed for that. People have allowed me to go to the intimate place where they are hiding behind a veil that they know I can see through. I help them lift that veil. I say that God allowed me to invade the camp. He always knew He would bring me out so that I could go back in and be able to serve my calling.'"

I've entitled this commentary "The Hero's Journey" because Jolinda is *exactly that—a hero*. The origin of the word *hero* comes from our earliest records and originally meant "protector" and "defender." A hero exhibits "great bravery in the course of action" and "selfless acts for the common good." A hero is one who, "in the face of danger, combats adversity through feats of ingenuity, courage, and/or strength" to achieve victory.

Joseph Campbell, one of the greatest mythologists of the twentieth century, wrote in his seminal work, *The Hero with a Thousand Faces*, about mythological heroes as metaphors for our own life experience. Jolinda's life is clearly not a myth. It is real—just like she is.

In mythology, one of the situations that heroes must confront is to go into the underworld to do battle. Jolinda's underworld was, literally, the notorious underworld of the inner-city streets on the South Side of Chicago, where she lived out a life of abuse, homelessness, jail, prison, drugs, alcohol, and, perhaps, the most difficult of all—surrendering up her children.

Jolinda's story is a woman's story of heroism. In her mid-teens, the most vulnerable age for girls, seeking friends, hungry for recognition and acceptance, needing affection, craving to be loved, she was targeted by not one but two predators, made pregnant not once but twice. At fifteen, Jolinda was a bright, promising student who was forced to leave school when she discovered she was pregnant and, thus, altered the trajectory of her future from budding scholar to becoming a single mother.

Jolinda bonded with each of her children and loved them as *her* children, regardless of who their fathers were. Then, to support them, she was forced by circumstances to go on welfare as well as sell drugs on the street—a crime for which she paid dearly. From there, her life spiraled downward into a cycle of debilitating substance abuse, homelessness, and physically abusive relationships until, again, as a mother and out of love for her children, one by one, she released them so that they might have advantages she was unable to provide.

Despite crippling fears and profound despair, Jolinda's remarkable resilience and love for her children kept her striving for a better life for herself and her children, doing the best she could.

While so many of her family and friends couldn't make it out and didn't make it out, no matter how dire her circumstances and profound her need to end her suffering, her love for her children and theirs for her did not allow her to give up—even when that meant risking her life in hand-to-hand combat to protect herself and her children.

I said to Jolinda some time ago, "I see the humanity of who you are reflected in your children as well. For example, as complex, as busy, and as high-profile a life as Dwyane leads, he would instantly drop everything in a moment for you and his siblings, as each of you would for him."

Her exceptional quality of selfless loving kept her always striving forward in her faith, which led to her encounter with God, and her surrender to the Lord and to herself, which allowed her, for almost three decades of her life, to dedicate herself in service to God and to her community.

Even as I write this, I find myself brought to tears reflecting on not only who Jolinda has become, but who Jolinda is. Over and over throughout her memoir and in the testimonies that follow, we have read how everyone, from judges who were lenient, to jailers and prison guards who were moved to help her, to Mr. Anderson and the landlord who offered her shelter without rent, to Pastor Darrell and his mother who implicitly trusted her—all responded to her by offering help and protection, often commenting to her that she was not like others in her circumstances. Yes, she is tough. Yes, she is strong—but she is also sensitive, tender, loving, generous, selfless, and always notable for her rigorous honesty.

No matter what, Jolinda was and is always respectful and considerate toward others. She has moral standards that are never compromised. To the best of her ability, she made every effort to maintain her appearance in public for her children and others so that she would always look like the respectable woman she knew herself to be. None of these attributes was ever taught to Jolinda; they are inherent in the fundamental dignity of who she is. It never occurred to her to do otherwise. No one, none of her experiences, could ever rob her of her dignity.

Because of who Jolinda is, beginning with her unconditional love for her children, herself, and continuing with everyone else with whom she interfaces, all are ennobled by her very presence. Through her example and wisdom, she enables all who know her to discover how to be and do our very best and how to live in God consciousness as she does.

The nineteenth-century American poet Ralph Waldo Emerson summarized who Jolinda is when he wrote: *The only person you are destined to become is the person you decide to be.*

Jolinda has chosen who she is.

In her daily prayer, when she sits and listens to God speak to her, she is also reminded of Psalms 46:10:

> *Be still and know that I am God.*
> *Be still and know that I am.*
> *Be still and know.*
> *Be still.*
> *Be.*

In the first book I wrote many, many years ago, *The Sound of the Soul*, there is a poem that closes the book by the Nobel laureate, Seamus Heaney. It's called "Personal Helicon." Helicon is a mountain said to be home of the Muses in Greek mythology. It is here because of the closing stanza:

> *Now, to pry into roots, to finger slime . . .*
> *Is beneath all adult dignity. I rhyme*
> *To see myself, to set the darkness echoing.*

On a personal note, this is why I created Vocal Awareness over sixty years ago—to see myself. In the same context, Jolinda has shared with me numerous times that she has learned even more about herself during the creation of this book.

As I teach in my Work, the Journey is never outward in life toward the *accomplishment or fulfillment of our goals. Rather, it is always and only* inward *to discovery of the Deeper Self.*

We all have an inner voice that only we are privy to. Jolinda shares hers with the world. These conversations between Source and Self are eye-opening and can lead to truly transformational growth.

As I close this commentary, I say directly to my dear friend: *Once again, thank you for your trust. Thank you for allowing me to share in the telling of your story. I am a much better man than I was before I began this journey with you.*

I conclude with some favorite quotations of mine that I believe offer a lovely perspective on the lessons in Jolinda's life scripture that can be a boon to us all.

> *Destiny is not a matter of chance, it's a matter of choice.*
> *It is not a thing to be, it is a thing to be achieved.*
> WILLIAM JENNINGS BRYAN

> *I long to accomplish a great and noble task, but it is my chief task*
> *is to accomplish small tasks as if they are great and noble.*
> HELEN KELLER

> *All men [persons] make mistakes,*
> *but only wise men [persons] learn from their mistakes.*
> WINSTON CHURCHILL

> *Not all who wander are lost.*
> J. R. R. TOLKIEN

Finally, once again, from JOSEPH CAMPBELL:

> *When everything is lost, and all seems darkness,*
> *then comes the new life and all that is needed.*

> *The artist is meant to put the objects of this world together in*
> *such a way that through them you will experience that light, that*
> *radiance which is the light of our consciousness and which all*
> *things both hide and, when properly looked upon, reveal. The*
> *Hero's Journey is one of the universal patterns through which*
> *radiance shows brightly. What I think is that a good life is one*
> *Hero Journey after another. Over and over again, [the hero is]*
> *called to the realm of adventure, called to new horizons. Each*
> *time, there is the same problem: Do I dare? And then if you do*
> *dare, the dangers are there, and the help also, and the fulfillment*
> *or the fiasco. There's always the possibility of a fiasco.*

> *But there's also the possibility of bliss.*

Acknowledgments

There are so many people that I want to acknowledge who helped me along on my Journey—who were there on some of the most difficult days I faced.

Some of you fed me. Gave me a place to stay where I was able to bathe and lay my head. I received comfort and guidance from some of you. Some even took time to talk with me and not judge me. I truly thank you from my heart.

My most enduring, intimate thanks and appreciation go to my Lord and Savior, Jesus Christ, who showed love despite the person I had become. He was a Friend who gave me comfort in the midst of my long-lasting addiction. He protected me from the choices that I made, which put me in dangerous situations. He was my Defender, my Waymaker. He was my way out.

The most powerful woman in the world who influenced me didn't sugar-coat the life I was living but kept it real. Who loved me, cried and prayed for me, and with me was my mom, Willie Mae Morris. I thank her for showing me how I could survive through the struggles that life brought my way. I thank her for showing me that I have this inner strength to be an extraordinary woman. She helped me see that

I could be a mother, grandmother, and all that that entails. She was a hard worker who made it through her Journey and showed me how to make it through mine as well. She was my mom. I could make it in mine and I did.

I now acknowledge you, my readers. You are very important to me. Some of you might not have experienced the struggles I had, but you might know someone who has. I believe this book can help inspire. I hope there is also something in *Conquering Me* that can help you on your Journey. I bless you all, my readers.

My next gratitude goes to me. Don't think it's vain for me to say this—just hear me out. This is a proud moment for me. I fought hard to overcome the struggles and challenges that had held me back, and in doing so, I overcame and conquered all obstacles, limitations, and inner battles I confronted. When I completely let go and allowed God to take care of me totally, my transformation began.

I realized He was not just fighting for me. He was fighting with me. I made a decision to surrender so I could fully serve and experience God soaring within me.

My beautiful children, grandchildren, and great-grandchildren, you are my why. Thank you for allowing me to be a part of your Journey— whether it's through a prayer, a word of encouragement, or using my Voice as a place of reason. God knew I would need all of you. Thank you.

My children's spouses: Thank you for being a part of my children and grandchildren's lives. My prayer is that you and your families continue to grow and deepen in your love for one another and God's love for you.

Thank you, Arthur, Viola (Bit-Bit), Jeanne, my siblings, Diane, Roslyn, Bebe, Rose, Eddie, and Roderick. Thank you, Yolanda, Edward Jones, Sr., and my nephew, Dahveed. Your role in my life and in the telling of this story is undeniable.

I'd also like to thank Indie Books International. Thank you to Henry DeVries, CEO of Indie Books International, and his incredible team for trusting that I had something to say and for treating me with respect.